SEND
THESE
TO ME

Send These to Me

IMMIGRANTS IN URBAN AMERICA
REVISED EDITION

John Higham

THE JOHNS HOPKINS UNIVERSITY PRESS
Baltimore and London

© 1975 by John Higham
© 1984 by The Johns Hopkins University Press
All rights reserved
Printed in the United States of America

Originally published by Atheneum, 1975,
as "Send These to Me: Jews and Other Immigrants
in Urban America"
Johns Hopkins Paperbacks edition, 1984

The Johns Hopkins University Press
Baltimore, Maryland 21218
The Johns Hopkins Press Ltd., London

Library of Congress Cataloging in Publication Data
Higham, John.
  Send these to me.

  Includes bibliographical references and index.
  Contents: The immigrant in American history—The
politics of immigration restriction—The transformation
of the Statue of Liberty—[etc.]
  1. Minorities—United States.   2. United States—
Emigration and immigration.   c. Antisemitism—United
States.   4. Nativism.   I. Title.
E184.A1H49   1984   305.8'00973   84-47960
ISBN 0-8018-2473-7
ISBN 0-8018-2438-9 (pbk.)

To Eileen

Contents

Introduction

This book was put together in 1973–74 as a preliminary attempt to understand historically the structure of ethnic relations in America. All but two of the chapters had originated as separate essays; but they had grown together in my mind sufficiently to make extensive revision, expansion, and updating seem worthwhile. This was, therefore, in large measure a new book when it appeared in 1975. It has now, in this second edition, become a little newer. Two of the less consequential chapters in the original version are gone. The story of immigration restriction in Chapter 2 has been carried down to the present in order to encompass the unexpected wave of immigration of the last ten years and its effects. I have added a new essay on assimilation (Chapter 8), which develops considerably some thoughts that were only lightly touched upon in the first edition. Otherwise I have left the book unchanged, for its argument and point of view seem more persuasive today than they did a decade ago.

Three themes provide the substance of these essays. One concerns broad relations between immigration and other dimensions of American life, such as the political system, the economy, education, and mass culture (Chapters 1, 2, and 8). Against that background, a second theme explores the efforts of social scientists and other intellectuals to formulate a general theory of American ethnic relations (Chapters 9 and 10). Here I write critically as well as historically. Third, I examine in Chapters 4 through 7 the particular case of the Jews, whose complex and fascinating experience seems to me to tell us much about urban America. Chapters 5 through 7 may also be read independently as a general history of American anti-Semitism. All three of my basic themes come together in Chapter 3, on the Statute of Liberty.

Readers of my first book, *Strangers in the Land* (1955), will find in the present volume certain changes of approach, which have animated my continuing search for a fuller understanding of ethnic America. *Strangers in the Land* was a narrative of conflicts shaped by powerful ideologies. This special interest in ideological conflict had focused my attention on extreme and fanatical expressions of ethnic discord: the frenzies of the mob, the nightmares of the propagandist, the repressive statute, and the moments of national frustration. Further reflection convinced me that ideological polarization has been dramatically significant in America only at times of crisis. Without losing interest in ideologies, I discovered the challenge of social history and began to explore the organization of American society as revealed in everyday behavior. That is why, in studying American anti-Semitism, I started by distinguishing sharply between its relatively weak ideological sources and its more substantial basis in the new social relationships of the Gilded Age.

Another feature of my early work that I have tried to correct in the essays gathered here was an overemphasis on economic causation. Like other historians schooled in the progressive interpretation of American history, I was persuaded that ideas and economic forces were the great levers of historical change and that they usually worked together. Yet potent ideas often clashed with powerful economic interests; and when the interests lost out, I had no way of explaining the strength and apparent autonomy of the ideas.[1] My growing attraction to sociological analysis did not in itself resolve the problem. Replacing economic interests with social structures meant a gain in breadth, but an awkward disjunction between ideas and institutions remained.

Gradually I learned from anthropologists—and from historians

1. John Higham, *Writing American History: Essays on Modern Scholarship* (Bloomington, Ind., 1970), 58–72.

influenced by anthropology—to apply the concept of culture to the study of ethnic experience. If culture refers to a pattern of symbolic meanings through which the members of a collectivity grasp their world, then the symbols of the culture can give to ideas and institutions a basic congruence. Within the medium of culture each sustains the other.[2] This approach left the problem of causation completely unsettled. Ethnic history acquired, however, a greater coherence as a study of divisions within and interactions between cultures.

Only readers who are themselves historians are likely to care about such methodological issues. The larger context this book addresses is a fundamental, long-standing debate that no one who writes about the ethnic theme in American life can avoid. The debate is about nothing less than the origins and destiny of the American people. On one side of this debate is the vision of an increasingly unified society, a vision that used to be concentrated most powerfully in the symbol of the melting pot. On the other side is a vision of persistent separateness, the vision of a society that is in some basic sense pluralistic or irreconcilably divided. Are the cleavages in American society more basic and persistent than the unities, or are the differences of a secondary order of importance? This book is a record of that debate, and also a contribution to it.

The debate has never been settled, and one hopes that it never will be. Ambiguity about an American identity has always been essential to the open and indeterminate character of American society. In the mid-1970's, however, when *Send These to Me* made its modest debut, the debate on unity and diversity in American life seemed almost to have ended, at least in academic discourse and in the mass media. This was the time of the "Roots Phenomenon," when Alex Haley's gigantic saga of a black family's survival through centuries of oppression capped the ethnic revival of the decade and riveted the attention of the largest audience ever assembled for a television program. A celebration of the incorruptible autonomy of the ethnic group had acquired such

2. Clifford Geertz, *The Interpretation of Cultures* (New York, 1973), 89–90.

moral authority that the idea of a national culture could hardly be taken seriously. Patriotism had gone out of fashion; the melting pot was a subject of mockery. In the discourse of intellectuals insistence on the integrity of particular concrete communities became so strident that notions of a national community of all Americans (however such a community might be defined) seemed too frail or deceptive to build upon.[3]

Obviously, this was not a good time to publish a history that was concerned with the linkages between ethnic groups, rather than the inviolable uniqueness of a single strain. It was the wrong time to argue, as I did, that pluralistic perspectives cannot enrich and humanize our history unless they are contained within a larger conception of social integration. It was a bad time to praise ambiguity.

Now times have changed. Today the middle ground I took in the old debate about the American people requires no apology. As the passions of hyperethnicity cooled in the late 1970's, a renewed appreciation of assimilation as a powerful and socially desirable force became noticeable among historians and sociologists. The assumption—so prevalent in the early 1970's—that assimilation is a process of loss was once more challenged by scholars who see it as a process of gain.[4] The understandable preoccupation of most ethnic historians with the distinctive experience of a single group no longer precludes a widening interest in comparisons and continuities between groups.

I hope it will be apparent to the most casual reader that my own sympathies are with the life of the debate itself rather than with any single voice or set of voices it enlists. Yet I, too, am one of the participants in the debate, and my own notions of the terms on which it can flourish obviously color the pages that follow. It may be useful, therefore, to note in conclusion certain governing convictions these studies have given me:

3. I am making free use here of some of my remarks in "Current Trends in the Study of Ethnicity in the United States," *Journal of American Ethnic History*, II (1982), 5–15.

4. For example, Arthur Mann, *The One and the Many: Reflections on the American Identity* (Chicago, 1979); Stephen Steinberg, *The Ethnic Myth: Race, Ethnicity, and Class in America* (New York, 1981).

1. Ethnic diversity is a profoundly important fact of American life, but not always a desirable condition. Ethnic differences, so often a delight, an incentive, and a bulwark, easily become dangerous and destructive. American society, therefore, has the task of modulating them by drawing forth their constructive potentiality. This is an unfinished, probably an endless, task, which requires new strategies as times change.

2. Because the most intense ethnic feelings are highly virulent, it is fortunate that ethnic identification is frequently mild. Its intensity varies greatly among members of a single group, between ethnic groups, and over time. Contrary to some claims, we are not all "ethnics." Everyone has some sense of ancestral belonging, but many Americans, much of the time, feel little ethnic identification. Their presence can forestall polarization either by muffling divisive issues or by shifting the issues to a more universal plane. Ethnic history should not overlook the bystanders.

3. The model of ethnic relations that is called "pluralistic integration" in the last chapter is destined to be the common ground on which more and more people of every kind will choose to stand. It is not by any means America's only tradition in ethnic relations. It will not appeal to the more militant champions of a particular ethnic heritage; nor will it satisfy those rationalists for whom all ethnic feelings are prejudices to expose or obstacles to overcome. But pluralistic integration is our best tradition. And the history of the twentieth century, for all of its pain and disillusion, gives us reason to believe that pluralistic integration will prevail.

JOHN HIGHAM
Baltimore
February, 1984

SEND
THESE
TO ME

Chapter One

The Immigrant in American History

In the late 1770's a well-to-do French farmer who had settled in the Hudson River Valley posed a question that has fascinated subsequent generations and reverberated through American history. "What then is the American, this new man?" asked St. John de Crèvecoeur in writing an affectionate sketch of his adopted country. Crèvecoeur's answer elaborated a claim already advanced by another recent arrival from Europe, Tom Paine. Paine's famous revolutionary pamphlet, *Common Sense* (1776), was the first stentorian call for independence from Britain. It declared, and Crèvecoeur heartily agreed, that the Americans were not transplanted Englishmen. They were a mixture of many European peoples, a nation of immigrants.

The idea that all Americans, except possibly the Indians, once were immigrants has never had unqualified acceptance. It was undoubtedly a minority view in Crèvecoeur's time. John Jay, writing the second of the *Federalist* papers, probably commanded wider assent. Jay defined Americans as "one united people—a people descended from the same ancestors, speaking the same language, professing the same religion, attached to the same principles of government, very similar in their manners and customs."[1] Many writers still describe America not as an eclectic

1. Winthrop D. Jordan, *White Over Black: American Attitudes Toward the Negro, 1550–1812* (Chapel Hill, 1968), 336–40; *The Federalist*, No. 2.

and cosmopolitan society, but as the creation of one dominating group. Today a unitary conception of America, emphasizing stability and power rather than migration and freedom, crops up on the left as well as on the right.

Both interpretations tell us something about the American conundrum; but neither Crèvecoeur nor Jay comprehended its complexity. Diversity and homogeneity intertwine so densely in American experience that neither theme alone can do it justice. This complicates enormously the problem of understanding immigration. The historian must thread his way between rival legends, each an amalgam of partial truths and potent myths. One legend puts the immigrant, and all he represents, at the center of American experience. Another relegates him to the periphery.

In recent years the legend of the American as immigrant has been widely stressed. One finds a classic statement in a posthumous little book written for and attributed to President John F. Kennedy, entitled *A Nation of Immigrants* (1964). The ideas summarized there influence serious scholarship as well. A British historian, making an excellent survey of American immigration, turns aside in his preface from a straightforward narrative to pay deference to the legend. Immigration, Maldwyn Jones tells us, is "America's historic *raison d'être* . . . the most persistent and the most pervasive influence in her development." Still more sweepingly, an eminent historian declared a few years ago that the immigrants *were* American history. An adequate description of the course and effects of immigration would require him to write the whole history of the country.[2]

In some senses, of course, immigration does ramify into every aspect of American life. Conceived as the quintessential act of mobility, or as the starting point of the great American success story, immigration exemplifies conditions general to the whole society. Since the common experience of all Americans is the memory of displacement from somewhere else, migration may be seen as the key to the American character. In the absence of a truly rooted national tradition, Americans have been united—it

2. Maldwyn Allen Jones, *American Immigration* (Chicago, 1960), 1; Oscar Handlin, *The Uprooted: The Epic Story of the Great Migrations That Made the American People* (Boston, 1951), 3.

might be argued—by their commitment to the future. And the future-looking orientation of the American people has shaped the most notable American traits: idealism; flexibility and adaptability to change; a dependence on the self and the immediate family more than the wider community; a high respect for personal achievement; a tendency to conform to the values of peers and neighbors instead of holding stubbornly to ancestral ways.[3]

These are plausible attributes of migration as a social process; but they do enlarge the immigrant, as a specific type, to the dimensions of myth. In view of such large conceptions of the matter, it is little wonder that scholars have been hard put to specify what particular features of American life derive in some distinctive way from immigration. Insofar as we conceive it as a kind of rite of passage to an American identity, it eludes us as a historical variable. By visualizing the immigrant as the representative American, we may see him building America; we cannot see him changing it. Whatever significance immigration may have in some inclusive or representative way, it has also been a major differentiating force. It has separated those who bear the marks of foreign origin or inheritance from others who do not. The importance of immigration in this more limited sense—as a source of distinctions, divisions, and changes within the United States—remains as yet only dimly grasped. We shall have to disentangle the special effects of immigration from the encompassing legend; and that will require all the light comparative history can shed.

Let us begin with the word. In 1809 a traveler noted, "Immigrant is perhaps the only new word of which the circumstances of the United States has in any degree demanded the addition to the English language." The word materialized simultaneously with the creation of a national government. In 1789 Jedidiah Morse's famous patriotic textbook, *American Geography*, mentioned the "many immigrants from Scotland, Ireland, Germany, and some from France" who were living in New York.[4] Paine,

3. George W. Pierson in *The Moving American* (Boston, 1972) gives a thoughtful exposition of these relationships.
4. Mitford M. Mathews, ed., *A Dictionary of Americanisms on Historical Principles* (Chicago, 1951), 863; Jedidiah Morse, *The American Geography* (Elizabethtown, N.J., 1789), 253.

Crèvecoeur, and earlier writers had referred only to "emigrants." But by 1789 our language was beginning to identify newcomers with the country they entered rather than the one they had left. Thus the term immigrant presupposed the existence of a receiving society to which the alien could attach himself. The immigrant is not, then, a colonist or settler who creates a new society and lays down the terms of admission for others. He is rather the bearer of a foreign culture.

Morse explicitly differentiated the "immigrants" from "the original inhabitants," the Dutch and English "settlers." The Dutch had planted in 1624 the settlement on the Hudson River that became the province of New York forty years later when it fell into the hands of the English. At the time of the American Revolution Dutch was still spoken fairly extensively in churches and homes in New York and New Jersey. By that time people of English origin composed the preponderant element, as indeed they did in all thirteen states. The best estimate identifies as English about 60 per cent of the white population of 1790.[5] Like the Dutch in New York, the English in all of the colonies before the Revolution conceived of themselves as founders, settlers, or planters—the formative population of those colonial societies— not as immigrants. Theirs was the polity, the language, the pattern of work and settlement, and many of the mental habits to which the immigrants would have to adjust. To distinguish immigration from other aspects of American history, we shall have to exclude the founders of a society from the category of immigrant.

The English seizure of the Dutch settlements illustrates another mode of ethnic aggregation that does not belong within the scope of immigration. It should not include peoples who are forcibly incorporated into the host society. Those groups join the society on terms that shape their subsequent experience in special ways. Americans tend to forget how many alien groups joined them involuntarily. The great American success story features the saga

5. American Council of Learned Societies, "Report of Committee on Linguistic and National Stocks in the Population of the United States," American Historical Association, *Annual Report*, I (1931), 124-25.

of the immigrant, for the immigrant chose America, however circumscribed was his choice and however involuntary his dislodgement from home. In the process of immigration the alien seeks a new country; and it encourages his aspiration. Most of the captured groups, on the other hand, do not fit the success story because their entry into the Anglo-American community did not depend on the real freedom and mobility that propelled the immigrant.

Two types of coercion have contributed to the peopling of the United States. The most obvious was slavery. The English founders imported African slaves who accounted in 1790 for about 19 per cent of the population of the new nation. Virtually from the beginning, blacks constituted an inferior caste in the American social order. Immigrants were expected sooner or later to blend with the rest of the society or go back where they came from. Blacks were permitted only a limited degree of assimilation, and they were unable to leave.

Meanwhile expansion and conquest engulfed many Indian tribes and other groups already established in the New World. Unlike the Negroes and the immigrants, these groups belonged to a particular place, to which they tried to cling in their encounter with the dominant American society. The Indians, after proving resistive both to assimilation and to enslavement, were steadily driven westward. Treated as foreign nations until 1871 and expected to die out, most of them became part of the United States only when they could not otherwise survive at all. With far less cruelty and destruction, the Anglo-Americans also overran various French and Spanish settlements. In 1755 they uprooted several thousand French Acadians from villages on the Bay of Fundy and dispersed them to other English colonies. Subsequent annexations took in, and left relatively undisturbed, the languid French settlements in the Illinois country, at St. Louis and, most important, New Orleans.[6] As a result of the War with Mexico (1846–1848) the Anglo-Americans took possession of a considerable Spanish population in the Southwest. The widely scattered

6. Marcus Lee Hansen, *The Mingling of the Canadian and American Peoples* (New Haven, 1940), 26–28; Clement Eaton, *The Growth of Southern Civilization, 1790–1860* (New York, 1961), 125–49.

"Californios" lost their patrimony and disappeared. In the Rio Grande Valley of New Mexico, on the other hand, tightly knit village settlements enabled the "Hispanos" to preserve their culture and their identity as ancient inhabitants of the place, proudly distinct from the "Anglos" around them and from the Mexican immigrants in adjacent states.[7]

Altogether, the United States has participated in almost all of the processes by which a nation or empire can incorporate a variety of ethnic groups. It has acquired a diverse people by invasion and conquest, by enslavement, and by immigration. The one incorporative process America has not attempted on a significant scale is a federation between contiguous but unlike peoples. This is a dangerous form of nation-building. It leaves entirely distinct ethnic groups in control of different parts of the country and so leads often to disruption and secessionist movements. In Canada, Nigeria, and the old Austro-Hungarian Empire, federation gave territorially based ethnic majorities a threatening veto power against one another. When the individual American states federated into a single national community in 1789, however, the event had no direct ethnic import. In every state of the American Union the dominant group sprang from approximately the same British ancestry. And by the time federation extended to Hawaii and Alaska, society there had been Americanized. Thus the American experience with federation has increased the variety of minorities without altering the distribution of ethnic power.

II

What then can be said about ethnic groups formed by the voluntary process of immigration? After taking account of the descendants of English colonizers, African slaves, and the more or less indigenous groups adopted in the course of expansion, what remains? Actually, a great deal. The 40 per cent of the white population of 1790 who were not English, plus the 46,000,000

7. Leonard Pitt, *The Decline of the Californios: A Social History of the Spanish-Speaking Californians, 1846–1890* (Berkeley, 1970), esp. 11, 130–31; Nancie L. Gonzalez, *The Spanish-Americans of New Mexico* (Albuquerque, 1969).

immigrants who have entered the United States since that time, have produced a very considerable part of the American people.[8] For example, in 1920, the best authorities estimated, nearly 15 per cent of the population of the continental United States might be ascribed to German immigration and another 10 per cent attributed to southern—i.e., Catholic—Ireland (Table 1).

Suggestive though such figures are, they leave us uncertain about the extent to which most people actually identify with the origins imputed to them. The effort in the 1920's to assign all Americans to specific national origins arose at a time of unusual anxiety over the menace of immigration to the whole social order. It assumed that nearly everyone had a clear ethnic identity: an uncomplicated attachment to a specific line of descent originating outside the United States. The assumption that we are all ethnics—an assumption shared by some who would disdain to think of themselves as immigrants—has never been testable because the boundaries of most American ethnic groups are so vague. A second attempt to determine the ethnic composition of the American people was made in 1972 by census-takers who asked a broad national sample, "What is your origin or descent?" If the respondents said they were "American," the interviewers probed for a more specific and earlier origin.[9] A large proportion of the white respondents, however—about four out of every ten—would not claim descent from any of the eight nationalities which the census-takers offered as possible choices. Some of this unclassified population can be assigned to small national strains, such as the Swedish and the Dutch; some were simply uncooperative. But a great many derived from an ancestry that was either too mixed or too remote from European antecedents to sustain any consciousness of an Old World heritage.

The size of the unclassified group in the 1972 ethnic survey is one indication of a gradual erosion that besets American immigrant groups after the supply of fresh immigration has dwindled. At some point the initial effort to constitute an organized group

8. For total immigration from 1820 to 1972 see U.S. Bureau of the Census, *Statistical Abstract of the United States, 1973* (Washington, D.C., 1973), 94.

9. U.S. Bureau of the Census, "Characteristics of the Population by Ethnic Origin: March 1972 and 1971," *Current Population Reports,* P-20, No. 249 (Washington, D.C., 1973), 11.

TABLE I.   *National and Racial Origins, Population of the*
United States: 1920 and 1972   (in thousands)

	1920 NATIONAL ORIGINS ASCRIBED	PER CENT	1972 NATIONAL ORIGINS DECLARED	PER CENT
British (inc.				
Anglo-Canadian)	42,066	39.5	29,548	14.4
German	15,489	14.6	25,543	12.5
Irish	10,653	10.0	16,408	8.0
Polish	3,893	3.7	5,105	2.5
Italian	3,462	3.3	8,764	4.3
French (inc.				
Fr.-Canadian)	3,029	2.8	5,420	2.6
Russian	1,661	1.6	2,188	1.1
Spanish (inc.				
Sp.-American)	1,313	1.2	9,178	4.5
Other white	13,140	12.3	77,031	37.6
Swedish	1,977	1.9		
Dutch	1,881	1.8		
Norwegian	1,419	1.3		
Negro	10,463	9.8	22,737	11.1
Indian	244	0.2	819	0.4
Asian	182	0.2	2,099	1.0

SOURCES: Adapted from Warren S. Thompson and P. K. Whelpton, *Population Trends in the United States* (New York, 1933), 90–91; Leon S. Truesdell, *The Canadian Born in the United States* (New Haven, 1943), 60; U.S. Bureau of the Census, *Statistical Abstract of the United States: 1973* (Washington, D.C., 1973), 30, 34; U.S. Bureau of the Census, "Characteristics of the Population by Ethnic Origin: March 1972 and 1971," *Current Population Reports*, P-20, No. 249 (Washington, D.C., 1973), 19. Data on racial groups are not included in the 1972 study of ethnic origins, although it encompasses a cross section of the entire population. I have therefore used the 1970 Census to fractionalize the 50.1 per cent who are grouped as "Other" and "No Report" in the 1972 study.

life is succeeded by a struggle to survive. A strong religious heritage, compact settlement, or pronounced phenotypical characteristics will check the decline. Intergroup conflict may reverse it. In the typical process of development, however, a substantial proportion of every generation after the first marries outside the group and becomes more interested in other associations. Those who lose close contact with their immigrant origins are assimilated into a partially de-ethnicized host society.

On the other hand, the triumph of assimilation is not nearly as complete or as rapid as the official ideal of the melting pot has sometimes persuaded us to think. For many, ethnic identity remains a viable option. Almost every ethnic group that has survived its formative encounter with American culture retains a loyal core, which keeps it alive and encourages a periodic rekindling of group consciousness. In recent years a renewed appreciation of the ethnic bond as a source of political power and personal integration has inspired scholars to look more closely than ever before at its persistence in American politics. Much research has shown that people usually inherit their political predispositions. They grow up with, and commonly pass on to their children, a set of values that defines their friends, their enemies, and ultimately themselves. To take an extreme example, the Irish were already enthusiastic Jeffersonians in 1800—"the most God-provoking Democrats this side of Hell," Uriah Tracy called them.[10] One hundred and seventy-two years later their stronghold—Massachusetts—was the only state the Democratic party carried.

The wider significance of these new studies is still obscure. One scholar, examining the history of New Haven, Connecticut, has hypothesized that ethnic voting becomes most salient in the second or third generation, when the emergent ethnic group has

10. Maldwyn Allen Jones, "Ulster Emigration, 1783–1815," *Essays in Scotch-Irish History*, ed. E. R. R. Green (London, 1969), 66. The Scotch-Irish and the Catholic Irish then formed a single element in America, united by a common hatred of the English. The findings of the ethnocultural school are conveniently summarized in Samuel T. McSeveney, "Ethnic Groups, Ethnic Conflicts, and Recent Quantitative Research in American Political History," *International Migration Review*, VII (1973), 14–33. See also John L. Shover, "Ethnicity and Religion in Philadelphia Politics, 1924–40," *American Quarterly*, XXV (1973), 499–515.

produced a middle class capable of providing skilled and visible leadership. Yet we also know that the attainment of middle-class status tends to weaken ethnic identity by tempting the recipients of that status into new residential and friendship patterns; occupation replaces ancestry as the foundation of social life.[11] There may be an irony here: ethnic voting intensifies as ethnic identity becomes problematical.

Between evidence of some striking continuities in ethnic life and contrary evidence of great flux and change, reconciliation seems impossible without appreciating the characteristic indistinctness of national and class boundaries in American society. "The distinctions among groups, whether identified as occupational class or ascribed status groupings, tend to merge, almost imperceptibly, into one another," a leading sociologist has concluded. "Thus the 'model' of urban pluralism that we see developing for the American case must necessarily take into account the relatively high permeability of the boundaries between groups and the corresponding tendencies toward fusion."[12] Due to this permeability, it has been possible to shed the outward marks of foreign origin without undergoing total assimilation. Some differences of attitude and world-view linger after the group itself has ceased to figure largely in a person's consciousness. In other countries minorities usually stand out more sharply. Either a more complete absorption is demanded, as in the case of Brazil, or a fuller separateness is tolerated, as in Canada. In the United States, Joshua Fishman has said, ethnicity has learned a great secret: "To exist and yet not to exist, to be needed and yet to be unimportant, to be different and yet to be the same, to be integrated and yet to be separate."[13]

11. Raymond E. Wolfinger, "The Development and Persistence of Ethnic Voting," *American Political Science Review*, LIX (1965), 896–908; Edward O. Laumann, *Bonds of Pluralism: The Form and Substance of Urban Social Networks* (New York, 1973), 89–109.

12. Ibid., 208–9.

13. Joshua A. Fishman et al., *Language Loyalty in the United States: The Maintenance and Perpetuation of Non-English Mother Tongues by American Ethnic and Religious Groups* (The Hague, 1966), 73. On Brazil see Richard M. Morse, "The Heritage of Latin America," in Louis Hartz et al., *The Founding of New Societies* (New York, 1964), 124. On Canada see below, p. 20.

Thus, leaving aside the special situation of the indigenous groups and the blacks, American society may be visualized as a cluster of immigrant-ethnic communities lapped by an expanding core population of mixed origins and indeterminate size. An inflow from the ethnic communities slowly enlarges the fuzzy perimeter of the core population. Cross-cut with memories of ancestral diversities, the host society becomes less and less capable of defining itself in an exclusive way. The Pilgrim and the Puritan have faded as American symbols. Craggy-featured Uncle Sam has gone too, and the Statue of Liberty has largely replaced Plymouth Rock. The newly minted term WASP became in the 1960's the only ethnic slur that could safely be used in polite company; for it was part of a largely successful assault on certain remaining bastions of ethnic exclusiveness.[14]

Although the immigrant sector has at times been large in America, it has never been overwhelming. Some other new countries present more striking statistics. For example, Canada's people in 1911 were 22 per cent foreign-born. In Argentina nearly one-third of the population in 1914 was foreign-born. Foreigners outnumbered natives in some provinces of Canada and Argentina by two to one. In Buenos Aires they comprised three-fourths of all adults.[15] Immigration never reached anything like those heights in the United States. At most, the proportion of the foreign-born was half as great as it was in Argentina. Immigrants rarely exceeded a third of the population in a state, and then only

14. The earliest references I have found occur in 1964. In Saul Bellow's exuberant novel, *Herzog* (New York, 1964), 309, Moses Herzog relishes "defying the Wasps, who . . . stopped boiling their own soap circa 1880, took European tours, and began to complain of the Micks and the Spicks and the Sheenies." In the same year and in the same sense E. Digby Baltzell introduced the term into the vocabulary of American social science in *The Protestant Establishment: Aristocracy and Caste in America* (New York, 1964). Quickly, in writers like Peter Schrag and Michael Novak, "Wasp" became synonymous with a desiccated, life-denying culture.

15. *The Canada Year Book*, 1914, pp. 63–65; Robin A. Humphreys, *The Evolution of Modern Latin America* (Oxford, 1946), 56–61; James R. Scobie, *Argentina: A City and a Nation* (New York, 1971), 33. Here and elsewhere I am indebted to the pioneering essay by Frank Thistlethwaite, "Migration from Europe Overseas in the Nineteenth and Twentieth Centuries," XI Congrès International des Sciences Historiques, *Rapports* (Stockholm, 1960), V, 32–60.

in an occasional frontier state during its early years. Wisconsin was 36 per cent foreign-born in 1850, Nevada 44 per cent in 1870, North Dakota 43 per cent in 1890.[16] But these levels fell off sharply in later decades. First- and second-generation immigrants combined never exceeded 35 per cent of the total American population (Table 2).

In some states and localities at certain periods the impact of immigration has indeed been massive. At the time of the American Revolution German stock alone comprised about a third of the population of Pennsylvania, to say nothing of the many Ulstermen from Northern Ireland. At the time of the Civil War more than half the residents of Chicago, Milwaukee, and St. Louis were foreign-born. In Milwaukee in the late nineteenth century 20 per cent of the adult population could not speak English. At the beginning of the twentieth century 75 per cent of Minnesota, 71 per cent of Wisconsin, 64 per cent of Rhode Island, 62 per cent of Massachusetts, and 61 per cent of Utah were people with at least one parent born outside the United States.[17] The great immigration of the early twentieth century concentrated heavily on the cities, so that three-quarters of the population of New York, Chicago, Cleveland, Detroit, and Boston consisted of first- and second-generation immigrants in 1910. But the immigrants never swamped the older Americans in any major city because the latter participated in the urban movement just as vigorously as did the immigrants. The proportion of foreign-born in the twenty-five principal cities actually declined steadily every decade after 1860.[18]

More important, the sheer size of the immigrant population is less striking than its truly extraordinary diversity. Other immigrant-receiving countries have tended to draw disproportionately from a few favored ethnic backgrounds. In a century of immigration to Argentina, for instance, 40 per cent of the newcomers came from Italy, another 27 per cent from Spain. The same

16. Niles Carpenter, *Immigrants and Their Children, 1920*, U.S. Bureau of the Census, Census Monographs, VII (Washington, D.C., 1927), 308.

17. Ibid., 25–26, 309; *United States Census, 1890: Population*, Part II, lxv.

18. Stephan Thernstrom, *The Other Bostonians: Poverty and Progress in the American Metropolis, 1880–1970* (Cambridge, Mass., 1973), 111–44; Carpenter, *Immigrants and Their Children*, 25.

TABLE 2.   *Foreign-Born and Their Children in the United States, 1790–1980*

| | FOREIGN-BORN | | NATIVES OF FOREIGN OR MIXED PARENTAGE |
	Number	Per Cent of Total Pop.	Per Cent of Total Pop.
1790	500,000[a]	12.8	
1800	600,000[a]	11.3	
1810	800,000[a]	11.1	
1820	1,000,000[a]	10.4	
1830	1,200,000[a]	9.3	
1840	1,400,000[a]	8.2	
1850	2,244,602	9.7	
1860	4,138,697	13.2	
1870	5,567,229	14.0	13.8
1880	6,679,943	13.3	16.5
1890	9,249,560	14.7	18.3
1900	10,444,717	13.6	20.6
1910	13,630,073	14.7	20.5
1920	14,020,203	13.7	21.5
1930	14,283,255	14.8	21.0
1940	11,656,641	8.8	17.5
1950	10,431,093	6.9	15.6
1960	9,738,143	5.4	13.6
1970	9,619,302	4.7	11.8
1980	14,079,906	6.2	

SOURCES: Niles Carpenter, *Immigrants and Their Children, 1920* (U.S. Bureau of the Census, Census Monographs, VII, Washington, D.C., 1927), 6, 308; *U.S. Census, 1970: Population*, I, part 1, p. 361; Ernest Rubin, "Immigration and the Economic Growth of the U.S.: 1790–1914," *R.E.M.P. Bulletin* (Research Group for European Migration Problems), VII (Oct.–Dec. 1959), 87–95; U.S. Bureau of the Census, *U.S. Census, 1980: Summary Tape File*, 3c.
[a] Provisional estimate by Ernest Rubin.

nationalities, together with a large Portuguese contingent, made up 76 per cent of Brazil's immigration.[19] Canada, between 1851 and 1950, got almost half its immigrants from the British Isles and a quarter of the remainder from the United States. Australia, too, recruited overwhelmingly from the British Isles. As recently as 1947 only 11 per cent of the Australian white population was traceable to other origins.[20] In contrast, the United States during the period 1820–1945 recruited 12 per cent of its total immigration from Italy, 13 per cent from Austria-Hungary and its successor states, 16 per cent from Germany, 10 per cent from Russia and Poland, 6 per cent from Scandinavia, and a third from the British Isles.[21] New England sustained a major invasion of French Canadians. Hundreds of thousands of Mexicans poured into the Southwest. About half a million Greeks reached the United States before the Second World War. Substantial concentrations of Japanese materialized in the San Francisco Bay area, of Finns in the lumber and copper towns of the Northwest, of Armenians in the orchards around Fresno, of Netherlanders in South Dakota and Michigan, of Portuguese in New Bedford, of Arabs in New York City. In some mining and mill towns one might find a dozen ethnic groups intermixed in more or less the same neighborhood.[22] No other country has gathered its people from so many different sources.

The very diversity of the immigration makes its impact difficult to measure. In some ways diversity limited that impact. Where one immigrant culture predominates, it can impart its own distinctive flavor to an area and perhaps affect decisively the allocation of power. Thus Chinese immigration created a deep and lasting social cleavage in Malaya and Thailand, as East Indians

19. United Nations Educational, Scientific and Cultural Organization, *The Positive Contribution by Immigrants* (Paris, 1955), 121, 149–52.

20. Norman B. Ryder, "Components of Canadian Population and Growth," in *Canadian Society: Sociological Perspectives*, ed. Bernard R. Blishen et al. (New York, 1961), 62; Charles A. Price, *Southern Europeans in Australia* (Melbourne, 1963), 9.

21. William S. Bernard et al., *American Immigration Policy: A Reappraisal* (New York, 1950), 311

22. Timothy L. Smith, "New Approaches to the History of Immigration in Twentieth-Century America," *American Historical Review*, LXXI (1966), 1267–68.

did in Guyana. In Argentina Latin immigration overwhelmed the Indian, mestizo, and Negro elements. A nation that had an Indian and mestizo majority in the mid-nineteenth century has become overwhelmingly white. Only tiny pockets of Indians survive, and the rural people who are identifiably mestizo have dwindled to perhaps 10 per cent of the total population.[23] In Canada immigration has strengthened the English culture to the disadvantage of the French, since the immigrants send their children to English-speaking schools and press for privileges that threaten the special status of French. But an influx as miscellaneous as that which the United States has received cannot easily alter preexisting relationships. Competing against one another, immigrants have ordinarily found themselves on all sides of the choices America has thrust upon them. Except in relatively isolated, rural areas, no immigrant enclave—no close-knit neighborhood or favored occupation—has been safe from invasion by some newer, less advantaged group. Employers learned to set one group against another and thus manage their labor force more easily, a policy they called "balancing nationalities."[24] Politicians learned to rally miscellaneous support, while exploiting ethnic division, by a strategy known as "balancing the ticket." Accordingly, the immigrants have never been arrayed solidly against the native population on economic issues, and no political party has ever captured the whole "foreign vote."

All of this is not to say that immigrants have exercised only fleeting and localized influence before melting away into America's great majority. Neither the commanding position of the majority group nor the fragmentation of the immigrants into many disunited minorities deprives them of a major role in American history. To delimit the scope of their role is rather to make possible a judgment of its distinctive import. Even so, the crux of the matter still eludes us unless—concentrating on the process of immigration—we can somehow separate what it may have *made possible* from what it merely *reinforced*. No one has

23. Scobie, *Argentina*, 32–33. A similar but less drastic trend in Latin America as a whole is tabulated in Fernando Bastos de Avila, *Immigration in Latin America* (Washington, D.C., 1964), 71–74.
24. Peter Roberts, *The New Immigration* (New York, 1912), 75.

yet wrestled hard with that question. But we can make a tentative start by noting that immigration occurred in two large and quite distinct phases.

Beginning in the 1680's, the English colonies in America attracted a sizable, voluntary inpouring of other ethnic groups, which continued without slackening until the American Revolution. Then it resumed in 1783 and continued strong until 1803. This First Immigration, as I shall call it, followed a sharp decline in English fears of overpopulation at home and a consequent falling off of English emigration. The proprietors of the newer colonies, notably Pennsylvania and Carolina, turned to foreign sources for the people essential to their promotional designs. Prior to 1680 the occasional Scot, Irishman, or Jew had left no special imprint on the long Atlantic seaboard except in the motley Dutch town of New Amsterdam. Now advertising, the promise of religious liberty, and other inducements attracted French Huguenots, Irish Quakers, German pietists. Their coming started a wider movement—particularly from Ireland, Scotland, Switzerland, and the Rhineland—which soon acquired its own momentum. Altogether, about 450,000 immigrants arrived in the course of the eighteenth century, over half of them Irish, predominantly Presbyterian, who suffered terribly from English landlords and English mercantilist policies.[25] The colonies, dependent on local initiative and competing with one another for people, became so avid for immigration that their Declaration of Independence in 1776 charged the king with obstructing it.

Actually, Britain permitted a latitude in the admission of foreigners to rights in her colonies that was inconceivable in the mother country or elsewhere in the world. Although the English maintained at home restrictions designed to prevent foreign immigration, their own society was too pluralistic to make a monolithic policy seem essential overseas. The crown therefore delegated the responsibility for colonization to private promoters.

25. I have modified the estimate ventured by J. Potter, "The Growth of Population in America, 1700–1860," *Population in History: Essays in Historical Demography*, ed. D. V. Glass and D. E. C. Eversley (London, 1965), 645, to take account of my longer time span and the figures given in R. J. Dickson, *Ulster Emigration to Colonial America, 1718–1775* (London, 1966), and Jones, "Ulster Emigration," loc. cit.

Within certain limits they could bring in "any other strangers that will become our loving subjects."[26] An Act of Parliament in 1740, which applied only to America, laid down a uniform procedure for naturalizing foreign Protestants and Jews. Catholics, though denied civil rights, could not be altogether excluded from so decentralized a society. The other great colonizing powers, Spain and France, kept authority centralized and policies uniform. They admitted only native-born Catholics to their overseas domains, so immigration to those parts did not begin until after the end of the colonial era.

The United States not only had a colonial immigration, but by the time of the American Revolution a significant portion of the immigrants of the preceding century had been fully accepted in the new society. The first major ethnic crisis in American history boiled up in Pennsylvania in the 1740's, when the mushrooming German settlements temporarily seemed an unassimilable alien mass. The threat soon passed, however. The Germans proved to be disunited; and the society in which they lived was itself too differentiated to exclude them systematically. A Schwenkfelder leader wrote wonderingly in 1768, "You can hardly imagine how many denominations you will find here. . . . We are all going to and fro like fish in water but always at peace with each other. . . . Dear Friend, think of the unlimited freedom . . . and you will understand in what dangers we are concerning our children."[27] The seduction of the children was in effect an enlargement of the core population. Consequently the founders of the new nation did not consist exclusively or perhaps even primarily of rebellious Englishmen, Germans, and the like. America's

26. Royal charter granted to the London Company, 1609, quoted in Emberson E. Proper, *Colonial Immigration Laws: A Study of the Regulation of Immigration by the English Colonies in America* (Columbia University Studies in History, Economics and Public Law, XI, New York, 1900), 8. See also Edward A. Hoyt, "Naturalization under the American Colonies: Signs of a New Community," *Political Science Quarterly*, LXVII (1952), 248–66.

27. Quoted in Dietmar Rothermund, *The Layman's Progress: Religious and Political Experience in Colonial Pennsylvania, 1740–1770* (Philadelphia, 1961), 190. See also James T. Lemon, *The Best Poor Man's Country: A Geographical Study of Early Southeastern Pennsylvania* (Baltimore, 1972), 15–22, 47–48.

"charter group" (to use a helpful phrase Canadian sociologists have coined) was already becoming a blend—a blend not of races but of closely related ethnic strains.

This widening of the Anglo-American community took on a special ideological significance when Americans needed, in 1776 and after, to differentiate themselves from Englishmen. The immigration of the eighteenth century enabled Paine and other formulators of the national legend to claim that Americans, unlike Englishmen, are a truly cosmopolitan people, the heirs of all mankind. Thus a universalistic and eclectic sense of national identity was created. In the long run this has probably been the most important single effect of the First Immigration. The English have tended to assume that all groups should retain their own cultural distinctiveness and remain at a comfortable distance from one another.[28] That assumption has survived and flourished in Canada, where the English permitted the French settlers (they were not immigrants) to keep their own special privileges. Accordingly, immigrant groups also received special concessions; Canadians came to describe their society as a "mosaic."[29] Neither Canada nor other countries that came out of the expansion of Europe have felt the deep commitment the First Immigration implanted in American culture: the commitment to breed a "new man."

III

The Second Immigration, like the First, lasted for a century. It ran from the 1820's to the stiff immigration restriction law of

28. Michael Banton, *White and Coloured: The Behavior of British People Towards Coloured Immigrants* (New Brunswick, N.J., 1960), 77–78, 90; Robin W. Winks, "Imperialism," *The Comparative Approach to American History,* ed. C. Vann Woodward (New York, 1968), 264.

29. Howard Palmer, "Mosaic vs. Melting Pot: Reality or Illusion," unpublished paper delivered at meeting of Canadian Association for American Studies, October, 1972, is the most perceptive and well-balanced discussion; but see also Allan Smith, "Metaphor and Nationality in North America," *Canadian Historical Review,* LI (1970), 247–75, and John Porter, *The Vertical Mosaic: An Analysis of Social Class and Power in Canada* (Toronto, 1965), 60–103.

1924. This human flood vastly extended the diversity its predecessor had created. During the first two decades of the nineteenth century war and other restraints on emigration had kept the transatlantic movement at a low level. The proportion of the foreign-born in the American population fell by the 1830's to about 8 per cent. Then a transportation revolution made America accessible from more and more remote points, while a population crisis in rural Europe and the breakdown of the traditional agricultural system put millions of people to flight. The tide surged to a high point in the 1850's, to a higher one in the early 1880's, and to a crest in the opening decade of the twentieth century.[30] Whereas the First Immigration had been entirely white and predominantly English-speaking, the Second brought a Babel of tongues and an array of complexions ranging from the blond Scandinavian through the swarthy south Italian to the West Indian Negro. And whereas the First Immigration had been very largely Protestant, the second was heavily Catholic from the outset; and by the end of the century it was increasingly Jewish and Eastern Orthodox.

Primarily because of immigration, the Roman Catholic Church as early as 1850 became the largest single religious body in America; and so it has remained. Immigration transformed the church into an ethnic fortress, in which immigrant peoples through their own ethnic parishes, their own parochial schools, hospitals, and orphanages resisted the onslaught of the surrounding Protestant culture on their faith and traditions.[31] As long as the Second Immigration lasted, Catholicism in America was mostly defensive and conservative: an anomaly, in spite of brave assertions to the contrary, in a Protestant country. Ultimately, however, Catholicism identified itself so closely with Americanism that Americanism ceased to be Protestant. By the 1950's informed observers of all faiths recognized that America was no longer distinctively or predominantly a Protestant country. This in itself was a major consequence of the Second Immigration.

30. Philip Taylor, *The Distant Magnet: European Emigration to the U.S.A.* (London, 1971).

31. Jay P. Dolan, "A Critical Period in American Catholicism," *Review of Politics*, XXXV (1973), 523-36.

Elsewhere in the western hemisphere immigration has tended to reinforce, rather than alter, the preexisting religious pattern.[32]

In the secular sphere the Second Immigration was perhaps most important in shaping an urban, industrial way of life. On this subject it is not possible to distinguish the influence of immigration sharply from that of other forces. Many influences intermingled in transforming the United States from a decentralized, rural republic to a consolidated, industrial nation. But a comparative approach underlines the special ways in which immigration met the demands of an urban, industrial order in the United States. To a degree unequaled elsewhere, the immigrants supplied an industrial labor force and an urban state of mind.

Initially, the promise of land and the wealth it contained lured many of the 50,000,000 people who poured out of Europe in the nineteenth and early twentieth centuries. Like the eastward migration across the Russian steppes, the overseas movement to North and South America, to Australasia, and to parts of Africa was in good part an insatiable land rush. Immigrants broke the soil and harvested the wheat of the Argentine pampas and the Canadian prairies; they cleared forests in southern Brazil; they dug gold in California and Australia; they spread rich farms over large parts of the American Middle West. Where they could acquire land, they took root. Increasingly, however, the newcomers in the immigrant-receiving countries gravitated toward the cities. This was especially so in the United States. In 1890, 62 per cent of America's foreign-born lived in urban places, as against only 26 per cent of the native whites born of native parents.

The urban immigrants played a unique role in the United States. Industrialization in the other immigrant-receiving countries before the First World War was quite limited. They needed immigrants not only for the hard labor that built the cities and the transportation network but even more to provide a wide range of commercial, technical, clerical, and professional skills. In Canada, for example, British immigration supplied a large pro-

32. Will Herberg, *Protestant-Catholic-Jew: An Essay in American Religious Sociology* (New York, 1955); Thomas T. McAvoy, ed., *Roman Catholicism and the American Way of Life* (Notre Dame, Ind., 1960). Cf. UNESCO, *Positive Contribution by Immigrants,* 140.

portion of skilled and clerical workers in the early twentieth century.[33] In Argentina European immigrants virtually created an energetic middle class in a nation that had been sharply divided between a creole aristocracy and apathetic mestizo masses. Seeking immigrants as the representatives of a higher civilization, the ruling elite intended them to "Europeanize" the native population, to produce, in Sarmiento's phrase, "a regeneration of the races."[34] The United States, on the other hand, already had its own vigorous middle class. What its more highly developed economy lacked was an industrial working class. The Second Immigration coincided with the industrialization of the United States and furnished the bulk of the manpower for it. Irish and French Canadians gave a tremendous impetus to the textile industry of New England. Germans, Jews, and Italians transformed the clothing industry of New York. A dozen nationalities collaborated in the blast furnaces and rolling mills of Pennsylvania and the meat-packing houses of the Middle West.

To make adequate use of the enormous supply of illiterate European peasants who became available around the end of the nineteenth century, it was necessary to simplify and routinize factory work. Accordingly, a dependence on unskilled immigrant labor encouraged the introduction of automatic machines and processes. In bituminous coal mining, machines which largely replaced the pick miner increased the proportion of unskilled labor. In cotton factories automatic looms that an inexperienced immigrant could operate did the work formerly requiring skilled weavers. Only in America did the immigrants constitute a mass proletariat engaged in manufacturing; and because they did, America was able to develop to the full a system of mass production.[35]

33. Lloyd G. Reynolds, *The British Immigrant: His Social and Economic Adjustment in Canada* (Toronto, 1935), 99–102.

34. Scobie, *Argentina*, 151–52, 172–179; Gino Germani, "Mass Immigration and Modernization in Argentina," *Latin American Radicalism: A Documentary Report on Left and Nationalist Movements*, ed. Irving Louis Horowitz et al. (New York, 1969), 315. See also F. B. Pike, "Hispanismo and the Non-Revolutionary Immigrant in Spanish America, 1900–1930," *Inter-American Economic Affairs*, XXV (1971), 3–30.

35. Brinley Thomas, *Migration and Economic Growth: A Study of Great Britain and the Atlantic Economy* (2nd ed., Cambridge, 1973), 165–72. See also the comments by Thomas and Oscar Handlin in UNESCO, *Positive Contribution*, 170–71, 191.

Adjustment to the standardized, mechanized life of the industrial city was a stressful, often lacerating experience, whatever resources a person brought to it. Particularly for those who started at the bottom of the ladder in an incomprehensible, alien society, the ordeal could be harrowing. In some respects, however, the immigrants were relatively well prepared to meet the challenge. The older Americans cherished ideals of individualism that were ill suited to the interdependent character of the new urban world. They were slow to respond to collective needs, slow to reach out for mutual support beyond the immediate family. The foreigners, remembering the intimate villages they had left, probably liked the big impersonal cities of America no better than most native Americans did. But the immigrant cultures were far less individualistic. In seeking means of self-protection—in striving to make their homes and jobs decent and secure—the immigrants had no inhibitions about resorting to collective action.

One means at hand was the trade union. First- and second-generation immigrants in the late nineteenth and early twentieth centuries dominated the labor movement, the most prominent leaders of which were Irish, German, and Jewish.[36] When fully mobilized, the immigrants could throw themselves into a strike with the selfless passion of a communal uprising. But most of the unions belonged to skilled workers from northern Europe, who held aloof from the southern and eastern European masses and took pride in the exclusiveness of their craft. Throughout industrial America intricate ethnic divisions dissipated class consciousness. The immigrants tended to identify not with a downtrodden class but with exemplars of success among their own people.[37]

36. Gerald N. Grob, *Workers and Utopia* (Evanston, Ill., 1962), 144–46; Moses Rischin, "The Jewish Labor Movement in America: A Social Interpretation," *Labor History*, IV (1963), 227–47. See also William Z. Ripley, "Race Factors in Labor Unions," *Atlantic Monthly*, XCIII (1904), 301–4.

37. David Brody, *Labor in Crisis: The Steel Strike of 1919* (New York, 1965); Victor R. Greene, *The Slavic Community on Strike: Immigrant Labor in Pennsylvania Anthracite* (Notre Dame, Ind., 1968); Clyde Griffen, "Workers Divided: The Effect of Craft and Ethnic Differences in Poughkeepsie, New York, 1850–1880," *Nineteenth-Century Cities: Essays in the New Urban History*, ed. Stephan Thernstrom and Richard Sennett (New Haven, 1969), 49–97.

For most immigrants, therefore, the trade union offered a less accessible or responsive channel for collective action than the political party.

In the cities immigrant politics was machine politics: a politics of loyalty, authority, reciprocal obligation, and personal service. Although the machine served self-interest, it worked through disciplined group effort and unquestioning obedience. Its style of operation, therefore, was antithetical to American individualism. Without the Second Immigration, the machine could hardly have become so distinctive and notable an American institution. And when its traditional ministrations could no longer cope with the immense needs of the urban masses—when the psychological "recognition" it gave and the favors and jobs it dispensed no longer appeased them—the political machines gradually adapted to the immigrants' requirements. Detroit's independent reform mayor, Hazen Pingree, showed in the 1890's how an aroused immigrant working class could be rallied to support a program of cheap transit fares and equalized taxes even against the opposition of the old-style bosses.[38] After 1910 the Democratic machines in major cities came increasingly under the control of politicians like Alfred E. Smith of New York, who recognized the value of welfare legislation to their organizations as well as their constituents. Through a new politics of welfare the Democratic party won the allegiance of more and more of the urban ethnic groups. In the process it broke the Republicans' grip on the industrial states and became after 1930 America's majority party.[39]

While coming to terms with the city in these ways, the immigrants were also forging an urban mass culture to replace the traditions they could not transplant intact. It is hardly surprising that heterogeneous people, cut adrift from their past and caught

38. Melvin G. Holli, *Reform in Detroit: Hazen S. Pingree and Urban Politics* (New York, 1969). For an excellent portrait of a traditional boss see Joel Arthur Tarr, *A Study in Boss Politics: William Lorimer of Chicago* (Urbana, Ill., 1971).

39. John D. Buenker, *Urban Liberalism and Progressive Reform* (New York, 1973); J. Joseph Huthmacher, *Senator Robert F. Wagner and the Rise of Urban Liberalism* (New York, 1968); John W. Allswang, *A House for All Peoples: Ethnic Politics in Chicago, 1890–1936* (Lexington, Ky., 1971).

up in the machine process, should have found the substance of a common life in the stimuli of the mass media. Beginning as early as 1835, when the Scottish-born journalist James Gordon Bennett started the raucous New York *Herald,* immigrants have pioneered in the production of mass culture. Hungarian-born Joseph Pulitzer modernized the sensationalism that Bennett began. Pulitzer's New York *World,* with its special appeal to immigrant readers, showed how a newspaper could speak for, as well as to, the urban masses. Meanwhile a transplanted Irishman, Robert Bonner, developed the promotional techniques that created in the late 1850's the first mass-circulation weekly, the New York *Ledger.*[40] Of the four outstanding editors at the turn of the century who expanded the magazine audience still further, two were foreign-born—S. S. McClure and Edward Bok. The prominence of immigrant editors in the creation of mass-circulation newspapers and magazines suggests that the need to adjust to a cosmopolitan society and an unfamiliar culture nurtured a burning passion to communicate and an instinctive feeling for what is immediately transmissible to an amorphous public. Americans became a nation of newspaper readers because what they shared was not a common past but rather the immediate events of the present: the "news."

Other immigrants and their children have thronged the popular stage, the music shops of Tin Pan Alley, the film studios of Hollywood. Spyros Skouras created a theatrical empire. Edward L. Bernays professionalized the field of public relations. The early history of radio broadcasting is in large measure a story of struggle between David Sarnoff's R.C.A. and William Paley's C.B.S.—one of them a first-generation Jewish immigrant, the other a second. A remarkable number of Hollywood moguls and popular comedians in the period between the two world wars were sons and daughters of Jewish immigrants.[41] Through their

40. Lambert A. Wilmer, *Our Press Gang: A Complete Exposition of the Corruption and Crimes of theAmerican Newspapers* (Philadelphia, 1859), 61, 79; Mary Noel, *Villains Galore: The Heyday of the Popular Story Weekly* (New York, 1954), 56-96.
41. Allen Churchill, *The Great White Way* (New York, 1962); Harold Clurman's review of John Lahr, "Notes on a Cowardly Lion," in the *New York Times Book Review,* November 23, 1969, p. 1; Earl Rovit, "Jewish

experience of displacement and assimilation, many second-generation immigrants gained a special capability for the arts of the
theatre: for playing a role, for transforming the self, for projecting an instant identity, and for achieving these effects in a milieu
of illusion and surprise.

There is, for example, a world of significance in the fact that
few entertainers in the early twentieth century rivaled the
dazzling fame of an immigrant specializing in the art of escape.
Harry Houdini, America's foremost magician, billed himself
"The World-Famous Self-Liberator." What captivated audiences
was Houdini's symbolic re-enactment of his (and their) crucial
experience—a very urban, very American liberation from old
traditions and confining circumstances. Escape was the recurrent
pattern of Houdini's formative years. His father fled Hungary to
escape arrest. At twelve the son ran away from home to escape
the crushing poverty of a family dependent on an unsuccessful
rabbi who never learned to speak English. At eighteen he eloped
with a Catholic girl whose parents would not accept him. As a
young magician he began to specialize in escapes because of the
enthusiasm of audiences for a stunt he called "Metamorphosis," in
which two people exchange positions across a seemingly impene-
trable barrier. Thereafter he acted out, more and more strenuously, the promethean fantasy of individual triumph over every
external constraint. He escaped from all handcuffs and straight
jackets; from iron collars, padlocked water tanks, safes, and
Chinese torture devices; from jail cells, the bottom of rivers, and
buried coffins.[42] Houdini's career, like the careers of many
makers of modern American mass culture, suggests how immigrants driven by the tremendous pressures for assimilation in the
late nineteenth and early twentieth centuries added a searing
intensity to the old American myth of freedom and mobility.

Humor and American Life," *American Scholar*, XXXVI (1967), 237–45;
Nathan Glazer, "The Immigrant Groups and American Culture," *Yale Review*, XLVIII (1959), 382–97; and Edward L. Bernays's perceptive comment
on his own early experience in *Biography of an Idea* (New York, 1965),
20–21.

42. Milbourne Christopher, *Houdini: The Untold Story* (New York,
1969).

So we come finally to a paradox in assessing the impact of immigration. Clearly, it has enhanced the variety of American culture. Its diversifying influence is imprinted in the American ideal of nationality, in the American religious pattern, and in the sheer presence of so many different human types. On the other hand, the diversities have given way time and again to pressures for uniformity, which have come not just from older Americans but which immigrants and their children have also shaped and inspired. Through the systems of mass production and mass communications, America and its immigrants assimilated one another within an urban, technological culture that overrode distinctions of place, class, and ethnic type.

Yet the distinctions were never obliterated, the assimilation never wholly satisfying or complete. Today many Americans are rebuilding ethnic identities, and are discovering that America no longer looks as monolithic as it did a few years ago. Other societies have had a simpler experience with immigrant groups, either absorbing them or acquiescing in their separateness. In American life these contrary impulses mingle, their tensions unresolved, their implications still unfolding.

Chapter Two

The Politics of Immigration Restriction

An almost unremitting effort to fix a satisfactory immigration policy runs through the second half of American national history. From the 1870's to the 1980's Congress has wrestled with the difficulties of regulating migration from other lands. A vast, chaotic, tremendously intricate mass of legislation accumulated. Although never the primary issue in national politics, immigration restriction sometimes aroused the concern of millions and the passions of substantial minorities. At other times interest declined almost to a vanishing point. Yet only for brief interludes was there any general belief that the problem had been settled. Wrangling, confusion, and a welter of special pressures crowd the legislative record. One finds little long-range, intelligent planning.

Why so much confusion and uncertainty? Why so untidy and labyrinthine a mass of legislation? One reason, surely, is the intrinsic complexity of immigration as a social issue. Immigration has touched all aspects of American civilization. Its impact is mostly indirect, often contradictory, and always difficult to measure. It has therefore called forth a veritable cacophony of criticism and acclaim. In addition, the immense variety in the sources of American immigration has given it a special complexity. A phenomenon that includes sudden inrushes of political refugees, an ebb and flow of migratory labor across various frontiers, continual fluctuations in the political strength of thirty or forty different voting blocs, and great differences in the economic capabilities and cultural predispositions of a still larger number of ethnic groups scarcely lends itself to simple rules or tidy management.

Certain features of American democracy have further complicated the search for a viable immigration policy. Americans generally have been unwilling to entrust much discretion to bureaucrats. In regulating immigration Britain and the Commonwealth countries have relied less on legislative prescription and more on administrative flexibility. Within certain broad terms laid down by Parliament, government authorities in Canada and Australia have enjoyed wide discretion to alter totals and quotas from day to day. The United States, a less deferential society, has been unwilling to allow officials shielded from the glare of publicity to make policy circumspectly. Congress, working in a turbulent milieu of competing pressures, has had to spell out rules and exceptions in detail. It has spawned a vast tangle of legislation which very few Congressmen have understood and which has repeatedly needed codification. Even so, the U.S. Immigration and Naturalization Service is continually besieged by clamorous individuals and groups who want to get people in or keep them out. In self-defense, it has elaborated its own rigid procedures, which in turn intensify demands for corrective legislation.

While exposing every aspect of immigration policy to sharp public controversy, the American style of democracy put a premium on values that made such controversies hard to resolve. The United States had been founded upon the belief that freedom is not just a national patrimony but a universal truth which Americans hold in trust for the rest of the world. Immigration restriction did not square easily with the belief that this is a land of opportunity for all, the conviction that American freedom has a universal relevance. Any restrictive policy, moreover, inevitably entails discriminations; and a system of discrimination that does not offend the democratic conscience has proved as yet unattainable. On the other hand, the growth of the world's population and its increased mobility made regulatory action unavoidable. In the modern world free migration would result in excessive population displacement toward countries with high wages or political stability. In this situation the restrictionists claimed to be the hard-boiled realists, though their "realism" was seldom free of prejudice and hysteria. Antirestrictionists tended to gloss over the dilemmas that immigration posed. Reluctant to admit that a problem existed, they flung the ancient ideals in their opponents' faces. For many decades neither side could bring our traditional principles into a creative relation with the facts of the modern world.

During the first century of United States history, ideals and circumstances reinforced one another. When a nation of immigrants shook off British rule, the very heterogeneity of the American people supplied their claim to a distinctive national character. "Europe, and not England, is the parent country of America," wrote Tom Paine in 1776,[1] and generations of patriotic orators after him declaimed the glory of a people who owed their greatness to diverse and multitudinous origins. This conception of Americans as a universal nationality carried two corollaries. One proposed for the United States the mission of providing an asylum, wherein the blessings of liberty would await all men. The other corollary, first enunciated by Jefferson, insisted on "the natural right which all men have of relinquishing the country in which birth or other accident may have thrown them, and seeking subsistence and happiness wheresoever they may be able, or may hope to find them."[2] In denying the old doctrine of perpetual allegiance, in affirming a mission to humanity, and in celebrating a diversity of origins, the Americans testified to the cosmopolitan principles of the Enlightenment on which their nation was founded. In actuality Americans were far less cosmopolitan than the glib phrases of the Enlightenment suggested. They assumed the unchallengeable predominance of a

1. Howard Fast, ed., *The Selected Work of Tom Paine and Citizen Tom Paine* (New York, 1943), 20. Throughout this chapter I have drawn on the fuller account of European immigration and its restriction contained in my book *Strangers in the Land: Patterns of American Nativism 1860–1925* (New Brunswick, 1955).

2. I-Mien Tsiang, *The Question of Expatriation in America Prior to 1907* (Baltimore, 1942), 26.

white Protestant northern European culture—the culture that had produced those ideals.

For a long time the favorable circumstances of the new nation obscured the disparity between ideology and culture. An under-populated country, confronting immeasurable natural resources and energized by the Protestant ethic, hungered for all the man-power it could get. Farmers pushing westward needed immi-grants to take over their half-cleared acres. Merchants needed immigrants to man their ships, to provide return cargoes for crops sent to Europe, to dig the canals, and to lay the railroad tracks. Mining enterprises and factory masters needed immigrants for the hard, dirty labor that native workmen scorned. Whole territories needed immigrants to qualify for statehood.

Periodically, the hectic pace of economic and geographical expansion broke down in severe depressions, but even as late as the Panic of 1873 these economic collapses did not seriously threaten the immigrants' general reception. Behind the continu-ing confidence in their economic desirability was an almost universal assurance of the resilience and homogeneity of Ameri-can society. In other words, an implicit faith in assimilation prevailed. All immigrant groups, despite their different back-grounds and (in some cases) their persistent separateness, were expected in due course to fuse with the older population auto-matically.

Several conditions sustained the American confidence in an effortless process of ethnic integration. Above all, the country did not suffer from deep class cleavages which immigration might aggravate. The American social structure combined an underly-ing cohesion with a remarkable degree of individual mobility. As native Americans climbed upward in a fluid society that did not sharply distinguish employer from employee, immigrants occu-pied the stations that others were vacating and then followed in their wake. Even the Protestant-Catholic division of the mid-nineteenth century, which created the Know-Nothing party and aroused demands for checking the political power of the immi-grants, did not upset confidence in their social assimilation. The process might take a while, but that was all right too. The Ameri-can people did not really demand a high level of national solidarity; they had enough already for their individualistic purposes. Moreover, this loose-knit, flexible society seemed quite safe from external dangers. After 1815, isolation was a fact more than a theory; and a deep sense of military security permitted the United States to work out its own group relations in a relaxed and tolerant way.

Although tariffs established some control over the importation of goods, in the field of immigration the federal government abided by the prevailing spirit of laissez faire. Before the 1880's immigration was neither hindered nor promoted by national action, except in two cases. Early in the nineteenth century the coerced immigration represented by the African slave trade was prohibited. Then for a short time, from 1864 to 1868, Congress tried to stimulate immigration by a statute authorizing employers to pay the passage and bind the services of prospective migrants.[3] Otherwise, the only federal enactments called for an official count of the number of entrants and decreed certain minimum living conditions aboard ship.

Individual states, however, did try to exercise some influence over immigration. Their intervention took two forms. Western and southern states in the mid-nineteenth century developed programs to lure new settlers from overseas. By the early 1870's, when this competition was at its height, a large majority of states employed promotional agents or offered other inducements. On the other hand, the seaboard states of the Northeast sought to protect themselves from the heaviest burdens of immigration. Their goals were modest, and their administration lax. Aiming only to provide an orderly reception, to help those in temporary difficulty, and to discourage the entry of the permanently incapacitated, the states of entry set up boards of immigration commissioners. Their members were charity leaders who served without pay. New York, whose experience provided the basis for later federal administration, established a central immigrant depot at the foot of Manhattan, maintained an immigrant welfare fund by collecting small fees from shipowners, and required the post-

3. Charlotte Erickson, *American Industry and the European Immigrant, 1860–1885* (Cambridge, Mass., 1957).

ing of a bond for any immigrant who seemed likely to become a permanent charity case.[4]

II

A change in public temper and policy began in the 1870's, but at the time the change seemed to apply only to one small and remote immigrant group. In California, the state with the most heterogeneous population in the Union, a movement directed solely against the Chinese rose to a pitch of violence unsurpassed in American immigration controversies. The Chinese had appeared during the Gold Rush, and from 1860 to 1880 they comprised about 9 per cent of the state's population.[5] White workers assailed their presence and drove them from the mines in the early 1850's.[6] The inflow slackened in the mid-sixties but increased markedly in the seventies. At the same time the completion of the Union Pacific Railroad (1869) marked the emergence of both great corporate wealth and a large floating labor supply. Mass demonstrations and mob attacks on the Chinese accompanied the growth of an agitation against the railroad and land monopolies that found the Chinese useful. European-born workers took the lead in the anti-Chinese movement.[7] When a general depression descended in the mid-seventies, an Irish demagogue, Denis Kearney, sparked the statewide triumph of a new Workingmen's party pledged to humble the rich and get rid of the Chinese.

4. Richard H. Leach, "The Impact of Immigration upon New York, 1840–60," *New York History*, XXXI (1950), 15–30; Charles P. Howland, ed., *Survey of American Foreign Relations, 1929* (New Haven, 1929), 427–30. There is a valuable chapter on regulations on both sides of the Atlantic in Philip Taylor, *The Distant Magnet: European Emigration to the U.S.A.* (London, 1971), 107–30.

5. *United States Census, 1890*, Vol. I: *Population*, 2, 401. The standard study is Mary Roberts Coolidge, *Chinese Immigration* (New York, 1909).

6. Rodman Paul, "The Origin of the Chinese Issue in California," *Mississippi Valley Historical Review*, XXV (1938), 181–96.

7. See, e.g., San Francisco *Argonaut*, January 9, 1886, p. 2; Joint Special Committee to Investigate Chinese Immigration, *Report* (S. Rep. No. 689, 44th Cong., 2d Sess., 1877), 56.

Sinophobia had far more than an economic appeal. Politicians of both major parties, newspapers, and most of the respectable middle-class public throughout the Far West soon succumbed to the hysteria because the Chinese aroused such deep cultural and racial antipathies among Americans of European descent. The Chinese did not come to the United States as free men. Transported and largely controlled by certain Chinese societies, they awakened fears of a new kind of slavery in a nation already convulsed by the struggle over African slavery; and the conviction that the Chinese could not become independent citizens was fed by images of Oriental despotism and depravity, commonly held throughout the United States before they arrived. Then too the wide gap between cultures was quickly infused with racial significance. The primitive race feelings ingrained in white America in the course of mastering blacks and Indians readily extended under these circumstances to the Chinese. A California statute of 1849, prohibiting blacks or Indians from testifying in the trial of a white man, was construed by the state supreme court only five years later to bar the testimony of Chinese as well. At one stroke they lost the protection of California law.[8]

Transatlantic migration had not put to any very severe test the cosmopolitan ideals of American nationality. Until the Chinese appeared in some numbers, immigration had brought the United States only people of northern European background. The Chinese—isolated, unfathomable, tightly organized—bore the stigma of color. As soon as their presence caused discomfort, no elaborate rationale was necessary to rouse against them the imperatives of white supremacy.

While a toll of riots and community expulsions mounted through the 1880's,[9] Democratic and Republican leaders in Washington vied with each other to appease the California electorate. The principal stumbling block was the Burlingame

8. Stuart Creighton Miller, *The Unwelcome Immigrant: The American Image of the Chinese, 1785–1882* (Berkeley, 1969); Gunther Barth, *Bitter Strength: A History of the Chinese in the United States, 1850–1870* (Cambridge, Mass., 1964); Alexander Saxton, *The Indispensable Enemy: Labor and the Anti-Chinese Movement in California* (Berkeley, 1971).

9. Jules A. Karlin, "The Anti-Chinese Outbreaks in Seattle, 1885–1886," *Pacific Northwest Quarterly*, XXXIX (1948), 103–30.

Treaty of 1868,[10] which pledged to China the right of unrestricted immigration and secured commercial privileges for the United States. The treaty permitted passage in 1875 of a law forbidding the importation of Chinese contract labor, but four years later a sense of honor impelled President Rutherford B. Hayes to veto a devious bill that would have negated the treaty. He tried, instead, to renegotiate it. Thereupon, a new treaty, applying only to Chinese laborers, permitted the United States to "regulate, limit, or suspend" their coming but "not absolutely prohibit it." The result was the act of 1882, "suspending" the entry of Chinese labor for ten years. Harsher laws, draconically administered, soon went well beyond treaty limits. A statute prohibiting the return of Chinese residents who happened to be out of the country preluded the election of 1888; and in 1892, the Geary law not only continued suspension for ten years more, but also required every Chinese in the United States to prove through white men's testimony his legal right to be here. At the turn of the century, suspension became permanent exclusion. Even Chinese immigration from our own island possessions, Hawaii and the Philippines, was prohibited. By then, the Chinese-American population was declining, and the problem seemed comfortably solved.[11]

Throughout, the Chinese issue was treated as quite separate and distinct from the question of European immigration. However, the social-economic situation that triggered the anti-Chinese movement in the seventies persisted, with widening implications. What troubled the Californians, apart from race and culture, was the onset of social stratification—the danger, as one of them put it, of the rise of a "caste system of lords and serfs."[12] The boasted fluidity of a frontier culture was giving way to an industrial system that separated workers from their boss and created

10. This treaty was drafted by Secretary of State William H. Seward, who had once joyfully predicted an influx of a million Asiatics a year into the trans-Mississippi West. See Henry Nash Smith, *Virgin Land* (1950), 166–67.

11. Howland, *Survey*, 494–500; Ellis Paxson Oberholtzer, *A History of the United States Since the Civil War* (New York, 1937), V, 57, 165–68, 323–25.

12. Elmer Clarence Sandmeyer, *The Anti-Chinese Movement in California* (Urbana, Ill., 1939), 32–33.

sharp class contrasts between rich and poor. In the 1880's the whole nation was beginning to worry about the same thing. The homogeneity and mobility that had long upheld the American faith in assimilation was threatened. As a result, a general movement to restrict immigration gathered strength through the eighties and early nineties, building to a climax in 1896.

In the flush times of the early eighties, immigration reached its highest point in the nineteenth century. Though the general reception was still enthusiastic, another point of view could now be heard. While conservatives clung to complacency, a growing company of reformers sounded alarms at the polarization of American society. Protestant advocates of a Social Gospel, a new generation of German-trained economists, and a host of municipal reformers charged immigration with increasing the rift of classes, complicating the slum problem, causing boss-rule, and straining the old moralities. These difficulties, like the immigrants themselves, centered in the recklessly expanding cities. But critics of land monopoly, such as Henry George, also argued that the supply of good vacant land in the West was giving out, thereby adding to the population pressure in the cities.[13] Realization was dawning that America's natural resources were limited. Thus, with the apparent passing of the frontier, a sense of "closed space" aggravated fears of a closed society. Many of the reformers who raised these issues were questioning the hallowed principles of laissez faire. Immigration restriction, therefore, appealed to them as a simple way of using the power of the state to deal with many interlocking social problems.

In 1882, when this criticism was just beginning, one special group of reformers prodded the federal government into establishing the first national controls over immigration. The directors of private welfare societies in eastern cities had long been concerned over the strain that immigration imposed on their own resources and their communities. A Protestant elite imbued with a spirit of civic responsibility, they ran the reception facilities in the port cities while lobbying for further state action to protect

13. Henry George, *Social Problems* (New York, 1886), 40–46, 161–62. See also Lee Benson, "The Historical Background of Turner's Frontier Essay," *Agricultural History,* XXV (1951), 72.

the urban poor. The charity leaders were aghast when the Supreme Court in 1875 struck down the existing regulations over immigration maintained by the seaboard states. State regulation, the Court held, infringes on Congress's exclusive power over foreign commerce. To escape the added burdens that now fell upon private philanthropy, welfare agencies begged the federal government to assume responsibility. For seven years unmoved, Congress finally passed the immigration law of 1882. This gave the Secretary of the Treasury executive authority over immigration but cautiously left the actual inspection of immigrants in the hands of the old state agencies. The United States was to accumulate an immigrant welfare fund by collecting fifty cents from each immigrant. Also, convicts, lunatics, idiots, and persons likely to become a public charge were denied admission. Thus, in building upon state precedents, the federal government took a limited, hesitant, but decisive step away from laissez faire.[14]

This preliminary action had hardly been taken when the depression of 1883–86 aroused a wider demand for regulating the incoming stream. Great strikes broke out, and—as if to demonstrate how deep the social chasm was becoming—the first mass movement of American workingmen, the Knights of Labor, spread through the industrial world. The Knights did not propose general restrictions on immigration as yet; they and the other labor unionists of the late nineteenth century were too close to their own immigrant past. But they resented fiercely the way that coal operators in Pennsylvania were bringing in carloads of foreigners to break strikes and hold down wages. In 1885, therefore, the Knights lobbied through Congress a contract labor law forbidding anyone to prepay the transportation of an immigrant to the United States in return for a promise of his services. Henceforth, every newcomer would have to convince immigration inspectors that he had no specific prospect of a job, yet was not likely to become a public charge.

While the unions attacked only a special kind of immigration, the labor upheaval frightened a large part of the urban middle class into a more general antiforeign reaction. Businessmen, seeing

14. All immigration legislation to 1907 is chronologically compiled in *Reports of the Immigration Commission*, XXXIX (Washington, D.C., 1911).

how prominently the immigrants figured in the new labor movement, concluded that the control of unrest depended on controlling immigration. Nonunionized workers and white-collar people began to suspect that the whole wave of industrial discontent was somehow foreign-inspired. A catastrophe in Chicago in 1886 catalyzed these fears. At a time when thousands of workers throughout the country were out on strike, a bomb exploded in the face of the police at a German anarchist meeting in Haymarket Square. An antiradical panic ensued, giving immigration restriction its first major impetus in public opinion.

The strife and tumult of the late nineteenth century came to a head in the 1890's in the midst of another, more severe depression. Now the restrictionist clamor, which had been confined largely to urban areas in the Northeast and Midwest during the eighties, spread into every part of the country. A new aggressive nationalism (itself a product of the social crisis) exacerbated the demand. Restriction became a defensive counterpart of the jingoist outbursts against England, Spain, and other countries during that troubled decade. Thus, the most serious outbreak of antiforeign violence in the nineties was a partly jingoist, partly nativist episode. In 1891, the leading citizens of New Orleans led a lynching party into the parish prison and systematically slaughtered eleven Italians who had just been found not guilty of a murder charge. When the Italian government reacted indignantly, there was feverish talk in the United States of a war with Italy. The incident proved second only to the Haymarket affair in stimulating restrictionist sentiment.

The emergence of Italians as an ethnic target calls attention to another aggravating factor in the 1890's. More and more of the people who crossed the Atlantic were coming from southern and eastern Europe. This "new immigration" seemed even more disturbing than the older immigrant groups. Italian, Slavic, and other peasants from beyond the Alps lived much closer to serfdom than did the folk of northwestern Europe; and the Jews from Russia and Rumania were seeing a world outside of the ghetto for the first time. By western European standards, the new immigrant masses were socially backward and bizarre in appearance. The "old immigration" still exceeded the new, and most restrictionist sentiment in the 1890's remained diffuse, reflecting a general concern over the whole foreign influx. In the urban and industrial areas, however, where the new groups piled up in squalid slums, they became vivid symbols of the problems of the time. Moreover, a number of eastern intellectuals began to argue that the southern and eastern Europeans were not only socially dangerous, but also racially unassimilable.

All in all, restrictionist pressure became so strong in the nineties that the real question is why it accomplished so little. Several circumstances seem to be involved. First, a good deal of the old confidence in assimilation persisted beneath the stormy surface of events. Free immigration and the ideals that validated it were cornerstones of American society; they could not be dislodged easily. Second, Republican votes proved insufficient to pass a truly restrictionist measure, and the Democratic party remained, at most, lukewarm toward the idea. Republican leaders offered restriction to American workingmen as a supplement to tariff protection. The Democrats, on the other hand, had a laissez-faire tradition. Moreover, they got much of their support from groups that were either intensely opposed to restriction or undecided. In the Northeast, the Democrats had always depended primarily on the votes of immigrant minorities. The other great source of Democratic strength, the South, hankered for a larger white population and had not yet quite made up its mind about the immigrants. Even at the climax of the restrictionist fever in 1896, more Congressmen from the South voted against restriction than from all other sections combined.[15] Finally, the restrictionists were severely handicapped by their own confusion. They disliked so many immigrants for such a variety of reasons that they had difficulty in agreeing on a plan of action.

Congress did pass one important law, but the act of 1891 did not attempt to reduce the number of immigrants in any way. Instead, it greatly strengthened the loose controls established in the preceding decade. The law of 1882 had left a conflicting division of authority between the states and the federal government. Now the whole job of inspection and regulation was vested in federal officials. Also, the act added further excluded cate-

15. *Congressional Record*, 54 Cong., 2d Sess. (1897), 2946–47.

gories to those of 1882 and 1885. Polygamists (i.e., unrepentant Mormons) and "persons suffering from a loathsome or dangerous contagious disease" were declared inadmissible; and the contract labor law was broadened to prohibit employers from advertising for help abroad and to exclude immigrants encouraged by such solicitations. Finally, the act prescribed practical means of enforcing existing regulations. It compelled steamship companies to carry back to Europe all passengers rejected by the United States inspectors, and it made the first effective provision for deporting aliens already in the United States. Aliens who entered illegally or became public charges might be deported within one year of entry. This statute provided a framework for administration for many years.

Yet, it left the central issue of quantity untouched, and here the proposals were various. Some wanted a temporary suspension of all immigration. Some proposed a stiff head tax of twenty dollars or more on each arrival. One of the most popular schemes would require a certificate from an American consul overseas attesting to the good character of each emigrant from his area. A consular inspection bill passed the House of Representatives in 1894 but ran into opposition in the Democratic Senate.

Ultimately, restrictionists rallied around a plan to exclude all male adults unable to read and write their own language. The literacy-test idea originated among the northeastern intellectuals who were particularly concerned about the new immigration. They argued that such a test would cut in half the influx from southern and eastern Europe, without seriously interfering with the older immigration from the more literate areas of Europe. Yet the intended ethnic discrimination would be accomplished by applying to every individual a single standard that reflected the premium American culture put upon education.

The ascendancy of the literacy test over other restrictive proposals was due to the pertinacity of Henry Cabot Lodge, its first and most influential congressional advocate, and to the supporting propaganda of the Immigration Restriction League. Organized by a group of Boston bluebloods in 1894, the League launched a whirlwind campaign to alert the country to the social and economic dangers of the new immigration. Since the congressional elections of 1894 installed Republican majorities in both Houses, the hour of victory seemed at hand. A literacy bill sponsored by the League passed Congress in the winter of 1896–97 by topheavy margins. As one of his last acts, President Grover Cleveland vetoed the bill.

His successor, William McKinley, was ready to sign; and the bill would undoubtedly have been reenacted speedily if the *fin-de-siècle* spirit of crisis and depression had not begun to dissipate as soon as the new administration took office. The first sign of a change had come already with McKinley's victory in 1896, which brought vast relief in conservative quarters and, incidentally, demonstrated that many of the immigrants supported the status quo. Then a dazzling resurgence of prosperity inaugurated a long period of good times and quieted the fierce industrial unrest of the preceding years. Even the jingoist impulse purged itself in the Spanish-American War. America seemed once again a land of opportunity for all. Consequently, some of the old confidence in assimilation came flooding back along with the whole revival of confidence in American society. Once again patriotic spokesmen boasted of the cosmopolitan makeup of the national character. Despite a phenomenal increase in the new immigration at this very time, restriction ceased to be a political possibility.

While politicians became apathetic toward restriction, two groups especially fell away from the movement. Businessmen now waxed enthusiastic about the enriching influx. A great expansion and simplification of factory processes increased the need for unskilled immigrant labor, and industrial leaders acquired a new assurance in their own ability to keep the foreign worker tractable and unorganized. Henceforth, organizations like the Chamber of Commerce and the National Association of Manufacturers lobbied vigorously against restriction. Meanwhile, urban reformers began to see the immigrant less as a cause and more as a victim of social evils. Although this shift in the reform outlook was far from complete, the general temper of early-twentieth-century progressives disposed them to concentrate on environmental conditions.

It should also be said, however, that most middle-class progressives had little in common with the conservative, boss-ridden, immigrant masses. The progressive spirit tended to weaken the late-nineteenth-century connection between restriction and reform but did not generate an adequate, countervailing philosophy of ethnic democracy. Consequently, the revival of a tolerant attitude toward immigration in the early twentieth century delayed the coming of restriction without revising its purpose and direction. The opportunity to think out a policy that might be both realistic and democratic was lost; and when antiforeign agitation again picked up, restrictionists simply carried on from the point at which they had paused.

III

The early-twentieth-century lull could not, in the nature of things, last for very long. The anguish and unrest of the preceding years might be temporarily relieved, but the social and economic problems then thrust forward were certainly far from solved. The age of Theodore Roosevelt and Woodrow Wilson made a modest start at solving them; but henceforth confidence in the future of American society would have to rest increasingly on the use of organized intelligence to preserve and fulfill what fortune initially provided. The eighteenth- and early-nineteenth-century faith that the American people could trust the laws of nature to operate automatically in their behalf would inevitably diminish in a complex industrial society. And with the extension of centralized direction over the national life, immigration would surely come under purposeful control.

Then too, the restriction issue could hardly remain quiescent indefinitely in view of the size and character of the transatlantic migration. The biggest inrush in American history was gathering force year by year. In the decade from 1905 to 1914 an average of more than a million people annually crowded past the immigration inspectors. After 1896 the great majority derived from southern and eastern Europe. Thereafter, the outflow from the more highly developed countries of northwestern Europe declined as the movement from distant lands increased. More and more remote cultures were drawn into the current; the first considerable number of Russian peasants, Greeks, Syrians, and Armenians appeared in the twentieth century. The bulk of southern and eastern European immigrants settled in the industrial area east of the Mississippi and north of the Ohio and Potomac rivers, where they were heavily concentrated in the mining and manufacturing centers. But a good many of them also spread throughout the Far West, and even the South had some 200,000 by 1910.[16] Whereas nativists in the nineties had very generally disliked the foreigner as such, the "new immigration" now stood out sharply as the heart of the problem. All of the regressive and antisocial qualities once imputed to the immigrants in general could now be fixed upon this more specific category. In fact, the major theoretical effort of restrictionists in the twentieth century consisted precisely in this: the transformation of relative cultural differences into an absolute line of cleavage, which would redeem the northwestern Europeans from the charges once leveled at them and explain the present danger of immigration in terms of the change in its sources.

The proponents of a literacy test had begun the elaboration of this distinction in the 1890's. No one, of course, either restrictionist or antirestrictionist, confessed that the special dislike of the new immigration arose basically from a human preference for homogeneity, which the unfamiliar customs and low standard of living of the new groups offended. Such an admission would have embarrassed the antirestrictionists, who needed to play down cultural differences, but it would also have discredited the restrictionists' posture of high-minded objectivity. Antirestrictionists concentrated on the economic need for foreign labor and on America's moral commitment to humanity.[17] Their opponents replied that such traditional considerations were out of date in the wholly new situation created by a new type of immigrant.

Accordingly, the most astute restrictionists applied themselves energetically to proving that the new nationalities endangered America as their predecessors had not. The earliest attacks

---

16. *United States Census, 1910, Abstract,* 197.

17. Thomas Wentworth Higginson, *Book and Heart* (New York, 1897), 163–64; Charles Parkhurst, "Value of Immigration," *Methodist Review,* LXXIII (1891), 709.

stressed a social and economic peril. Pennsylvania coal miners denounced the Italian, Hungarian, and Polish labor arriving among them as a degraded, servile class whose presence frustrated efforts to improve wages and conditions. Economists and a growing number of labor leaders generalized the argument into a plea for saving "the American standard of living."[18] The economic case was systematized by the United States Immigration Commission of 1907–11, whose forty-two-volume report comprised the most massive investigation of immigration ever made. The Commission worked out, in vast detail, an unfavorable contrast between the northwestern and southeastern Europeans in the United States *at that time*. The latter were more highly concentrated in cities and in unskilled jobs and were more inclined to return to Europe. These figures obscured significant differences between particular nationalities and did not take account of a marked improvement in the social-economic caliber of northwestern European immigration since the time when it had led the way.[19] Other critics, beginning with the Immigration Restriction League, produced even more misleading figures, correlating the new immigration with the growth of slums and with a high incidence of crime, disease, and insanity.[20]

A second line of argument concerned a racial menace. Here, the case against the new nationalities was harder to build. In popular parlance, race meant color. Since no very clear-cut difference of complexion was apparent between native Americans and any European group, the old instincts of white supremacy did not extend to the new immigration as easily as they did to the Chinese. To a large extent, race lines would have to be manufactured. Their construction was a gradual process, long impeded by the democratic tradition. Ultimately, however, the racial attack on the new immigration emerged as a powerful ideological weapon of the restriction movement.

18. Richmond Mayo-Smith, *Emigration and Immigration: A Study in Social Science* (New York, 1890); U.S. Industrial Commission, *Report on Immigration*, XV (1901).

19. Brinley Thomas, *Migration and Economic Growth: A Study of Great Britain and the Atlantic Economy* (Cambridge, Eng., 1973), 153–54.

20. *Publications of the Immigration Restriction League* (1895–97).

For a starting point, restrictionist intellectuals had a romantic, traditionalist concept of race that was different from the popular spirit of white supremacy. Throughout the nineteenth century patrician writers often acclaimed the American people as the finest branch of the Anglo-Saxon race. The Anglo-Saxon myth was somewhat inconsistent with the cosmopolitan ideal of nationality; but originally no race feelings (in the sense of biological taboos) were involved. In the Anglo-Saxon sense "race" meant essentially the persistence of national character; it expressed a cultural nationalism. In time, however, Anglo-Saxonism expanded and sharpened. It became permeated with race feelings. Increasingly, Anglo-Saxon culture seemed to depend on the persistence of a physical type. Nationalism was naturalized; and "race" in every sense came to imply a biological determinism.

Darwinism was a preliminary influence in the confusion of natural history with national history. By suggesting that a biological struggle underlies all of life, Darwinism encouraged Anglo-Saxon theorists to think of nations as species engaged in a desperate battle for survival. Toward the end of the nineteenth century, a number of patrician intellectuals turned the Anglo-Saxon tradition into a defensive attack on immigrants and an aggressive doctrine in foreign policy. They summoned Anglo-Saxon America to protect herself at home and to demonstrate her mastery abroad. Consequently, the victory of imperialism in 1898 gave racial nationalism an unprecedented vogue. Ideas that had been the property of an intellectual elite permeated public opinion.

Yet, race thinking still did not satisfactorily define the danger of the new immigration. Why would they or their children not respond favorably to the American environment? Indeed, what were the racial differences between southeastern Europeans and old-stock Americans? Darwinism was little help in answering these questions. Answers came only in the early twentieth century through new scientific and pseudoscientific ideas imported from Europe. The dazzling development of modern genetics around 1900 revealed principles of heredity that seemed entirely independent of environmental influences. Genetics inspired many scientists, led by Sir Francis Galton in England and Charles B.

Davenport in the United States, to hope for the improvement of society by preventing the inheritance of bad traits. Under the banner of "eugenics," these biological reformers gave a presumably scientific validation to immigration restriction; for how could a nation protect and improve its genes without keeping out "degenerate breeding stock"?

Simultaneously, a new school of anthropology was reeducating Anglo-Saxon nationalists on the racial composition of European man. William Z. Ripley's *The Races of Europe* (1899) conveyed to American readers a tripartite classification of white men recently developed by European scholars. The new race lines conformed not to national groups, but to physical types: the Nordics of northern Europe, the Alpines of central Europe, and the Mediterraneans of southern Europe. The latter two corresponded roughly to the new immigration. A number of writers combined the new anthropology with eugenics to produce a racist philosophy of history. Probably the most influential of these was Madison Grant, whose pretentious tract, *The Passing of the Great Race* (1916), delivered a solemn warning that the Nordics were making their last stand against the inferior races pouring in from southern and eastern Europe.

These ideas did not develop autonomously. Their importance was chiefly in giving clarity, definition, and some intellectual substance to fears and anxieties that were much more broadly based. The new racism seems to have reflected a wider tendency to make racial categories ever more rigid and impermeable; for this was also the period when lynchings and other measures to degrade and isolate southern Negroes reached an all-time high. Moreover, allegations of a racial peril in the new immigration rationalized an underlying concern about cultural homogeneity. At the deepest level, what impelled the restriction movement in the early decades of the twentieth century was the discovery that immigration was undermining the unity of American culture and threatening the accustomed dominance of a white Protestant people of northern European descent. The science of the day, together with America's traditional susceptibility to race feelings, made the language of race an impelling vehicle for thinking and talking about culture.

The mounting sense of danger—even dispossession—among millions of native-born white Protestants in the period 1910–30 is not hard to understand. A people whose roots were in the towns and farms of the early republic saw great cities coming more and more under the control of strangers whose speech and values were not their own. A people who unconsciously identified Protestantism with Americanism saw Catholic voters and urban bosses gaining control of the industrialized states. A people whose religion was already badly damaged by modern ideas saw the compensating rigors of their life-style flouted in the saloons and cabarets of a more expressive, hedonistic society. In reaction, the older America mounted a cultural counteroffensive through the prohibition movement, immigration restriction, and a sharpened racism.[21]

At first the counteroffensive made headway slowly. Statewide prohibition took hold in the South after 1907 but spread widely in the Midwest only after 1912. In Congress an effort to pass the literacy test failed in 1906. No further attempt was made until six years later. Not until 1914 did the restriction movement regain the momentum it had in the mid-nineties. The main reason for this slow recovery was the generally optimistic spirit of the first years of the twentieth century—an optimism reflected in the progressives' absorption with internal reform and the industrialists' unconcern with foreign radicalism. Another constraint was imposed by the ballots of the new immigrants. By the early twentieth century their voting strength in northeastern industrial areas was attracting Republican as well as Democratic politicians. Republicans could sometimes offset Democratic strength in the big cities by appealing to Jews, Slavs, Italians, and French Canadians who fell out with the Irish. Consequently, the G.O.P. could not afford to identify itself with restriction as openly as it had in the nineties. The immigrants made use of their growing influence whenever restriction bills came up. No legislative issue was closer to their hearts, and congressional committees had to face troops of immigrant representatives whenever hearings opened. Jews

---

21. John D. Buenker, *Urban Liberalism and Progressive Reform* (New York, 1973); Alan P. Grimes, *The Puritan Ethic and Woman Suffrage* (New York, 1967), 111–117.

generally took the lead; a National Liberal Immigration League under Jewish auspices did much to rally the opposition to the literacy bill in 1906 and in succeeding years.

Against this opposition, the restrictionist forces drew on three centers of strength. Patrician race thinkers supplied intellectual leadership. A stream of books and articles urged the eugenic implications of immigration policy and the danger of "race suicide." Meanwhile, a second group, the trade unions, lobbied energetically against the business apologists for immigration. The American Federation of Labor had moved far enough from its immigrant past by the early twentieth century to adopt an uncompromisingly restrictionist position. But its agitation did not count for much in actuality. The Congressmen who might have done labor's bidding were swayed by the stronger pressure of the immigrants; the big cities and industrial centers voted regularly and overwhelmingly against restriction.

Most of the support for restriction in Congress came from a third sector. From 1910 to 1952, the common people of the South and West formed a massive phalanx in favor of rigid legislation. This regional grouping represented a major shift in the alignment of forces. Initially, restriction sentiment had congealed in the Northeast, where the impact of immigration was most quickly and directly felt. In the 1890's the South and West had responded to the issue slowly and uncertainly. But in the twentieth century, while industrial and immigrant opposition thwarted northeastern restrictionists, the South and West emerged into the forefront of the movement. Appropriately, the political leadership passed from Henry Cabot Lodge of Massachusetts, who retired into the background after 1906, to more demagogic men like "Cotton Ed" Smith of South Carolina, Albert Johnson of Washington, and Pat McCarran of Nevada.

The essential explanation is to be found in racial and cultural defensiveness. The Deep South and the Far West, where the new regional lineup started, had long been the areas of most intense race feelings. Even without the sophisticated rationale of the new racial science, southerners and westerners could regard the unfamiliar peoples of southeastern Europe as less than completely white. Moreover, the Deep South and the western frontier had long been the sections with the most militant consciousness of having to fight to maintain a culture against external enemies. As racial lines hardened in the early twentieth century and the torrent of immigration mounted, community leaders from Seattle to Savannah raged at the great alien cities of the East and Midwest for polluting the purity of an Anglo-Saxon country and corrupting an individualistic, Protestant culture.

The first operative demonstration of the new racial emphasis came in 1905 with the outbreak of an anti-Japanese movement on the West Coast. Restrictionist leaders sensed that the Japanese issue might enable them to get the kind of general legislation they wanted. As matters turned out, the immigration law enacted in 1907 began the process of Japanese exclusion but otherwise contained only administrative reforms. Nevertheless, it was significant that Asiatic and European immigration were now, and would henceforth be, treated as different phases of a single question, not as entirely separate from one another.

Anti-Japanese sentiment had grown quietly on the West Coast for several years before it exploded. It inherited all of the attributes of the old anti-Chinese movement except mob violence. Before the 1890's, Japanese immigration to America was almost nonexistent, largely because Japan did not legalize emigration until 1885. During the nineties, the shrinkage of the Chinese-American population produced a demand for Japanese workers in large-scale agricultural enterprises and in construction work. Thousands of Japanese came in, many of them arriving indirectly via Hawaii. Again, as in the 1870's, a demagogic labor movement in San Francisco, this time the Union Labor party, mobilized the forces of hate.[22]

Yet, if history repeated itself, it also added a complicating factor not present in the earlier Oriental issue. Unlike helpless China, Japan became a formidable international rival. Her stunning victory over Russia in 1905 made her a world power, capable of menacing America's new stakes in the Far East. This, in one sense, aggravated the anti-Japanese movement and, in another sense, restrained it. Californians felt threatened not only by Japanese "blood" but also by Japanese military and naval power.

22. Roger B. Daniels, *The Anti-Japanese Movement in California and the Struggle for Japanese Exclusion* (Berkeley, 1962), 31–32.

Every representative of the "Yellow Peril" was counted a potential spy or saboteur. Significantly, the agitation against the Japanese in California came to a head in 1905 when the new situation in the Pacific first became apparent. On the other hand, these international ramifications exercised a brake on legislation. Responsible federal officials realized that Japan could not be dishonored with impunity, as China had been. Offensive treatment of Japanese immigrants might damage America's far eastern policy.

The whole problem introduced a new motif in immigration policy. In the Far East, America's historic isolation from world politics was passing. The sense of military security that had sustained the public's acceptance and the federal government's indifference toward immigration was diminishing. Considerations of national security and international relations were intruding upon what had been a purely domestic question. In time, the international rivalries of the twentieth century would have a shaping effect on the whole of immigration policy.

Realizing that a proud and sensitive Japan threatened America's far eastern empire, President Theodore Roosevelt tried to temper the anti-Japanese hysteria.[23] On the one hand, he maneuvered to check discrimination by state and local governments; on the other, he undertook to secure through diplomacy the exclusion that Californians wanted to compel by law. As a result, San Francisco rescinded a provocative school ordinance segregating Japanese pupils. In return, Congress in the immigration law of 1907 authorized the President to deal with Japanese immigration. He then arranged an informal gentlemen's agreement with Japan, by which the latter promised to issue no more passports to laborers coming to the United States. This ended the possibility of a substantial Japanese invasion. But the agreement left the West Coast acutely dissatisfied because it permitted the entry of several thousand Japanese a year, notably "picture brides" who added to the labor force and produced a growing Japanese population. After Roosevelt, the Wilson and Harding administrations continued to withstand pressure for a Japanese exclusion

23. Thomas A. Bailey, *Theodore Roosevelt and the Japanese-American Crises* (Stanford, 1934).

law, though they failed to prevent new discriminatory legislation in the western states.

Since America still seemed safely isolated from Europe before the First World War, the campaign to restrict the new immigration went forward without international inhibitions or incentives. From 1911 (when the United States Immigration Commission made its report) to 1917, a general bill that included a watered-down literacy test was continually before an increasingly race-conscious Congress. Despite vociferous support from the South and West, the bill did not become law until the eve of America's entry into the war. In even years, Congress stalled for fear of antagonizing the foreign vote in the November elections. In odd years, the bill passed by large majorities but succumbed to a presidential veto. Taft, in 1913, argued that America needed the immigrants' labor and could supply the literacy. Wilson, in 1915 and 1917, appealed to the cosmopolitan ideal of America as a haven for the oppressed.

Enacted finally over Wilson's second veto, the immigration law of 1917 was the first general and sweeping victory for the restrictionists in their thirty-five-year crusade. In addition to tightening administration in many ways, the act set three key precedents. First, it excluded adults unable to read some language. When immigration revived after the war, this barrier proved of little value in reducing the size of the influx; too many southeastern Europeans had by then learned how to read. Nevertheless, the adoption of the literacy test had great symbolic significance. Second, the law mapped out an "Asiatic barred zone" which completely excluded practically all Asiatic peoples except Chinese and Japanese. Since the Chinese were already shut out, Japan alone remained outside the rigid pattern of Oriental exclusion. Third, the act implemented the old distrust of foreign radicalism by excluding members of revolutionary organizations and by directing the deportation of aliens who preached revolution or sabotage at any time after entry. This was a crucial step forward in a trend, extending down to the 1950's, which progressively curtailed the civil liberties of aliens.[24]

24. William Preston, Jr., *Aliens and Dissenters: Federal Suppression of Radicals, 1903–1933* (Cambridge, Mass., 1963); Will Maslow, "Recasting Our Deportation Law: Proposals for Reform," *Columbia Law Review*, LVI (1956), 309.

Though the whole law grew out of prewar trends, the First World War created the extra margin of support that carried it past a veto. And before long, the war generated a climate of opinion that made these restrictions seem perilously inadequate. Although the war temporarily deferred further action by interrupting migration automatically, the European holocaust unleashed the forces that brought immigration restriction to its historic culmination.

The struggle with Germany stirred public opinion like a cyclone. America's isolation from European affairs, taken for granted in 1914, dissolved. Though statesmen tried to restore it after the war, henceforth it would have to be a deliberate contrivance rather than a natural condition. No longer could the American people feel providentially exempted from any international crisis. The new sense of danger came with such devastating force that it produced very little of the caution and restraint that had marked Roosevelt's Japanese policy. Instead, in every section of the country, men reacted toward all ethnic minorities as Californians had reacted toward the Japanese. Suddenly conscious of the presence of millions of unassimilated people in their midst, Americans quaked with fear of their potential disloyalty. Roosevelt himself signalized the change; for now he led the clamor for repressing any kind of divided loyalty.

The chief victims during the war years, the German-Americans, were soon thereafter restored to public favor, but the new emotional climate was not a passing phenomenon. Other minorities inherited the hysteria because it arose from a structural change in American nationalism. Known at the time as 100-per-cent Americanism, the new spirit demanded an unprecedented degree of national solidarity; loyalty and social conformity became virtually synonymous. The slack and gradual processes of assimilation characteristic of the past no longer seemed tolerable. Thus the war destroyed most of what remained of the old faith in America's capacity to fuse all men into a "nation of nations." The development of social stratification had weakened that faith; racial and cultural cleavage had narrowed it; and international stresses dealt it a final blow.

Once immigration revived in 1920, stringent restrictions seemed instantly imperative. Outside of immigrant groups and a few sympathetic social workers, the question no longer concerned the desirability of restriction, but simply the proper degree and kind. Even big business conceded the value of a "selective" policy. Furthermore, the 100-per-cent-American impulse created by the war greatly intensified the racial attitudes evolved in earlier years. For the first time the demand for Japanese exclusion met a general sympathy in eastern opinion; and everywhere a large sector of both the public and the intelligentsia echoed Madison Grant's pleas for preserving Nordic America from the mongrel hordes of southeastern Europe.

Two laws resulted. The first of them, though frankly a makeshift designed to hold the gate while a permanent plan was worked out, established the underlying principle of national quotas based on the preexisting composition of the American population. The law of 1921 limited European immigration to 3 per cent of the number of foreign-born of each nationality present in the United States at the time of the last available census, that of 1910. This would hold the transatlantic current to a maximum of 350,000 and assign most of that total to northwestern Europe. Ethnic affiliation became the main determinant for admission to the United States.

Restrictionists remained dissatisfied, partly because of administrative snarls in the law but chiefly because it was not sufficiently restrictive. In fact, a good many people were pressing for complete suspension of immigration. After three years of bickering, a permanent law passed on a landslide of southern, western, and rural votes. The only opposition came from industrial areas in the Northeast and Midwest.[25] Owing to considerations of Pan-American goodwill and to the southwestern desire for Mexican "stoop-labor," the act of 1924 left immigration from the western hemisphere unrestricted; but it perfected the structure of Oriental exclusion and drastically tightened the quota system for the rest of the world.

What excited most interest at the moment was the exclusion of aliens ineligible for citizenship (i.e., Orientals), a provision that summarily abrogated the gentlemen's agreement. Secretary of State Charles Evans Hughes protested against this affront to

25. Philadelphia *Public Ledger*, April 13, 1924, p. 14.

Japan when the bill came up, but its congressional sponsors replied that there was no discrimination in treating the Japanese like the rest of their race. Above all, an intensely nationalistic Congress was determined to take immigration out of the realm of diplomatic negotiation and deal with it by a sovereign assertion of American law. When the Japanese ambassador forcefully endorsed Hughes's protest, Congress exploded in wrath at the "insolent" demand that "we surrender our very independence of action as an independent nation."[26] The Japanese public reacted still more violently, and the cordial relations recently developed between the two countries were largely undone.

In revising the quota system for European immigration, Congress debated two plans and adopted both. The first plan based national quotas on the foreign-born population of the United States in 1890 instead of 1910 and cut the quotas from 3 to 2 per cent of that base population. By moving back the census base to 1890, the law allotted about 85 per cent of the total quota immigration to northwestern Europe.[27] Although this scheme accomplished the practical purpose of reducing the new immigration to very small proportions, some of the shrewdest racists saw its theoretical drawbacks. There was a certain crassness about shifting to an old census in order to achieve a desired discrimination; and was it not artificial to apportion quotas according to the distribution of the foreign-born when one wanted to protect the old native stock? Accordingly, a Pennsylvania Senator, David A. Reed, and John B. Trevor, a patrician New Yorker who belonged to the circle of Madison Grant, proposed assigning the quotas in accordance with the contribution of each national stock to the present American population. Practically, this "national-origins" scheme would yield about the same ratio between northwestern and southeastern Europe as would the 1890 census. The new principle had the advantage, however, of being geared directly to the preservation of America's racial status quo, an object which the other plan served only crudely and indirectly.

26. Rodman Paul, *The Abrogation of the Gentlemen's Agreement* (Cambridge, Mass., 1936), 58–81.
27. John B. Trevor, *An Analysis of the American Immigration Act of 1924* (New York, 1924), 62.

Moreover, by counting everybody's ancestors (instead of the number of foreign-born at some arbitrarily chosen census date), one could claim to offer exact justice to every ethnic strain in the white population.

The national-origins idea came up at the last moment. Since even its sponsors admitted the difficulty of formulating precise statistics on the origins of America's polyglot people, the completed law provided for using 1890-based quotas until 1927. Thereafter, a total quota of 150,000 would be parceled out in ratio to the distribution of national origins in the white population of the United States in 1920.

Few people understood the national-origins proviso very clearly, for it slipped into the law at the time when public interest was focused on the imbroglio with Japan over Oriental exclusion. Only afterward did significant differences between the 1890 quotas and the prospective national-origins quotas become apparent. Both schemes would yield about the same quotas for southeastern European nationalities, but they differed sharply in the distribution of quotas among northwestern European countries. Under national origins, according to Trevor's preliminary estimates, Great Britain would receive 57 per cent of the total quota immigration, whereas on the 1890 basis she received 21 per cent. The final computations of a board of statistical experts cut down the British quota somewhat but still left her with more than all the rest of northwestern Europe combined.[28] A howl went up from German, Irish, and Scandinavian groups in the United States, who charged that the national-origins principle discriminated against other Nordic peoples in the interest of the Anglo-Saxons. This pressure, which was strongest in the Midwest, threatened for a time to bring about the repeal of the national-origins clause. But Reed and Trevor lashed back at the "alien blocs" for trying to break down the immigration laws, and after two postponements, their plan went into effect in 1929.[29] The main architecture of American immigration policy was now complete.

Some unfinished business remained on the restrictionist agenda,

28. *Current Opinion*, LXXVII (1924), 623–34; Howland, *Survey*, 461–67.
29. Robert A. Divine, *American Immigration Policy 1924–52* (New Haven, 1957), 26–51.

but the few modifications in policy during the ensuing decade were minor or temporary. Immediately upon the passage of the law of 1924, restrictionists began a campaign to extend the quota system to the western hemisphere.[30] Mexican immigration, so far as it was recorded, reached a high point of 89,000 in 1924. Small farmers in the Southwest cried out against the advantage this cheap labor supply gave to the big cotton planters; and race zealots throughout the country determined to stop the inflow of "colored blood," whatever the cost in Pan-American goodwill. The State Department, fearing Mexican retaliation against American business interests, opposed the restrictionists forthrightly. In 1929 the department forestalled congressional action by adopting a system of administrative restriction with Mexico's cooperation. Merely by a rigid enforcement of old regulations, such as the public charge proviso of 1882 and the contract labor ban of 1885, the consuls who issued visas to prospective Mexican immigrants drastically reduced their number. While this policy increased immigration restriction, it avoided provocation and preserved some flexibility. During the manpower crisis of the Second World War the government was able to stimulate and assist the temporary migration of Mexican labor.

The Mexican experience furnished a precedent for tightening restriction generally when the Great Depression struck. Fearful of any addition to the appalling army of unemployed, President Herbert Hoover in September 1930 instructed consuls to deny a visa to anyone who might sooner or later become a candidate for relief. This very strict interpretation of the public-charge proviso, although somewhat modified in the mid-thirties, continued throughout the depression. It caused some criticism in liberal circles but never became a real political issue. The precipitous drop in immigration that occurred under this policy (though partly a natural result of the depression) provided an effective answer to the congressional restrictionists who tried unsuccessfully to impose a statutory reduction of 90 per cent on all immigration.

Certainly, these moves indicated no slackening of America's

30. Letter from James J. Davis to Calvin Coolidge, May 29, 1924 (Coolidge Papers, Library of Congress); Madison Grant, "America for the Americans," *Forum*, LXXIV (1925), 355.

purpose to maintain its human blockade. Even the most harrowing of the immigration problems of the thirties, the plight of refugees fleeing from Hitler, evoked a minimal response. For a while, consuls showed special consideration to refugees, but they still had to pass all the hurdles in existing laws. Roosevelt called an international conference on the subject, but he did not raise a hand when a bill to admit 20,000 refugee children as nonquota immigrants died in committee. In 1940 apprehensions over the possible entry of spies resulted in stringent new regulations which reduced the admission of refugees far below the level permitted by American quotas. Relative to population, the United States was much less of an asylum for the oppressed than were Britain, France, and the Netherlands.[31]

I V

Yet, again, as in the breathing spell of the early twentieth century, the forces that had created the nation's immigration policy were shifting far more than the surface of affairs revealed. A partial revision of attitudes can be observed throughout the 1930's and, in the late forties, the rigid legislative mold showed signs of cracking.

As early as the late 1920's, a decline of racism in intellectual circles set in. The eugenics movement waned; the Nordic cult lost its vogue. The change reflected the emancipation of American thought from biological determinism. The belief that iron laws of heredity control the course of history gave way to an increasing tendency to see human problems in distinctively human terms. The New Deal not only revived, but redoubled the old progressive emphasis on environment, while Hitler's demonstration of the fruits of racism inflicted a moral shock on every sensitive mind. Ruth Benedict popularized the relativity of culture, social psychologists elaborated the scapegoat theory of "prejudice," and it became intellectually fashionable to discount

31. David S. Wyman, *Paper Walls: America and the Refugee Crisis 1938-1941* (Amherst, Mass., 1968).

the very existence of persistent ethnic differences.[32] The whole reaction deprived popular race feelings of a powerful ideological sanction.

All the while, the processes of assimilation were at work. The cleavage between the peoples of the new immigration and the older American population gradually diminished. Familiarity increased; social differences became less pronounced. The ending of mass immigration relieved the worst fears of old-stock Americans, and it also facilitated assimilation by depriving the ethnic minorities of constant, large-scale reinforcements. The circulation of the foreign-language press, for example, peaked in the 1920's, then entered a sharp decline in the following decade. The Second World War not only mingled nationalities but also reduced class differences substantially; and the immense economic growth that followed the war enabled millions of second-generation immigrants to move into the mainstream of American life. The expansion of unionism that came with the rise of the Congress of Industrial Organizations opened one avenue of ethnic integration; the flight to the suburbs created another; education built a third. The sons and daughters of immigrants during these years actually advanced beyond the social-economic status of their parents to a greater degree than did white Americans whose parents were born in this country.[33] Although the intensity of ethnic feeling lessened, the new nationalities became more influential. Resentment at the quota system still rankled, and a more liberal immigration policy retained strong ethnic appeal.

Perhaps even more important in reshaping public opinion on immigration was a gradual change of attitude among old-stock Americans. The effort to maintain a unitary American culture was largely abandoned. The belief on the part of many white Protestant citizens of native antecedents that their way of life

---

32. Ruth Benedict, *Patterns of Culture* (1934). There is a suggestive critique of this trend in William Petersen, "The 'Scientific' Basis of Our Immigration Policy," *Commentary*, XX (1955), 84.

33. Joshua A. Fishman et al., *Language Loyalty in the United States: The Maintenance and Perpetuation of Non-English Mother Tongues by American Ethnic and Religious Groups* (The Hague, 1966), 52–55; Peter Blau and Otis Dudley Duncan, *The American Occupational Structure* (New York, 1967), 232–38.

constituted a standard deserving the official sanction of American institutions gave way to a more pluralistic, heterogeneous pattern. How this came about, and at what psychic cost, we have hardly begun to discover. But the fact that American ideals had always claimed to be universal and nonethnic certainly facilitated the shift toward an eclectic culture. The major churches lost interest in prohibition and started describing America not as a Protestant country but as a "Judaic-Christian civilization." By the time of the Second World War the American soldier could no longer be called "Yank," his cognomen in the First World War and before. He was now a G.I.—a self-deprecating, reluctantly regimented product of the American assembly line. After the war cultural leadership was assumed by an intellectual community drawn from a variety of ethnic backgrounds and largely estranged from all of them.[34]

During the 1940's and 1950's the Cold War muted the effects of this cultural transformation; its full impact on immigration legislation was delayed. Temporarily, considerations of national security and international conflict took precedence over all other aspects of the immigration question. Yet the global crisis had mixed effects. It spurred some to liberalize immigration laws in ways that could strengthen America's leadership of the "free world." Others were preoccupied with building more barriers against Communist ideas. Consequently a tendency to admit a larger number of immigrants collided with a countermovement to gird against disloyalty.

Minor legislative changes in the 1940's reflected both sets of pressures. In the Smith Act of 1940, a security-conscious Congress strengthened deportation procedures and required all of the 4,000,000 people who were not citizens to register. Three years later, a desire to invigorate the wartime alliance with China punched the first hole in the wall of Oriental exclusion; the Chinese got a token immigration quota of 105.[35] After 1945, as the Cold War mounted, it revived the old wish to provide asylum for

34. Gilman Ostrander, *American Civilization in the First Machine Age, 1890–1940* (New York, 1970), 29–30; Milton M. Gordon, *Assimilation in American Life: The Role of Race, Religion, and National Origins* (New York, 1964), 224–32.

35. Fred W. Riggs, *Pressures on Congress: A Study of the Repeal of Chinese Exclusion* (New York, 1950).

the oppressed; but it also quickened fears of disloyalty. The former predominated in the Displaced Persons Act; the latter culminated in the McCarran Acts.

The immediately urgent problem after the war was the fate of a million half-starving eastern Europeans who feared to return to their homes in Communist lands and were dependent upon Allied authorities in central Europe. Since the national-origins law hindered American cooperation in a joint international effort to resettle these people, President Harry S. Truman, in 1947, recommended admitting displaced persons outside the quotas. The shrieks of restrictionists against this "alien torrent" forestalled any action until the following year. Then, an act to admit 202,000 D.P.'s was hedged by numerous restrictive provisos. But the conservatives were fighting a losing battle. In the election of 1948, Truman and other northern Democrats capitalized on ethnic and liberal indignation at the restrictions in the law. In 1950, a generously amended act passed. The two measures—the first significant refugee legislation in American history—enabled 410,000 people to come to the United States outside of the quota system.[36]

Despite this modification the restrictionist tradition remained strong. Liberals and the most affected ethnic groups clamored for a principle of restriction that would be fairer than the national-origins quotas, but after thirty years they had become an institution. Congress even required that the displaced persons be charged against future annual quotas for their respective nationalities instead of being admitted separately, as Truman recommended. The restrictionists also enjoyed the advantage of a remarkable leader, Senator Pat McCarran. A wily, determined legislative in-fighter and an ardent nationalist, McCarran through seniority wielded great power over appointments and appropriations; and he cherished an intensely personal hostility toward Truman.[37]

36. See Divine, *American Immigration Policy*, 110–45; Eugene Kulischer, "Displaced Persons in the Modern World," *Annals of the American Academy of Political and Social Science*, vol. 262 (1949), 166–77; Richard Ferree Smith, "Refugees," loc. cit., vol. 367 (1966), 43–52.

37. Willard Shelton, "Powerful Pat McCarran," *The Progressive* (May 1952), 23; Marquis Childs in the Los Angeles *Daily News*, June 18, 1952, p. 34.

Conscious of the growing pressure for reform, McCarran boldly seized the initiative. First, he drove past a presidential veto the Internal Security Act of 1950, which ordered all aliens who had ever been Communists or members of front organizations excluded and deported. Meanwhile, McCarran's Judiciary Subcommittee worked out an omnibus bill, recasting into a single matrix the entire immigration code. It made hundreds of changes, but none of them major. Congressmen from immigrant districts raged against the bill not because it would admit fewer newcomers, but because it seemed unlikely to admit more. In 1952, the McCarran-Walter Act passed over a stinging veto. Again, the South cast the most solid restrictionist vote, with the West not far behind.[38]

Part of the mystifying political genius of the 300-page law was that it offered something for every taste. It repealed the ban on contract labor, but added other qualitative exclusions. It relaxed slightly the ban on ex-Communists imposed in 1950, but expanded the government's deportation powers and intensified its surveillance of aliens. The law showed more sympathy for divided families than previous acts had done, but not as much as reformers wanted. It terminated Oriental exclusion by assigning token quotas to all Asian countries, but set up new racial restrictions by putting all immigrants of Oriental ancestry under those quotas regardless of their place of residence or birth. Above all, the McCarran-Walter Act retained the old principle of national-origins quotas for Europe, based on the census of 1920 and totaling 150,000.[39] And that, to both supporters and opponents, was the crux of the matter.

During the ensuing decade opposition to the national-origins quotas slowly accumulated. Reformers insistently pointed out that the quotas were unrealistic as well as unjust. Britain received 42 per cent of all the quota visas but never used as many as half of them. Most immigrants entered outside the quotas. The major

38. Divine, *American Immigration Policy*, 164–91.
39. For more extended discussion of these provisions, see Donald R. Taft and Richard Robbins, *International Migrations: The Immigrant in the Modern World* (New York, 1955), 412–14, 421–24, 431–38; Marion T. Bennett, *American Immigration Policies: A History* (Washington, D.C., 1963), 133–93.

churches, both Protestant and Catholic, assailed the national-origins system. Organized labor, now thoroughly infiltrated by the groups against whom the quotas were aimed, abandoned its traditional antiforeign stance and called for liberalization of the law. Intellectuals viewed the quotas either as a quaint anachronism or as a national disgrace. In presidential elections the candidates of both parties promised to overhaul the McCarran-Walter Act. Successive administrations did extract from Congress minor amendments—a refugee relief act in 1953, another one in 1957, a law in 1961 in behalf of orphans and divided families—all authorizing additional nonquota admissions.[40] On the basic issue, however, Congress was immobilized by the overrepresentation of rural areas and the seniority of small-town Congressmen on key committees. The outstanding congressional expert now on immigration was Representative Francis Walter, a conservative Democrat long associated with patriotic causes; and the threat of Walter's opposition blocked all attempts to revamp the quota system.

The Supreme Court in 1962 handed down its famous reapportionment decision, *Baker* v. *Carr,* presaging a significant shift of congressional power toward metropolitan areas. Francis Walter died the following year. By 1964 the civil rights movement was at flood tide, and President Lyndon Johnson's smashing victory in the fall elections burst the legislative stalemate. Making immigration reform part of his civil rights program, Johnson put relentless pressure on Congress. "We have no right to disparage the ancestors of millions of our fellow Americans in this way," Johnson told Congress.[41] By 1965 the question was no longer whether ethnic discriminations would be expunged, but who would get the credit for doing it.

All sides agreed that the changes should not allow the total

40. Cabell Phillips, "That Phony Refugee Law," *Harper's Magazine,* (April, 1955), 70; *New York Times,* September 27, 1953, sec. 4, p. 10, and February 9, 1956, pp. 1, 14. See also the various articles in a special immigration issue of *Law and Contemporary Problems,* XXI (Spring, 1956).

41. "Amending the Immigration and Nationality Act," *Department of State Bulletin,* LII (1965), 146–47. See also Abba Schwartz, *The Open Society* (New York, 1968), 29, 112–24; "End Racist Immigration," *Christian Century,* LXXXI (1964), 1003–4.

annual immigration to rise substantially above its current level, which was a little less than 300,000. The administration bill proposed that the national-origins quotas should be gradually converted into a single pool of visas over a five-year period. Congress, however, produced a law that terminated differential national quotas forthwith. It also abolished all discrimination against Asians. Its object was to put all the countries of the world on an equal footing.

The Immigration Act of 1965 fixed an overall limit on the number of immigrants each year who were not immediate relatives of United States citizens: 120,000 from the independent countries of the Western Hemisphere, 170,000 from the rest of the world. The ceiling on immigration from the Western Hemisphere (to go into effect in 1968) was the most controversial proviso of the law; it was adopted over the opposition of the State Department to gain the votes of certain conservative senators. Of the quota for the rest of the world, no more than 20,000 admissions would be allowed to any one country. None of those numbers, however, applied to the immediate families of citizens; they might enter without restriction. Thus, by abandoning all national and racial preferences and by assigning an overriding priority to family unification, the new law lifted the shadow of racism from American immigration legislation. It marked the culmination of a fundamental change in national policy that had begun with the Displaced Persons Act of 1948. By 1965 so many loopholes in, and exceptions to, the national origins quota system had been devised that two out of every three immigrants were entering outside the quotas; and when those quotas were finally swept away, the dwindling minority of Congressmen who still favored the preservation of ethnic and racial priorities seemed pretty much resigned to the change.[42]

42. Edward M. Kennedy, "The Immigration Act of 1965," *Annals of the American Academy of Political and Social Science*, vol. 367 (September 1966), 137–49; David M. Reimers, "An Unintended Reform: The 1965 Immigration Act and Third World Immigration to the United States," *Journal of American Ethnic History*, III (1983), 9–28; *New York Times*, August 27, 1965, p. 9, September 20, 1965, p. 1.

V

For several years controversy over immigration to the United States almost ceased. The Senate Subcommittee on Immigration and Naturalization lapsed into somnolence. It held no hearings for nearly a decade, and a reporter who visited its spacious chambers in 1975 found them bare.[43] The only aspect of U.S. policies that provoked any widespread criticism in the late 1960's was the encouragement they gave to the so-called brain drain— the migration of young engineers, physicians, and scientists from the Third World to affluent countries like the United States, which offered a richer market for their skills. In the nineteenth and early twentieth centuries the proportion of professional people who moved from one country to another had been very small. International migration was then overwhelmingly a quest for opportunity on the part of disadvantaged classes. Of the immigrants to the United States in the period 1908–1923 who declared any occupation at all, only 2.6 per cent had been professionals. In an increasingly technical world, however, some kinds of expert knowledge became highly portable, and the United States took advantage of that by giving preference, within the various quotas, to immigrants with needed skills. The new law of 1965 specifically reserved for professional persons alone 10 per cent of the immigrant places available outside the Western Hemisphere. Was the United States draining the world's poorest countries of the very people they could least afford to lose?[44]

The problem of the brain drain largely corrected itself in the 1970's as the shortages of American doctors, nurses, and technicians disappeared. The new current of the seventies was not a disproportionate influx of professional people, but rather a dra-

43. *New York Times*, September 29, 1975, p. 17.
44. Justus M. van der Kroef, "The U.S. and the World's Brain Drain," *International Journal of Comparative Sociology*, XI (1970), 220–39. On levels of professional immigration, compare William S. Bernard, *American Immigration Policy: A Reappraisal* (New York, 1950), 44, with U.S. Bureau of the Census, *Statistical Abstract of the United States: 1973*, p. 96.

matic increase in the number of poor, unskilled immigrants who found their way to the United States from non-European countries. A new wave of immigration was under way, the first sizable one since the early 1920's. By the late 1970's official statistics showed an average of half a million immigrants per year (Table 3). According to the best available estimate, another half million annually slipped into the United States illegally.[45] This large scale, clandestine immigration was the feature of the new wave that caused widest concern.

The national and racial sources of the new wave also set it apart from earlier migrations. After the reforms of 1965 had swept away the old racial barriers, Mediterranean countries such as Portugal and Italy produced a much larger share of European emigrants. In the 1970's Europe as a whole was eclipsed by a swelling emigration from Latin America and Asia. Whereas northwestern Europe and Canada accounted for 52 per cent of the legal immigration of the 1950's, their combined share in the 1970's was only 10 per cent. By 1972 the leading countries of origin were Mexico, the Philippines, Italy, Cuba, and Korea, in that order.[46] Government policies in the late 1970's that gave a special welcome to anti-Communist refugees from Indochina and Cuba further augmented the flow from the Third World.

In certain areas where the new immigrants have clustered, their presence has been sharply divisive. American blacks in Miami and in southern California resented the aid and sympathy that Cubans and Vietnamese received and the considerable success their enterprise reaped. In Texas, concern over the burden that illegal Mexican immigrants might put on community services inspired a state law in 1975 denying money to local school districts for the education of illegal aliens. Nevertheless, the striking fact about public opinion in the 1970's and 1980's was its relative mildness, even during years of heavy unemployment.

45. Census Bureau estimate cited in James Fallows, "Immigration: How It's Affecting Us," *Atlantic*, 252 (November, 1983), 101. See also Joyce Vialet, *Illegal Aliens: Analysis and Background* (Congressional Research Service, Library of Congress, Washington, D.C., 1977).

46. *Statistical Abstract: 1973*, p. 96; U.S. Department of Justice, Immigration and Naturalization Service, *1980 Statistical Yearbook*, p. 4.

TABLE 3. *Recent Immigration by Area of Last Residence*

	1951–55	1956–1960	1961–65	1966–1970	1971–75	1976–1980
Europe	628,235	700,058	531,270	598,400	422,194	378,174
Asia	45,613	105,068	104,305	317,159	590,223	997,955
America	392,353	604,591	795,080	921,294	878,027	1,104,502
Africa	5,216	8,876	9,631	19,323	27,948	52,831
Australasia	3,825	9,151	9,946	15,176	12,090	13,504
Total	1,087,638	1,427,841	1,450,312	1,871,365	1,936,281	2,557,033

SOURCES: U.S. Bureau of the Census, *Historical Statistics of the United States, Colonial Times to 1970* (Washington, D.C., 1975), pt. 1, series C89–119; U.S. Department of Justice, Immigration and Naturalization Service, *1980 Statistical Yearbook*, p. 4.

67

Neither the racial composition nor the total size of the new wave aroused national anxieties. There was some vigorous lobbying for stricter numerical limits by environmentalists who were alarmed by runaway population growth in the Third World. Their organization, the Federation for American Immigration Reform (FAIR), did not, however, dominate the new immigration debate. Controversy focused on specific practical problems rather than general principles or total numbers.

The chief problem was the growth of an elusive, floating population, perhaps several million all told, who had no proper papers, who worked willingly for low wages to the disadvantage of unskilled Americans, and who lived in constant fear of deportation. Although illegal immigrants came from far and wide, some of them entering as visitors or students, the great majority simply walked across the border from Mexico. Since Mexico also furnished more legal immigrants in the 1970's than did any other country, and the illegal flow from other parts of Latin America was substantial, Hispanic groups emerged as the most visible, outspoken opponents of a crackdown on illegal immigration.

From a Mexican point of view what U.S. newspapers began about 1970 to describe as an "ever-deepening crisis" was wearily familiar. Mexican peasants had long moved freely between the two countries in response to the seasonal labor needs of big farmers and to the expansion of railroads into sparsely populated areas of the Southwest. Stimulated by official encouragement during times of labor shortages, the habit of going north for work took root in large parts of Mexico. U.S. efforts to control the traffic by fees and examinations simply diverted much of it into illegal channels. After World War II the demand for transient, vulnerable immigrants to do hard, unskilled work spread from the Southwest to other parts of the United States because native Americans—black as well as white—were less and less willing to hold such jobs in restaurants, hotels, laundries, hospitals, and sweatshops. What was new about illegal immigration was simply its scale and its wide dispersion throughout urban America. In moving from the fields to the cities the illegal immigrant gained a new visibility. He became the American equivalent of the "guest worker" in Western Europe, but without the protections the latter enjoyed.[47]

The illegal influx entered an explosive phase during the 1970's, owing not only to the demand for uncomplaining, low-cost labor but also to severe population pressures in Latin America and to changes in U.S. law and policy. After 1968 the government restricted entry from everywhere in the Western Hemisphere so sharply as to make legal immigration possible for only a fraction of a vast human movement. In ending the historic exception for the Western Hemisphere, Congress created a system that was impossible to enforce under existing conditions.

Concerted efforts to formulate a more workable policy began with the Carter administration. From the outset Labor Secretary F. Ray Marshall treated the control of illegal immigration as essential to the administration's goal of lowering unemployment. The Carter program, as submitted to Congress in August, 1977, called for fining employers who knowingly hire illegal aliens. It also proposed a scheme of registration by which people already living in the United States illegally could become permanent residents with full civic rights. By linking amnesty for workers with sanctions against employers, Carter hoped to restore respect for law and "avoid having a permanent 'underclass' of millions of persons who have not been and cannot practically be deported."[48]

This package of reforms proved no easier to enact than previous changes in immigration policy. Congress merely authorized a Select Commission on Immigration and Refugee Policy to study the whole matter further. Under the chairmanship of the Rev.

47. *New York Times*, October 17, 1971, pp. 1, 58; Lawrence A. Cardoso, *Mexican Emigration to the United States, 1897–1931* (Tucson, 1980); Gerald M. Rosberg, "Legal Regulation of the Migration Process: The 'Crisis' of Illegal Immigration," in *Human Migration: Patterns and Policies*, ed. William H. McNeill and Ruth S. Adams (Bloomington, Ind., 1978), 336–76. See also John Crewdson, *The Tarnished Door: The New Immigrants and the Transformation of America* (New York, 1983).

48. Quoted in Elizabeth Midgley, "Immigrants: Whose Huddled Masses?" *Atlantic*, 241 (April, 1978), 15. See also Otis L. Graham, Jr., "The Problem That Will Not Go Away: Illegal Immigration," *Center Magazine*, X (July–August, 1977), 62–66.

Theodore M. Hesburgh, the Commission tried to build support for ways and means of enforcing existing laws humanely while allowing a modestly compensating increase in the ceiling on legal immigration. Its findings added to the bipartisan credibility of the Carter proposals, which then gained a qualified endorsement from the Reagan administration. The Commission's recommendations passed the Senate in 1982 and again in 1983 in the form of the Simpson-Mazzoli Bill. Both times, however, the bill was sidetracked in the House by the intense opposition of Hispanic legislators, together with the unwillingness of agricultural interests to limit the availability of cheap labor and the deep distrust many sorts of Americans felt toward any new governmental regulations of employment.[49]

Thus the immigration debates of the late 1970's and early 1980's revealed a growing public concern over the breakdown of law. At least until 1984, that concern was too diffused and disunited to overcome the concentrated resistance of a newly mobilized ethnic group, which appealed to old ideas of American freedom and to the tolerant, pluralistic attitudes dominant in public opinion in the middle decades of the twentieth century. In June, 1984, however, the demand for reform brought the Simpson-Mazzoli Bill to the verge of enactment. As the bill squeaked through the House of Representatives, public opinion polls showed strong majorities for penalizing companies that knowingly hired illegal aliens but much weaker support for the accompanying amnesty that would grant most resident aliens legal status.[50] It seemed unlikely that the Simpson-Mazzoli Bill, with its precarious balance between sanctions against employers and amnesty for illegal residents, would end the struggle to make the new immigration policies of 1965 effective and continuously relevant in a changing world.

49. *New York Times*, December 27, 1982, p. B12, and October 6, 1983, p. 1. See also Lawrence H. Fuchs, "Immigration Reforms in 1911 and 1981: The Role of Select Commissions," *Journal of American Ethnic History*, III (1983), 58–89.
50. *New York Times*, June 21, 1984, pp. 1, D21–22; "Closing the Door?" *Newsweek*, CIII (June 25, 1984), 18–24.

Chapter Three

The Transformation of the Statue of Liberty

Not like the brazen giant of Greek fame,
With conquering limbs astride from land to land,
Here at our sea-washed, sunset gates shall stand
A mighty woman with a torch, whose flame
Is the imprisoned lightning, and her name
Mother of Exiles. From her beacon-hand
Glows world-wide welcome; her mild eyes command
The air-bridged harbor that twin cities frame.

"Keep, ancient lands, your storied pomp!" cries she
With silent lips. "Give me your tired, your poor,
Your huddled masses yearning to breathe free,
The wretched refuse of your teeming shore.
Send these, the homeless, tempest-tost to me,
I lift my lamp beside the golden door!"[1]

For nine frustrating years, from 1877 to 1886, a committee of
New York business and society leaders collected funds to pay for
a pedestal on which a gigantic Statue of Liberty might stand in
New York Harbor. The statue itself, the inspiration and creation
of a French sculptor, Frédéric Auguste Bartholdi, was under
construction in Paris. It was to be a gift to America from the

1. A photocopy of the original manuscript in the possession of the American Jewish Historical Society appears in Heinrich Edward Jacobs, *The World of Emma Lazarus* (New York, 1949), 178.

French people, a symbol and pledge of friendship between the two republics. Americans needed only to erect it properly; yet the task almost exceeded the limits of the sluggish public spirit of the day.

At one point, in 1883, when the statue was almost ready to ship and the pedestal only half finished, the Pedestal Fund Committee organized a temporary art exhibition as a fund-raising device. Prominent families lent some of their treasures, and a number of artists and writers gave original drawings and letters for a portfolio which was put up for auction. Emma Lazarus, one of the few proper New Yorkers with some literary credentials, contributed to the portfolio an original sonnet. She called it "The New Colossus"—a reference to the Colossus of Rhodes, a statue of the sun god which once stood in the harbor of Rhodes and was known in ancient times as one of the Seven Wonders of the World.

On the evening of December 3 the art exhibition opened. A chorus of fifty voices, supported by Theodore Thomas's orchestra, sang a "Hymn to Liberty," especially composed in honor of Bartholdi's statue. William M. Evarts, former Secretary of State and chairman of the Fund Committee, read the Lazarus sonnet.[2] Although the exhibition was adjudged a financial success, the auction was a bit disappointing. The entire portfolio, including the sonnet, sold for $1,500, about half the sum the committee hoped it would bring.[3]

A finely bred, bookish young lady, Emma Lazarus rarely wrote in a patriotic vein. But this occasion touched obliquely a new and vital concern of hers. Until 1881 she had produced derivative, self-consciously literary verse, the tinkling melodies then fashionable in the world of genteel culture. Belonging to one of the oldest and most secure of New York Jewish families, she had abandoned the synagogue in her youth and had pretty largely lost a sense of Jewish identity. Then the horrifying outbreak of anti-Jewish pogroms in Russia in 1881, and the sight of the first bedraggled refugees arriving in New York, gave her a theme and a mission.

2. "The Pedestal Fund Art Loan Exhibition," *The Art Amateur*, X (January, 1884), Supplement, 41–48.
3. Loc. cit., X (February, 1884), 58; *The Critic*, III (1883), 491.

With a new passion, she wrote henceforth mainly as a champion of the Jews. She became the first modern American laureate of their history and culture.[4] To her the Statue of Liberty, facing seaward, could hold out to all uprooted folk the same message of succor that she, Emma Lazarus, was expressing to and for her fellow Jews.

Yet Lazarus took no further interest in the Statue of Liberty once her poem was written. The most authoritative study reports that she never mentioned the statue again. Nor did her contemporaries pay much heed to "The New Colossus." When she died in 1887, four years after its composition, obituaries failed to mention it.[5] The reviewers of her collected works, which appeared in 1889, concentrated on her specifically Jewish poems. One critic conceded that "her noble sonnet" on the Bartholdi statue had given many their "first apprehension of the glory in even the more sordid elements in our American life."[6] Others ignored the poem completely. The most influential critic of the period, Edmund Clarence Stedman, who was a friend and admirer of Emma Lazarus, included several of her poems in his widely read anthologies, but "The New Colossus" was not among them. After the turn of the century Miss Lazarus herself was largely forgotten outside a small Anglo-Jewish literary circle.[7]

In 1903, on the twentieth anniversary of the writing of "The New Colossus," another shy, poetry-loving spinster who belonged to the old New York aristocracy, Georgina Schuyler, secured permission to put a bronze tablet containing the entire poem on an interior wall of the statue's pedestal. This she did

4. Allen Guttmann, *The Jewish Writer in America: Assimilation and the Crisis of Identity* (New York, 1971), 21–25.

5. Hertha Pauli and Ernst Bosch, *I Lift My Lamp: The Way of a Symbol* (New York, 1948), 303, 320. See also the tributes printed in *The Critic*, VIII (1887), 293–95, 317–18.

6. "The Poems of Emma Lazarus," *The Literary Review*, XX (1889), 36. Cf. Solomon Solis-Cohen, "The Poems of Emma Lazarus," *The American*, XVII (1889), 295–97; "The Poems of Emma Lazarus," *The Spectator*, LXIII (1889), 608–9.

7. Edmund Clarence Stedman, *An American Anthology, 1787–1900* (Boston, 1900), and *A Library of American Literature From the Earliest Settlement to the Present Time* (New York, 1889); Warwick James Price, "Three Forgotten Poetesses," *Forum*, XLVII (1912), 361–76.

primarily as a memorial to Lazarus, whom she evidently had known and admired. The event passed without ceremony or public notice.[8] In fact, the poem rested there for another thirty years without attracting any publicity at all.

This long neglect is remarkable, for the ideas that the poem expressed were deeply ingrained in American tradition. The concept of America as a refuge from European oppression supplied one of the original, fertilizing elements of our national consciousness. Jefferson, Emerson, Lowell, and many a lesser patriot had voiced its continuing appeal. In the late nineteenth century, however, pride in America's receptive mission dimmed. A gradual liberalization of political institutions throughout most of Europe blurred the once sharp image of the immigrant as one who had been unfree in his native country. Meanwhile, the new problems of an urban, industrial age inspired a strong movement in America to restrict immigration. By 1886, when the New Colossus was unveiled upon her completed pedestal, there was already considerable alarm about the huddled masses pouring through the golden door. The lavish dedication ceremonies transpired without a single reference to the Lazarus sonnet and without serious attention to its theme. Instead, President Grover Cleveland discoursed grandiloquently on the stream of light that would radiate outward into "the darkness of ignorance and man's oppression until Liberty enlightens the world." And the New York *World*, which sparked the final, successful fund-raising campaign to pay for the pedestal, declared that the statue would stand forever as a warning against lawlessness and anarchy and as "an emblem of that true fraternity which binds us . . . to every struggling nation that dares to strike for freedom."[9] The rhetoric of the inaugural concentrated almost exclusively on two subjects: the beneficent effect on other countries of American ideas, and the desirability of international friendship and peace.

8. Pauli and Bosch, *I Lift My Lamp*, 321. On Georgina Schuyler see Francis Greenwood Peabody, *Reminiscences of Present-Day Saints* (Boston, 1927), 253–73.

9. Andre Gschaedler, *True Light on the Statue of Liberty and Its Creator* (Narberth, Pa., 1966), 148; New York *World*, October 29, 1886, p. 4. In the same vein see also John Greenleaf Whittier, "The Bartholdi Statue," *The Critic*, VI (1886), 225.

Not only the uneasy mood of the time but also the statue itself resisted the generous construction Emma Lazarus placed upon it. The creators of the monument did not intend a symbol of welcome. Bartholdi and the French liberals who supported his work prized America not as an asylum but as an example of republican stability. They constructed a passive figure, austere and stern-visaged, a model of frozen perfection. Their primary objects were to commemorate France's participation in the War of American Independence and to strengthen Franco-American friendship. The statue had been devised as an exhibit at the Philadelphia Exposition of 1876, which marked the one hundredth anniversary of American independence. Only the raised arm, holding a torch, was completed in time for that occasion. But the Exposition publicized the project, and in doing so fixed in American minds the original identification of the statue with national independence.[10] The meaning of the statue would have to change profoundly before Americans could see its uplifted torch as a beckoning light to the huddled masses of the Old World.

The immigrants themselves wrought that transformation as they arrived in this country in the years after the statue was erected. The vast majority debarked at New York, and to every exultant heart and straining eye this first American presence was a profoundly moving sight. The immigrants perceived the statue as waiting for them, big with promise. They saw it not as a beacon to other lands but as a redemptive salutation to themselves. The memory of that awesome moment and the unspoken greeting it contained was a thing to cherish, a thing to tell one's children about. In 1906 Edward A. Steiner, an immigrant writer who obviously had not heard of Emma Lazarus's poem, predicted that a great poet would someday put into words the inspiring emotions that millions of immigrants felt on encountering "this new divinity into whose keeping they now entrust themselves."[11]

10. Gschaedler, *True Light*, 44–45, 63, 72.
11. Edward A. Steiner, *On the Trail of the Immigrant* (New York, 1906), 60. See also Broughton Brandenburg, *Imported Americans: The Story of the Experiences of a Disguised American and His Wife Studying the Immigration Question* (New York, 1904), 204, and Louis Adamic, *Laughing in the Jungle: The Autobiography of an Immigrant in America* (New York, 1932), 40.

Decades passed, however, before the immigrants' interpretation of the statue penetrated the official culture of the United States. While a bitter controversy over immigration pitted older against newer American groups, the Statue of Liberty remained for most citizens an aloof, impersonal symbol, conveying a warning rather than a welcome to the outside world. Native-born Americans were not unaware of the special meaning the statue had for immigrants. Within a year of its dedication, a leading illustrated news magazine published a large handsome drawing of immigrants gazing joyfully at Bartholdi's Colossus from the steerage deck of an incoming vessel.[12] But the perception remained inert; it lacked any mythic power. The early custodians of the statue (the Light-House Board, then the War Department) attempted no interpretation of it. The National Park Service, which took jurisdiction in 1933, clung to the traditional motifs—Franco-American friendship and liberty as an abstract idea. On the statue's fiftieth anniversary, in 1936, patriotic organizations and public schools promoted a nationwide celebration which kept the usual themes steadily at the fore. Speaking at the base of the statue, President Franklin D. Roosevelt, a little bolder than most, at least mentioned the immigrants' search for freedom. But he quickly assured his hearers that it was a thing of the past. "We have within our shores today the materials out of which we shall continue to build an even better home for liberty."[13]

Ironically, it was the termination of mass immigration that eventually made possible a general acceptance of the meaning Emma Lazarus and the immigrants attached to the Statue of Liberty. After the restrictive Immigration Act of 1924, immigration as a mass movement receded into history. Meanwhile, the children of immigrants from southern and eastern Europe grew up into full participation in American life. To ease their Americanization, public school curricula devoted increasing attention

12. *Leslie's Illustrated Weekly Newspaper*, LXIV (1887), 324-25.
13. Walter Hugins, *Statue of Liberty National Monument: Its Origin, Development, and Administration* (U.S. Department of the Interior, National Park Service, 1958), 7-24, 45-47, 76-77; John J. Heimburger, "Statue of Liberty: An American Tradition," *School Life*, XXII (October, 1936), 35-36; B. D. Zevin, ed., *Nothing to Fear: The Selected Addresses of Franklin Delano Roosevelt, 1932-1945* (Cambridge, Mass., 1946), 71.

to the immigrants' love for and contributions to America. By 1926 fourth-grade children in St. Louis, Missouri, were studying the Statue of Liberty with the object of understanding what it meant to immigrants. By then some of the textbooks on American history included photographs of immigrants saluting the statue as they entered New York Harbor.[14] That immobile figure, fixed on her pedestal, gradually joined the covered wagon as a symbol of the migrations that had made America.[15]

In the late 1930's, more than fifty years after its composition, Emma Lazarus's poem finally attracted public interest. The event that called it forth from obscurity was a recurrence of the very problem that had moved the poet in the first place: the plight of Jewish refugees. Their efforts to escape Nazi barbarism coincided with a growing revulsion of American opinion against racism and with a steady movement of the United States toward war with Germany. In contrast to the situation in the 1880's, when Americans were turning away from a cosmopolitan, humane outlook, the circumstances of the late 1930's united a particular concern for the Jews with a broader movement to strengthen ethnic democracy. Immigration policy did not change significantly. But a nation striving to overcome its own ethnic hatreds, to dignify influential minority groups, and to gird for war against Hitler needed to define itself anew as a bastion against persecution.[16]

Louis Adamic, a Yugoslavian-American journalist, did more than anyone else to popularize "The New Colossus." About 1934 he launched a one-man crusade to elevate the status of the recent immigrant groups and to propagate an eclectic sense of American

14. St. Louis, Missouri, Board of Education, *Social Studies for Kindergarten and Grades I–VI* (Curriculum Bulletin No. 6, St. Louis, 1926), 176–77; Charles A. Beard and William C. Bagley, *The History of the American People* (New York, 1923), 501; Grace A. Turkington, *My Country, A Textbook in Civics and Patriotism for Young Americans* (Boston, 1923), 38–39; Howard C. Hill, *Community and Vocational Civics* (Boston, 1928), 121. Earlier editions of the Beard and Bagley book in 1921 and 1922 had nothing on the Statue of Liberty.

15. The two symbols actually converged on the cover of Eugene C. Barker et al., *The Story of Our Country* (Evanston, Ill., 1941).

16. James Benet, "Mother of Exiles," *New Republic*, LXXXIX (1936), 108–9; Louis Adamic, *America and the Refugees* (Public Affairs Pamphlet No. 29, 1939); *The Atlantic*, "We Americans" (Boston, 1939).

nationality. His immediate object was not to revise the immigration laws but to get American history rewritten along lines that would recognize the contributions of the newer ethnic groups. After 1938 he adopted the Lazarus sonnet as the keynote of practically everything he wrote or said. He quoted it endlessly in books, pamphlets, and public lectures.[17] During the 1940's the words of the poem became a familiar litany in mass circulation magazines, children's stories, and high-school history texts.[18] In 1945 Georgina Schuyler's commemorative tablet was moved from the second-story landing to the main entrance of the statue. Beginning in 1948, the *World Almanac* included the poem as a regular feature. Curiosity about its forgotten author awakened. Now she seemed less a Jewish than an American poet, a human statue of liberty. According to the title of one rapturous biography, she was *Emma Lazarus, Woman with a Torch*.[19]

The acclaim resounded in spite of a nagging difficulty in the text of the famous sonnet. To call America "Mother of Exiles" was splendid. To describe the immigrants as "huddled masses yearning to breathe free" was well enough. To label them "wretched refuse," however, was downright offensive. The condescension may have been innocent enough. Possibly, as a recent defender of Lazarus has argued, she was using "wretched" and "refuse" in a non-pejorative sense. "Wretched" had once meant distressed or afflicted, rather than despicable; "refuse" had meant

17. Louis Adamic, "Thirty Million New Americans," *Harper's Magazine,* CLXIX (November, 1934), 684–94; *My America, 1928–1938* (New York, 1938), 195; *From Many Lands* (New York, 1940), 292; *Two Way Passage* (New York, 1941), 49. See also R. Alan Lawson, *The Failure of Independent Liberalism, 1930–1941* (New York, 1971), 151–54.

18. A few examples may suffice: Francis Rowsome, "When Liberty Was Imported," *American Mercury,* LVII (1943), 72–79; "She's Still a Thriller," *Rotarian,* LXXIV (May, 1949), 16–19; Donald C. Peattie, "Liberty," *Reader's Digest,* LV (September, 1949), inside back cover; Myrtle Roberts, *Pattern for Freedom: A History of the United States* (Philadelphia, 1953), 474–75; Matilda Bailey, *The World of America: The Mastery of Reading* (New York, 1956), 117–19.

19. Bernard Postal, "The Sonnet of Liberty," *Coronet,* XLVIII (May, 1960), 82; Eve Merriam, *Emma Lazarus, Woman with a Torch* (New York, 1956). One article, Ann Batchelder's "Emma in Retrospect," *Ladies' Home Journal,* LVIII (June, 1941), 153, avoided any mention of her Jewish writings and affiliation.

what is rejected regardless of value, not what is worthless. In the 1880's, however, the words were already laden with disparagement. *Life,* a popular magazine, contrasted "the refuse of foreign populations" with "the very flower of manhood and womanhood" who "composed the nucleus of the nation."[20] Lazarus's unguarded phrase must have hurt. But the poem was too keenly needed to be damaged greatly by a phrase. Readers slid over the words, hearing only their music, dwelling on images of travail and redemption.

The unquestioning enthusiasm for Emma Lazarus's poem was closely entwined with an enormous growth in the popularity of the statue itself as a national symbol. Like the Liberty Bell in Philadelphia, the statue continued to be an embodiment of the national idea; but its special identification with millions of immigrants humanized the statue to a degree unequaled by any other monument. Attendance soared in 1940 and again in 1941. The *New York Times* called the statue "our No. 1 symbol." A National Park Service superintendent reported that visitors almost always treated it with profound respect.[21]

The boom rolled on through the postwar years. In 1954 nearly 800,000 visitors crowded the little ferries that shuttled back and forth from Manhattan to Bedloe's Island. The U.S. Postal Service that year produced a veritable explosion of statuesque symbolism. Having first appeared on a postage stamp in 1922, as one among a variety of notable American scenes, the Statue of Liberty was featured in the 1940's on a one-cent "National Defense" stamp and on a special overseas airmail stamp. These earlier uses paled in comparison with a literally dazzling display of the statue on the new three-cent, eight-cent, and eleven-cent stamps of the standard series inaugurated in 1954. Here a glow of divinity enveloped Bartholdi's mundane figure. Behind its diademed head a radiant

20. Letter, Samuel H. Monk to Editor, *Times Literary Supplement,* August 14, 1969, p. 907; *Life,* XII (July 19, 1888), 30. See also the debates of the California constitutional convention of 1850, quoted in Leonard Pitt, "The Beginnings of Nativism in California," *Pacific Historical Review,* XXX (February, 1961), 27.

21. "Our No. 1 Symbol," *New York Times Magazine,* June 22, 1941, p. 13; "Life Visits the Statue of Liberty," *Life,* X (June 2, 1941), 94–97; "Living with a Goddess," *American Magazine,* CLIX (June 1955), 49.

halo lit the sky; and within the halo appeared the motto, "In God We Trust."[22]

Meanwhile planning began for a national museum of immigration in the base of the statue. After some years the museum materialized; and its location further confirmed the new identity the statue had taken on. So long as millions of immigrants entered "the golden door," the Statue of Liberty was unresponsive to them; it served other purposes. After the immigrant ships no longer passed under the New Colossus in significant numbers, it enshrined the immigrant experience as a transcendental national memory. Because few Americans now were immigrants, all could think of themselves as having been immigrants. The Statue of Liberty helped them to do so. Since it belonged to all the people and on the broadest level symbolized the nation as a whole, the statue connected the special heritage of newer Americans with the civic principles of all Americans. Fundamentally, the new meaning engrafted on the Statue of Liberty in the second quarter of the twentieth century worked to close the rift that mass immigration had opened in American society.

Yet the revival of the myth of America as a refuge for the oppressed was not merely retrospective, not simply a healing message for domestic purposes. The reality of asylum in America never entirely disappeared, and the celebration of the immigrant experience in the mid-twentieth century encouraged fresh efforts to live up to the ideals of "The New Colossus." In 1965 Congress repealed the discriminatory features of the Immigration Law of 1924. President Lyndon B. Johnson, signing the new law at the base of the Statue of Liberty, alluded to the Lazarus poem and declared that the nation was returning "to the finest of its traditions." In the same spirit the President used the occasion to announce a large-scale program for reception of refugees from Cuba.[23] Emma Lazarus would have approved.

22. U.S. Postal Service, *Postage Stamps of the United States* (Washington, D.C., 1970), 45, 103, 117, 145–46.
23. *Washington Post*, October 4, 1965, pp. A6–7.

Chapter Four

Abraham Cahan: Novelist Between Three Cultures

Northeast from the tip of Manhattan, a mile and a half from the point where the immigrants landed, the Jewish East Side of New York began. By the turn of the century, it extended northward from Henry Street to Tenth Street and eastward from the Bowery almost to the East River. Within these teeming blocks, some of them the most crowded in the world, 150,000 Jews lived on the threshold of American life.[1] Every year thousands more arrived, while other thousands poured out from the great ghetto to the colonies it had spawned in Brooklyn, Harlem, and the Bronx.

There was never, in the history of American immigration, anything quite like the old East Side. Not as colorful as the adjacent Italian quarter around Mulberry Street, not as exotic or cohesive as San Francisco's Chinatown before the earthquake, not as prosperous as the German sections of Milwaukee and St. Louis, nor as poor and squalid as the Irish North End of Boston a half-century earlier, the Jewish East Side had the qualities of each and exhibited, withal, a spectacular energy uniquely its own. Here abilities that had been pent up for centuries within the tradition-bound villages of eastern Europe were suddenly set free. Here the largest, most diversified, and most authentic Yid-

1. New York *World*, August 3, 1902, p. 7.

dish-speaking community in America confronted trials and opportunities on a scale that only New York could present.

The thirty-year period from the mid-1880's to the First World War was the great age of the Lower East Side. Russian and Polish Jews had preempted certain streets before the Civil War, but the settlement was small and unimportant until 1880. From then until 1914 it grew by leaps and bounds. All over eastern Europe a general economic revolution uprooted petty Jewish tradesmen and artisans. In Russia pogroms and official persecution hastened the exodus. The world war halted this migration; the restriction laws of the early 1920's stopped it for good. Since then, the old East Side has faded. More and more non-Jews moved across the Bowery, diluting the Yiddish atmosphere of the area, and by 1930 it held a smaller Jewish population than it had in 1900.[2] Except for a tenacious remnant, its former inhabitants have spread through the city, the hinterland, and beyond. The East Side reached its zenith, therefore, just at the moment when Abraham Cahan, on the eve of the First World War, was writing his one major novel, *The Rise of David Levinsky*. Published in 1917, it is the unrivaled record of a great historical experience.

No one knew the East Side better than Cahan. As a struggling immigrant, he had worked in its tenements and taught in its schools. He had helped to organize its earliest Jewish unions and had participated in all the labor conflicts of its clothing industry. He had founded, and from 1902 to his death in 1951, edited, its outstanding newspaper, the *Jewish Daily Forward*. This he built into the most widely read Yiddish paper in the world. To the cultural life of the East Side he had already contributed short stories, three novels, and a constant stream of literary criticism. *The Rise of David Levinsky* was therefore only one of Cahan's achievements; but it is the most accessible of them, and it may be the most enduring.

The story is first of all a classic account of the Americanization

2. *New York Times*, March 18, 1928, sec. 10, p. 12; Zalmen Yoffeh, "The Passing of the East Side," *Menorah Journal*, XVII (1929), 265–75. The best history of the East Side is Moses Rischin, *The Promised City: New York's Jews, 1870–1914* (Cambridge, Mass., 1962), which may be supplemented by a superb album of photographs and other mementos, *Portal to America: The Lower East Side, 1870–1925*, ed. Allon Schoener (New York, 1967).

of the immigrant. A young man is uprooted from a traditional society and becomes a restlessly driven individualist. Although relatively few immigrants underwent so profound a deracination, Levinsky's experience differed from that of many eastern European Jews chiefly in degree. The story has been told frequently enough, but ordinarily in a simpler form than we encounter it here. One conventional version extols the progress of the immigrant; another laments his disintegration. But David Levinsky's "rise" is simultaneously a fall, and the reader participates in both.

What Cahan emphasizes is neither anguish nor ecstasy but an ultimate emptiness. Levinsky copes with change too well to lose control, yet change is too massive to leave him unscathed. Repeated manipulation of himself and of others to take advantage of shifting circumstances gradually leaches away the emotional core of his being. He loses a capacity to maintain any deep loyalty or enduring relationship. A character in another story of Cahan's sums up the point: "I have money and I have friends, but you want to know whether I am happy; and that I am not, sir. Why? Because I yearn neither for my country, nor for Zelaya, nor for anything else."[3]

As an impoverished boy in Russia, living in a corner of a basement room, Levinsky absorbed two of the deepest values of orthodox Jewish culture. Placed in a Talmudic seminary, he developed a passionate hunger for learning. To commune with God by memorizing and construing sacred texts was man's supreme vocation. The other anchor of Levinsky's life was his mother, whose affection transmitted to the fatherless boy the intensity of Jewish family life. In orthodox communities, love was sanctioned only within the limits of the family. There—a result rather than a cause of marriage—it preserved continuity and stability.[4]

Cracks were appearing, however, in this tight little world, so long impervious to external ways. The city in which Levinsky grew up in the 1860's and 1870's harbored a number of western-

3. Quoted in Joan Zlotnick, "Abraham Cahan, a Neglected Realist," *American Jewish Archives*, XXIII (1971), 36. See also Isaac Rosenfeld, "America, Land of the Sad Millionaire," *Commentary*, XIV (1952), 131–35.

4. Mark Zborowski and Elizabeth Herzog, *Life Is With People: The Culture of the Shtetl* (New York, 1962).

ized Jews, who wore modern clothes, read modern books, and neglected the synagogue. Their sons and daughters attended Russian government schools, associated freely with one another, and married for love. An older boy, rebellious and cynical, whispered subversive thoughts in Levinsky's ear. Before he left his native city, his religious passion was growing worldly. A brief exposure to modern life had destroyed for him the bars that orthodoxy put between the sexes; he succumbed to romantic love and sexual desire. Although he did not know it, his Americanization had begun. Like many other eastern European Jews, Levinsky's estrangement from traditional roots started in Europe.[5]

What remained of his religion collapsed in New York. "The very clothes I wore and the very food I ate had a fatal effect on my religious habits." The hunger for learning survived in secular form. A Talmud-trained capacity for feverish mental labor now went into the pursuit of a liberal education. But to attend college a homeless boy must first save money, and money could be had by bending, with the concentration of a scholar, over a sewing machine in a sweatshop. Somehow, the means became the end; an appetite for business success overpowered his cultural ambition. Levinsky attributes his change to an accident, a trivial affair that provoked him to retaliate against his German-Jewish employer. Cahan, who never steps beyond Levinsky's angle of vision, leaves the matter at that; we are free to speculate on its deeper sources. In any case, the American experience, so stimulating and manifold in its possibilities, coarsened Levinsky's character in the very process of liberating it. Since he could not forget what he had betrayed, the path of commercial achievement ended in spiritual loss and emptiness. Similarly, since he could not attain the idealistic women he sought, the path of romantic love ended in lonely bachelorhood.

While illuminating a profound conflict of values in American-Jewish life, Levinsky's story also reflects problems of adjustment that faced immigrants from many lands and backgrounds. They had to cope, in the hurly-burly of an American city, with an unaccustomed tempo of life. Stimulation mingled with confusion,

5. David Singer, "David Levinsky's Fall: A Note on the Liebman Thesis," *American Quarterly*, XIX (1967), 696–706.

opportunity with exploitation. Success in such a setting depended on assimilation, and this never came easily or automatically. To understand an unfamiliar, unpredictable environment, an immigrant had to distinguish between appearance and reality, between the civic rhetoric he heard in a schoolroom and the behavior he observed outside it. Since his native habits were often an encumbrance, adaptability might damage his inner integrity. Whether he was struggling to keep up with native American slang or, at a more advanced stage, to acquire a proper decorum, he lived insecurely in an ever-shifting milieu. If the immigrant were a woman, shut up in the home, and condemned to learn a new language and new ways from her children while pledging her own happiness to them, the strains of assimilation might become tragically intense. It is no accident that the mother in many an immigrant novel is a doomed figure, and that Cahan's one character of true nobility is Dora, clinging to a boorish husband for the sake of a daughter who proves unworthy of her mother's self-denial.

These glimpses of the psychological meaning of success and assimilation emerge, in *David Levinsky*, from a rich context of social history. Although Cahan's insight into individual character is striking, the force of his book comes at least as much from the New York Jewish scene re-created in all its dense variety. Levinsky's life touched virtually every segment of New York's Jewish society. The sweatshops, of course, are here, and so are the crowded flats where the kitchen served as a dining room and a bedroom for the extra boarder. Here, too, are the cafés, where the Yiddish *littérateurs* sat hours on end, drinking glasses of steaming tea. Here are the Russian revolutionists, periodically visiting New York to raise funds and sympathy, as Leon Trotsky did in 1916. Here is the decayed Hebrew poet, dabbling in real estate, fumbling in his declining years to revive the celebration of the Passover Seder in an amused and irreligious family. Here are the feverish speculators, making and losing fortunes in New York real estate at an informal curb exchange. Here is the sedate orthodox merchant, one of a class of pious, well-to-do Jews who stayed in the familiar ghetto, living comfortably in big old houses that survived from an earlier era. Here, by contrast, are mordant sketches of "uptown" parvenu society and of the marriage market at the Catskill resorts.

On this Russian-Jewish panorama, German Jews frequently appear. Having arrived in America one or two generations earlier, they controlled the power and prestige in American-Jewish affairs; the deluge from eastern Europe bore hard upon them. Cahan exhibits their relations with the eastern European Jews more perceptively than any historian has yet done. Instead of a simplified image of either panicky disdain or big-brotherly sympathy, we observe the German Jews behaving in a diversity of roles: to their eastern European kinsmen they were employers, philanthropic mentors, business enemies, social arbiters whose favor might be courted, and eventually even friends.

At the center of the whole spectacle is the development of a great industry—the mass production of women's garments. *The Rise of David Levinsky* belongs not only in the genre of immigrant fiction but also among the best novels of American business. During the Progressive Era, many of the leading American novelists—Theodore Dreiser, Frank Norris, Robert Herrick, and others—were focusing on the great tycoon, embodiment of the American worship of success.[6] Cahan shared their view of the bitter fruits of business success; like them he presented the conquests of the marketplace as morally debasing. The other important novelists who explored this theme, however, did not pay much attention to the functioning of business itself. Whereas Dreiser and others concentrated on the businessman's personal life-style, Cahan also wrote, in the guise of fiction, a significant chapter in American economic history.

The ready-made clothing industry, centered in New York, had emerged as early as the 1830's. Well before the Civil War German Jews occupied a prominent position in the industry. Some of them, beginning as storekeepers, became wholesale manufacturers by sending material out to contractors. By 1880 these Jewish entrepreneurs dominated the New York clothing

6. Kenneth S. Lynn, *The Dream of Success: A Study of the Modern American Imagination* (Boston, 1955); Van R. Halsey, "Fiction and the Businessman: Society Through All Its Literature," *American Quarterly*, XI (1959), 391–402.

industry, and in the sweatshops their contractors operated, the new Jewish immigrants, pouring in from eastern Europe, went to work.

Women's wear, the most volatile section of the industry, was also the newest; most types of women's clothes were exclusively home-made or custom-made until the late nineteenth century. This field, where style and variety were at a premium, the Russian Jews made their own. During the 1890's Russian-Jewish tailors, setting up their own tiny factories outside the contracting system, drove most of the big German-Jewish firms out of the women's cloak and suit trade.[7] *The Rise of David Levinsky* tells the story of how they did it.

This, of course, was an extraordinary ethnic accomplishment, and Cahan was not immune to its appeal. In spite of the unsparing social criticism with which the book abounds, David Levinsky obviously speaks for the author in expressing a quiet pride in the collective achievement of his people. That business success should redound to the credit of a group, while demoralizing the individual members responsible for it, may betray an inconsistent point of view. But the inconsistency—if it be such—goes down deep in American values, which have always been ambiguous in appraising success. What Cahan's novel may lack in that resolution of themes characteristic of the highest literature is amply made up by the comprehensiveness, the balance, and the integrity of its vision.

II

Until the twentieth century serious American literature almost totally ignored the immigrant. In the 1870's and 1880's "local color" writers such as George Washington Cable and H. H. Boyesen occasionally took note of ethnic minorities other than the Indian and Negro. But the local colorists merely glossed the surface of the subject, exploiting its quaintness and charm.

7. John R. Commons, "Immigration and Its Economic Effects," *Reports of the United States Industrial Commission,* 19 vols. (Washington, 1900–1902), XV, 320–24.

Beyond these scattered, external vignettes, our literary record told virtually nothing about one of the most distinctive and important aspects of American civilization.

In large measure this neglect was due to prevailing canons of taste. The nineteenth-century American reading public wanted its heroes and heroines well-born and properly bred. It might sometimes accept a noble savage like Huckleberry Finn, but he must be an authentic child of nature, untainted by European vices. A combination of lower-class status and European birth seemed incompatible with the moral purity on which American cultural authorities insisted. When Abraham Cahan began in the 1890's to write unsentimental stories about East Side life, he faced resistance from publishers and outraged protests from many Americanized Jews who felt their own respectability threatened.

By the turn of the century, cultural standards were changing, however. The gradual movement toward an ever-more consistent and thoroughgoing realism brought Cahan essential support and encouragement. William Dean Howells, who was opening doors for so many literary innovators, launched Cahan as a novelist virtually singlehandedly. On discovering Cahan's first short story in a minor American magazine, Howells sent for him and urged him to attempt a novel. Much heartened, Cahan produced a grim tale about a husband and wife alienated by the process of Americanization; he submitted the manuscript to Howells. The latter sent it to publisher after publisher until he persuaded one to take it. When the book, entitled *Yekl: A Tale of the New York Ghetto*, appeared in 1896, Howells completed his services by writing a review that acclaimed Cahan as an author "who will do honor to American letters."[8] This was the genesis of the first full-fledged immigrant novel in English—the first, that is, by a naturalized writer who saw life through the eyes of his own people in reporting their American experience to an American audience.

Thereafter the way was not easy; *Yekl* sold poorly and was soon forgotten, in spite of Howells's promotion. But incentives to look squarely at all of America's peoples gradually increased.

8. Rudolf and Clara M. Kirk, "Abraham Cahan and William Dean Howells: The Story of a Friendship," *American Jewish Historical Quarterly,* LII (1962), 27–57. The complete text of Howells's review is given on pp. 51–52.

After 1900 progressivism, like the realism that preceded and accompanied it, inspired a sympathetic interest in the social problems of the newcomers. Native American novelists such as Upton Sinclair and Ernest Poole illuminated the exploitation of immigrant workingmen.[9] In 1913 the most gifted native American interpreter of immigrant experience, Willa Cather, published *O Pioneers*, in which she turned back from more genteel subjects to the nationalities she remembered from her Nebraska childhood. About the same time *McClure's Magazine*, which had rejected *Yekl* in the nineties, asked Cahan to do some sketches of East Side life. He supplied a series of four stories, which he later expanded into *The Rise of David Levinsky*.[10]

Although cultural changes in America may explain the emergence of an English-speaking audience for Cahan's fiction, those changes cannot account for the way he wrote, for the rareness of his kind of insight, or for its total absence from earlier American literature. What qualities in Cahan equipped him to produce a unique masterpiece of social criticism?

Howells's review of Cahan's first book obliquely suggested an answer. "He sees things with American eyes," Howells noted, "and he brings in aid of his vision the far and rich perceptions of his Hebraic race; while he is strictly of the great and true Russian principle in literary art." To be more precise, Cahan stood at a crossroads of three cultures. Ordinarily, the special contribution of a "hyphenated" writer is a double vision, juxtaposing two cultures. In Cahan's case a third culture, which was Russian, supplied an extraordinary detachment and breadth of view. Through the lens of this third culture Cahan gained critical distance from *both* his ethnic subculture and his adopted country. He could see their complementary failings without overlooking their distinctive achievements.

Cahan's theme of success, and its morally debasing effects, was distinctively American. In this sense he wrote in the tradition of

9. Upton Sinclair, *The Jungle* (New York, 1906); Ernest Poole, *The Harbor* (New York, 1915).

10. Abraham Cahan, "Autobiography of an American Jew," *McClure's Magazine*, XL (1913), 92–106; XLI (1913), 73–85, 116–28, 131–32. See also Cahan's unfinished autobiography, *Bletter von Mein Leben*, 5 vols. (New York, 1926–1931), V, ch. 6.

The Rise of Silas Lapham and *Sister Carrie*. Although not attracted by money, Cahan in other forms knew firsthand the terrible struggle for success. During one period in his life, from 1897 to 1902, he broke out of the Jewish community and concentrated fiercely on becoming a recognized American writer. He returned to Yiddish journalism partly because his work did not sell—Cahan's realism was still too pungent for American taste at the turn of the century—and partly because he was offered a free hand in running the *Jewish Daily Forward*.[11]

Cahan's subject matter, of course, was Jewish, and his approach owed much to the Yiddish culture of the eastern European Jews. From Yiddish literature and tradition Cahan derived his close but self-critical identification with the life of his people.[12] But his artistic sensibility was Russian. His capacity to treat all kinds of people with pity and calm impartiality came from the great Russian realists, from Tolstoy and Chekhov and their contemporaries. Because of his allegiance to the standards of Russian literature, Cahan achieved a perspective that was neither wholly American or wholly Yiddish, but in some measure universal.

The great struggle of Cahan's early life was for a Russian education. Born in a Lithuanian village near Vilna in 1860, he was the son of a poor Hebrew teacher, a dreamy, soulful man. His parents sent him to Hebrew schools like those that David Levinsky attended. Unlike Levinsky, however, Cahan developed a passion for Russian culture at an early age and became completely immersed in it before he had to emigrate in 1882. As a boy he taught himself the Russian language, then attended a Russian public school against his parents' will. By tutoring he earned money to buy secular books, and by discarding his traditional Jewish garb he gained access to the Vilna public library. There he steeped himself in the great Russian writers.[13]

11. Melech Epstein, *Profiles of Eleven* (Detroit, 1965), 73–85. On this period see also Moses Rischin, "Abraham Cahan and the New York *Commercial Advertiser*," *Publications of the American Jewish Historical Society*, XLIII (1953), 10–36.

12. "Introduction," *A Treasury of Yiddish Stories*, ed. Irving Howe and Eliezer Greenberg (Greenwich, Conn., 1968), 35–53.

13. The first two volumes of Cahan's autobiography have been translated into English as *The Education of Abraham Cahan* (Philadelphia, 1969).

The initial effect of Cahan's Russification was not literary; it was political. While studying at a governmental teachers' college, he heard of the revolutionary movement and joined it. This completed his westernization; in socialism he found a new religion. It was also socialism, rather than anti-Semitism, that expelled him from Russia. When the police discovered his participation in a revolutionary group, Cahan escaped in disguise to America. Here he soon embarked on a career of socialist journalism. But after the first excitement of these experiences passed, Cahan's interest in literature reawakened. He reread *Anna Karenina* in 1888, discovered Chekhov a while later, then went back to Tolstoy again. Filled with a hunger for artistic truth, Cahan abandoned plans for a philosophical treatise on Darwinism and socialism. Instead, he devoted his spare time to fiction utterly untouched by any polemical intent. "Life-likeness clothed in the simplest forms of expression, and artistic sincerity reflecting the self-criticisms and the melancholy moods of the Russian people" became, in his own words, his literary credo.[14]

Yet American circumstances would not permit Cahan to function simply as a Russian-American writer. The Jewish identity he had cast off in Russia proved an essential American vesture. Simply to agitate for socialism in America, a Russianized intellectual had to rejoin the Jewish community. At first, radicals like Cahan who came to the United States in the early eighties spoke only Russian. But few Russians emigrated, and few Jews understood Russian. To win a popular following, the intellectuals had to identify themselves with the Yiddish-speaking working class. Cahan began lecturing in Yiddish the very year of his arrival, and soon embarked on a career of Yiddish journalism that lasted, with only brief intermissions, to the end of his days.[15] Eventually, his socialism faded into a cherished memory, but his renewed affiliation with Jewish life never wavered.

As the best Yiddish editor in America, Cahan acquired a devoted and discerning sense of the moods and interests of the

14. Abraham Cahan, "The Younger Russian Writers," *Forum*, XXVIII (1899), 119.
15. Epstein, *Profiles*, 61–67; Morris Hillquit, *Loose Leaves from a Busy Life* (New York, 1934), 17, 34–36.

Jewish immigrants; as an English-language journalist, contributing to general New York newspapers within a few years of his arrival, he became the first interpreter of the East Side to native-born America. One of his most exciting discoveries, in this role of cultural ambassador and ethnic spokesman, was Yiddish literature. In the late nineteenth century, Yiddish—previously a vernacular tongue with no cultural prestige—became a medium of significant artistic expression. Often under the influence of Russian realism, Yiddish poets, dramatists, and storytellers reproduced with poignant fidelity the folk-life of the people. The lowly "mama-gab," which westernized intellectuals like Cahan once disdained, revitalized their ethnic heritage.[16]

Cahan did more, perhaps, than anyone else to encourage Yiddish literature in America. In the 1890's, as editor of a socialistic weekly, he publicized European Yiddish writers and offered an outlet for the best talent in the New York ghetto. Later, in the *Jewish Daily Forward*, he published the work of virtually every notable Yiddish writer. Instead of trying to purify Yiddish by making it more German, Cahan insisted in his newspaper and strove in his own writing to reproduce the plain speech of the masses. All this experience contributed to *The Rise of David Levinsky*. Although created in English and cast in a Russian mold, it contained the essence of Yiddish culture and experience.

I I I

For several decades this memorable novel received more respect than attention. Authorities on American-Jewish culture regularly acknowledged its importance; but historians of American literature rarely noticed it, and the general audience for whom Cahan wrote knew little about it. Never a best seller, the book had a modest sale of 8,000 copies during the first two years of publication. A cheap edition, issued by a reprint house in 1928, did

16. Hutchins Hapgood, *The Spirit of the Ghetto: Studies in the Jewish Quarter of New York* (New York, 1902), 199–229; Nathaniel Buchwald, "Yiddish," *Cambridge History of American Literature*, ed. William P. Trent et al., 4 vols. (New York, 1917–1921), IV, 598–609.

fairly well for a few years. In 1943 the book went out of print.[17]

Until recently, the situation of the American Jew did not encourage a widely sympathetic reading of *David Levinsky*. A mass exodus of eastern European Jews from the immigrant ghettos of the big cities was under way by the time Cahan wrote. In escaping from confinement to poverty and foreignness, millions of Jews collided against rising barriers of discrimination. They were, therefore, defensive about the immediate past and eager to decontaminate Jewish life from the color and flavor of the ghetto. Under these circumstances, David Levinsky's dispassionate self-examination was an embarrassment. Instead of seeing the nuances and varieties of character that Cahan had painted, instead of appreciating his implicit criticism of American business life, uneasy readers thought he had perversely documented all the anti-Semitic stereotypes. A genteel professor, reviewing the book in a highbrow magazine in 1917, wondered indignantly if the author realized how revolting Levinsky was; and a nervous liberal assured social workers that the book misrepresented American-Jewish life.[18]

Burdened with the same "second-generation" anxieties, the American-Jewish novel moved away from the world of Abe Cahan. Other themes came to the fore: the rebellion of the young against their elders, intermarriage, psychological insecurity, anti-Semitism. By the 1930's novelists who stayed in the vein of realistic social criticism had become angry and hortatory. The Jewish slumdweller, deprived of most of his specific Jewishness, was converted into a faceless prototype of all persecuted minorities.[19]

After 1950 the problems that weighed so heavily on the second generation ceased to be oppressive. Discrimination vastly diminished. The strains of extreme mobility let up. A third generation,

17. Memo, Hugh Van Dusen, Harper & Row, Torchbooks, to John Higham, June 21, 1960.

18. H. W. Boynton, "Outstanding Novels of the Year," *Nation*, 105 (1917), 600–1; *Book Review Digest*, 1917, p. 85. On the other hand, John Macy published a glowing and perceptive appreciation: "The Story of a Failure," *The Dial*, LXIII (1917), 521–23.

19. Allen Guttmann, *The Jewish Writer in America: Assimilation and the Crisis of Identity* (New York, 1971); George C. Clay, "The Jewish Hero in American Fiction," *Reporter*, XVII (September 19, 1957), 43–46.

more self-assured, came on the scene, and it wanted to learn what its fathers tried to forget. Now, as never before, the life of the New York ghetto in the early twentieth century stirred the hearts of English-language readers. But those who described it in the era of mass suburbia drew on the softened contours of memory. The ghetto was reborn in a shimmer of nostalgia.[20] To see it whole, there was still no substitute for the level gaze, the amalgam of intimacy and detachment, and the deep sense of history that belonged to Abraham Cahan.

20. See especially Harry Golden, *Only in America* (New York, 1958) and subsequent books, and Alfred Kazin, *A Walker in the City* (New York, 1951).

Chapter Five

Ideological Anti-Semitism in the Gilded Age

To general American historians, anti-Semitism has never seemed a subject of major importance. No decisive event, no deep crisis, no powerful social movement, no great individual is associated primarily with, or significant chiefly because of, anti-Semitism. Accordingly, historians have rarely taken more than a passing interest in studying it. A single notable exception to the prevailing inattention occurred in the 1950's, but the controversy ended in a most unfortunate way. Instead of clarifying the fundamental issues, it diverted research away from the whole subject.

Investigation of anti-Semitism in the American past did not rise above an antiquarian level until the late 1930's and 1940's,[1] when Carey McWilliams published *A Mask for Privilege* and C. Vann Woodward brought out his fine biography of Tom Watson. McWilliams's book established the outlines of what may be called the progressive interpretation of American anti-Semitism. The main elements of that interpretation were, first, an aroused sensitivity to the divisiveness of "prejudice"; second, a preoccupation with its conservative or reactionary manifestations; third, an economic interpretation of its origins. The Hitler fury in Europe and the stirring of a native fascism at home suddenly gave an

1. Lee J. Levinger's *Anti-Semitism in the United States: Its History and Causes* (New York, 1925) was a study of current events, since it confined itself to the postwar period.

ominous significance to earlier American anti-Semitism. Impelled by muckraking zeal, researchers studied anti-Jewish effusions during the Federalist era, the Civil War, and other periods.[2] On the whole, these inquiries displayed the progressive tendency to associate prejudice with conservatism and privilege, so that even Tom Watson—in Woodward's biography—seemed to lapse into a generally reactionary outlook as he plunged into ethnic strife. Woodward did not explain why that happened, but McWilliams indulged freely in the progressive inclination to utilize an economic interpretation of history as a weapon of exposure. McWilliams traced American anti-Semitism to the industrial revolution of the 1870's. It was sparked, he said, by the assault of big business on America's democratic heritage.[3] Anti-Semitism was "a mask for privilege."

After 1948, when McWilliams's book appeared, the drift of scholars was away from progressive interpretations of American history. Also, a remarkable improvement in most phases of American ethnic relations in the years after the Second World War discredited the immediate postwar fear of a renewed outburst of anti-Jewish feeling. As the anxieties that spurred the scholarship of the thirties and forties subsided, suspicions arose that the extent of American anti-Semitism was being exaggerated and its locus misplaced. Revisionists came forward with the argument that anti-Semitism had a much more limited and marginal place in American history. In an important essay published in 1951, effectively inaugurating the newer interpretation, Oscar Handlin declared that anti-Semitism was insignificant until well

2. Leonard A. Greenberg, "Some American Anti-Semitic Publications of the Late 19th Century," *Publications of the American Jewish Historical Society*, XXXVII (1947), 421-25; Morris U. Schappes, "Anti Semitism and Reaction, 1795–1800," ibid., XXXVIII (December, 1948), 109-37, and *A Documentary History of the Jews in the United States, 1654-1875* (New York, 1950); Bertram W. Korn, *American Jewry and the Civil War* (Philadelphia, 1951); Edward N. Saveth, *American Historians and European Immigrants, 1875-1925* (New York, 1948), 65-89; C. Vann Woodward, *Tom Watson, Agrarian Rebel* (New York, 1938).

3. Carey McWilliams, *A Mask for Privilege: Anti-Semitism in America* (Boston, 1948). A more temperate example of the liberal economic interpretation is in Abram L. Sachar, *Sufferance Is the Badge: The Jew in the Contemporary World* (New York, 1940), 534-39.

into the twentieth century. As late as the 1890's the Jewish stereotype involved "no hostility, no negative judgment." This flat denial of nineteenth-century anti-Semitism was inconsistent with other aspects of his thesis; Handlin made some slight emendations when he incorporated the essay into his popular book, *Adventure in Freedom*. Nevertheless, as the title of that book suggested, a mellow, optimistic point of view now enfolded virtually the whole sweep of American-Jewish history.[4] Here we observe a relaxation of the ethnic fears of 1933 to 1948. Here too we see emerging the broad tendency in the scholarship of the 1950's to reemphasize harmony and unity in American society.

In the shift from a progressive to a neoliberal interpretation of American history, a warm, almost nostalgic attitude toward the past was linked with two other characteristics. Neoliberal scholars undertook a skeptical reappraisal of the tradition of dissent in America; as a result they looked into liberal rather than conservative quarters for soft spots in the national culture. In doing so, they paid more attention to the role of ideas and less to economic forces; the economic interpretation of history so influential in the thirties lost much of its old rebellious appeal. These changes, too, had a shaping effect on Handlin's essay of 1951. The essay described the emergence in the 1890's of a new image of the Jew as an international money power striving to control the world economy. Handlin traced this image not to reactionary sources but rather to agrarian radicals, and he attributed it chiefly to a rural habit of mind—a parochial suspicion of the city. Not long thereafter, in a critical reexamination of American reform movements, Richard Hofstadter underlined the connection between anti-Semitism and the Populist mentality, concluding in fact that Populism "activated most of what we have of modern popular anti-Semitism in the United States."[5]

4. See Oscar Handlin, "American Views of the Jew at the Opening of the Twentieth Century," *Publications of the American Jewish Historical Society*, XL (June, 1951), 325, 328, and *Adventure in Freedom: Three Hundred Years of Jewish Life in America* (New York, 1954), 184.

5. Richard Hofstadter, *The Age of Reform: From Bryan to F.D.R.* (New York, 1955), 80. See, in a similar vein, Harry L. Golden, "Jew and Gentile in the New South," *Commentary*, XX (November, 1955), 403–12, and Victor C. Ferkiss, "Populist Influences on American Fascism," *Western Political Quarterly*, X (1957), 350–73.

Thus one set of assumptions gave way to another in the charting of American anti-Semitism. Assurance of its weakness replaced fear of its strength. A "mask for privilege" became a by-product of reform. And economic causation yielded to psychological and ideological explanations.[6] One might have supposed that the clash between progressive and neoliberal interpretations would inspire a thorough reinvestigation of the role of anti-Semitism in American history. Instead, the controversy narrowed into a fierce little quarrel over the nature of the Populist movement.

Although everyone tacitly agreed that anti-Semitism was at most a minor facet of Populism, no other aspect received such anxious scrutiny. The specific issue was the extent to which Populists should be blamed for fostering the myth of a international Jewish conspiracy. The scholars' real concern, however, was not with the nature of anti-Semitism; it was with the integrity of Populism as bearer of a radical and democratic heritage. Young historians, born and bred in the city, were reevaluating the "agrarian radicalism" that an older, less urbanized generation had fondly chronicled, and the charge of anti-Semitism dramatized the issue of their own intellectual antecedents. By the early 1960's intensive research on the Populists had taken most of the sting out of the charge, whereupon the quarrel subsided.[7] Preoccupation with Populism—an essentially democratic movement —relegated anti-Semitism again to obscurity.

6. Of course, not all scholarship can be so classified. See, for example, the notably objective review of colonial attitudes toward Jews in Jacob R. Marcus, *Early American Jewry*, 2 vols. (Philadelphia, 1951–1953), II, 514–27.

7. Pro Populist writings included: C. Vann Woodward, "The Populist Heritage and the Intellectual," *American Scholar*, XXIX (1959–60), 55–72; Paul Holbo, "Wheat or What? Populism and American Fascism," *Western Political Quarterly*, XIV (1961), 727–36; Walter T. K. Nugent, *The Tolerant Populists: Kansas Populism and Nativism* (Chicago, 1963); and a spate of articles by Norman Pollack, including: "Hofstadter on Populism: A Critique of 'The Age of Reform,'" *Journal of Southern History*, XXVI (1960), 478–500; "Handlin on Anti-Semitism: A Critique of 'American Views of the Jew,'" *Journal of American History*, LI (1964), 391–403; and "The Myth of Populist Anti-Semitism," *American Historical Review*, LXVIII (1962), 76–80. The whole dispute is recanvassed in a symposium, "Papers on Populism," printed in *Agricultural History*, XXXIX (1965), 59–85. See also William F. Holmes, "Whitecapping in Mississippi," *Mid-America*, LV (1973), 134–48.

To get a firmer grip on anti-Semitism as a historical force with a shape and significance of its own, we need some general rules of procedure. The rest of this chapter will propound and illustrate certain guiding principles relevant to an objective history of American anti-Semitism. In formulating those principles, it will be useful to apply them to the formative era of the late nineteenth century, for the conflict in interpretation has centered upon the period from 1870 to 1900, when the exceptionally fortunate position which American Jews had secured in the eighteenth and early nineteenth centuries was seriously weakened. During those years two types of anti-Semitism became visible. The first is social anti-Semitism: a pattern of discrimination. The second is political or ideological anti-Semitism: a power-hungry agitation addressed to the entire body politic, which blames the major ills of society on the Jews. The principles of interpretation set forth here apply to both types; but we shall be concerned largely with ideological anti-Semitism. A full discussion of the rise of social discrimination is reserved for the following chapter.

To begin to understand the attitudes involved in either social or ideological anti-Semitism, it is necessary first of all to guard against the categorizing tendency that distinguishes too sharply between anti-Semites and philo-Semites or between liberals and conservatives. Stated positively, this premise simply means that most people waver between conflicting attitudes and seldom enjoy an undivided state of mind. Even the supposedly inflexible sort of judgment which the ethnic stereotype represents can incongruously combine both positive and negative charges. Because stereotypes are stylized responses, we too often assume that they are simple ones—either black or white. But a stereotype may express ambivalent emotions. It may blend affection and contempt, as the southern image of the Negro has often done. It may mingle pity and censure, as eastern views of the Indian did in the last century.[8]

In the case of the Jew, especially diverse and conflicting attitudes have always existed side by side in American minds. The Jewish stereotype took two entirely different forms, one reli-

8. Roy H. Pearce, *The Savages of America: A Study of the Indian and the Idea of Civilization* (Baltimore, 1953).

gious and the other economic; and in either case attractive elements mingled with unlovely ones. Seen in religious terms, the Jew was a portentous figure, at once the glorious agent of divine purpose and the deserving victim of His vengeance. In this orthodox Christian view, the Jews were God's Chosen People, miraculously preserved and sustained; yet they were also an unfaithful people who suffered justly for their betrayal. There is no doubt that the clerical spokesmen for an Old Testament, Puritan culture felt an awe-struck sympathy and identification with the archetypal people of God. Americans in the Puritan tradition devoutly believed that, like ancient Israel, they too were a nation in covenant with God. Moreover, the millennial passages of scripture assured them that the conversion of the Jews to Christianity would mark the beginning of the millennium. Still the "chosen and favorite people of the Most High," as Ezra Stiles described them, the Jews were destined to be a "glorious nation and a blessing to the world" in the approaching millennial age.[9] In this vein a prominent philo-Semite in the 1880's described Jews as "descendants of those from whom we derive our civilization, kinsmen, after the flesh, of Him whom we esteem as the Son of God and Saviour of men."[10] Yet Christian orthodoxy also presented the Jews as rebels against God's purpose. The justice of their ruination supplied the test for many a sermon.[11]

A similar duality complicated the economic stereotype of Jews: they represented both the capitalist virtues and the capitalist vices. On the favorable side, the Jew commonly symbolized an admirable keenness and resourcefulness in trade. In this sense his economic energy seemed very American.[12] In another mood,

9. Edmund Wilson, *A Piece of My Mind* (New York, 1956), 90–102; Jacob R. Marcus, *The Colonial American Jew, 1492–1776*, 3 vols. (Detroit, 1970), III, 1143.

10. Zebulon Vance, *The Scattered Nation* (New York, 1904).

11. "The Jew," *Yale Literary Magazine*, XII (August, 1847), 419–22; Clarence H. Faust and Thomas H. Johnson, eds., *Jonathan Edwards: Representative Selections* (New York, 1935), 155; Ethan Smith, *View of the Hebrews*, 2nd ed. (Poultney, Vt., 1825), 14; Osborn W. Trenery Heighway, *Leila Ada, the Jewish Convert* (Philadelphia, 1853), 111–17, 226; John Marsh, *An Epitome of General Ecclesiastical History*, 7th ed. (New York, 1843), 163–65, 449.

12. Rudolf Glanz, "Jew and Yankee: A Historic Comparison," *Jewish Social Studies*, VI (1944), 3–30.

however, keenness might mean cunning; enterprise might shade into avarice. Along with encomiums on the Jew as a progressive economic force—a model of commercial energy and integrity— went frequent references to conniving Shylocks. The earliest published plays containing Jewish characters (1794, 1823) portrayed Shylock types, and by the 1840's the verb "to Jew," meaning to cheat by sharp practice, was becoming a more or less common ingredient of American slang.[13] In the early nineteenth century the bright side of these judgments outshone the tarnished. Later, in an increasingly secularized society, the whole religious image declined, and the unattractive elements in the economic stereotype grew more pronounced. The latent conflict between favorable and unfavorable attitudes came more clearly into the open.

In the late nineteenth century a remarkably friendly attitude toward Jews still prevailed widely. Protestant ministers and Reform rabbis frequently exchanged pulpits. Rising Jewish capitalists joined in general community affairs and built lavish homes in the most exclusive neighborhoods.[14] The traditional American image of the Jew as a constructive economic force—a model of commercial enterprise, energy, and integrity—still provided material for popular orators and storytellers.[15] On the other hand, a distrust that expressed itself in the negative side of the economic stereotype steadily gained ground during the post–Civil War decades. Since this distrust clashed with the prevailing temper of American culture, anti-Semitic attitudes were often covert and usually blurred by a lingering respect. Many Americans were both pro- and anti-Jewish at the same time.

13. Stephen Bloore, "The Jew in American Dramatic Literature (1794–1930)," *Publication of the American Jewish Historical Society*, XL (1951), 345–60; Mitford M. Mathews, ed., *A Dictionary of Americanisms on Historical Principles*, 2 vols. (Chicago, 1951), I, 905; "Present State of the Jewish People in Learning and Culture," *North American Review*, LXXXIII (1856), 368.

14. *Public Opinion*, III (August 27, 1887), 423; Stuart E. Rosenberg, *The Jewish Community in Rochester, 1843–1925* (New York, 1954), 105–6.

15. Hezekiah Butterworth, *In Old New England: The Romance of a Colonial Fireside* (New York, 1895), 46–78; New York *Herald*, September 15, 1891; Zebulon B. Vance, *The Scattered Nation* (New York, 1904). For background see Selig Adler, "Zebulon B. Vance and the 'Scattered Nation,' " *Journal of Southern History*, VII (August, 1941), 357–77.

This duality was particularly evident among the rural radicals whom Handlin singled out for special emphasis. No other sector of native American opinion had such strong incentives to seek a Jewish scapegoat. At a time when Jews and their admirers boasted of their wealth, farmers and workingmen were struggling vainly to curb the accumulation of power and wealth by a business plutocracy. Just as Wall Street provided an *institutional* symbol of that plutocracy, so the Jews offered an *ethnic* symbol of the same giant adversary. As Shylocks, the Jews stood not only for plutocracy in general but also for the financial power of gold in particular. Professor Handlin has made an important contribution in pointing out that the men who crusaded passionately against the gold standard in the 1890's sometimes attributed their repeated setbacks to the Jews.

Yet the Populists and other currency reformers who saw the "Shylocks of Europe" pitted against the "toilers" of America[16] were also the very groups most deeply swayed by the ideals that had made the United States a beloved homeland for thousands of Jews. The whole agrarian crusade of the late nineteenth century drew vitality from the best traditions of American democracy and Christianity. James B. Weaver, the Populist candidate for President, spoke feelingly of maintaining America's mission as an asylum for the oppressed of all nations. His fellow reformers appealed constantly to the doctrines of the Declaration of Independence and to "the great bond of brotherhood which lies at the base of Christianity."[17] When such men struck at the Jews, they violated their own motivating principles.

As a result, the reformers displayed a divided state of mind that defies easy classification. Ignatius Donnelly, the fiery Minnesota agitator whose utopian novel, *Caesar's Column*, forms the linchpin in Handlin's argument, epitomized this inner conflict. The Jews he regarded as "a noble race" perverted by the terrible

16. J. Sterling Morton and Albert Watkins, *Illustrated History of Nebraska*, 3 vols. (Lincoln, 1905-1913), III, 244; *Arena*, XVI (September, 1896), 699.

17. James B. Weaver, *A Call to Action: An Interpretation of the Great Uprising, Its Source and Causes* (Des Moines, 1892), 281-82; Milford W. Howard, *The American Plutocracy* (New York, 1895); [Ignatius Donnelly], *Caesar's Column: A Story of the Twentieth Century* (Chicago, 1890), 3.

persecutions Christians had inflicted upon them. While viewing the Jews as a repulsive incarnation of materialism, Donnelly urged a spirit of charity toward them. "We should not feel incensed against the nut-gathering tribe. . . . It is their instinct. They can no more help the cast of their minds than they can the cast of their features, and one generally fits the other."[18] Similar rationalizations of inner conflict may be found elsewhere in Populist literature, as for example in an anti-Semitic pamphlet entitled *Tit for Tat*, in which an anonymous midwestern radical argued that the Jew was simply turning the tables on his erst-while persecutors in gaining a ruinous economic monopoly over the Christian world.[19]

Although the dilemma of these democratic anti-Semites may seem especially poignant, a comparable ambivalence extended far beyond reform groups. At one moment an editorial in the great New York *Tribune* might describe Jews and Christians as united by a common spiritual heritage and steadily outgrowing old animosities; at another moment the same paper might comment: "There must be some other cause than their religion which makes these people dreaded as permanent inhabitants by every country to which they come." A Boston newspaper combined positive and negative judgments in a single sentence: "It is strange that a nation that boasts so many good traits should be so obnoxious."[20] Most of the anti-Semitism in native American circles in the late nineteenth century was entangled with a persistent sympathy, and this circumstance must be steadily recognized if we are to avoid exaggerating or underrating the phenomenon.

A second cardinal principle too little attended in the study of anti-Semitism is the importance of the role that the minority group itself plays in the conflict situation. Though prejudices distort reality, they also reflect it. In emphasizing the powerful

18. Ibid., 37; Ignatius Donnelly, *The American People's Money* (Chicago, 1895), 67, 136–37.

19. Professor Pal. Sylvanus, *Tit for Tat: Satirical Universal History; How Mr. Solomon Moses Is Persecuting His Old Persecutors* (Chicago, 1895). See also Semper Veritas, *An Appeal to the Jews, to Stimulate Them to Obtain a Higher State of Civilization; and Other Miscellaneous Matter for the Advancement of Moral Discipline* (San Francisco, 1878).

20. New York *Tribune*, September 27, 1891, p. 6, and June 28, 1882, p. 4; *Boston Saturday Evening Gazette*, quoted in *Jewish Messenger*, XLVI (August 1, 1879), 2.

irrational forces that enter into ethnic hostilities, one should not sentimentally ignore the objective differences and irreducible irritations that set the stage for conflict. Both the New Deal and the neoliberal interpretations had a common tendency to clothe the Jew in innocence—to concentrate almost entirely on the anti-Semite's need for a scapegoat. A deeper historical understanding must take account of the factors within Jewish history that have served to magnetize external antagonisms.

In this connection it should be observed that the unusual ambition and competitive drive for which the Jews are widely admired were not unmixed blessings in the late nineteenth century. These incentives propelled them upward in American society with amazing rapidity. Jewish wealth became conspicuous; Jewish power was an easy inference. In the innocence of their pride Jewish spokesmen publicized with glowing words the economic success some of their people enjoyed. One asserted in a popular magazine, for example, that the Jews controlled the finances of San Francisco. Another alleged that on Jewish holidays the business of the exchanges almost ceased.[21]

Meanwhile, the fame of the European Rothschild family vividly stimulated the imagination of a public avid for news of the very rich. During the Gilded Age the Rothschild name suggested, in the words of a contemporary biographer, "visions of untold wealth and unrivalled power, which appear so startling and amazing as to be more appropriate to romance than real life." The New York *Tribune* took for granted its readers' awareness of the "immense influence wielded by the Jewish princes of finance upon the Western Governments of Europe."[22] Unfortunately, the Rothschilds, who specialized in government loans, became involved in one of the most unpopular financial transactions the United States Treasury ever undertook. When

---

21. Gustav Adolph Danziger, "The Jew in San Francisco: The Last Half Century," *Overland Monthly*, XXV (April, 1895), 382; Henry Hanaw, *Jew Hating and Jew Baiting: An Essay* (Nashville, 1894), 8; Isaac Markens, *The Hebrews in America* (New York, 1888), passim.

22. John Reeves, *The Rothschilds: The Financial Rulers of Nations* (Chicago, 1887), 1. See also Joel Benton, "The Rothschilds," *Munsey's Magazine*, VII (April, 1892), 37–40; New York *Tribune*, September 19, 1891, p. 6, and constant references by Populist publications, such as *National Economist* (Washington), October 8, 1892, p. 6.

President Cleveland's efforts to save the gold standard culminated in 1895 in a secretly negotiated contract to buy gold in Europe, three names appeared on the contract: J. P. Morgan and Company, August Belmont and Company, and N. M. Rothschild and Sons. By singling out the Rothschilds as the key figures in the transaction, silverites found all the evidence they needed of how the Jewish money power profited from American distress.[23]

At the very time the Rothschilds were exercising the American imagination and German Jews in considerable numbers were climbing the social ladder, the arrival of a mass immigration from eastern Europe further complicated the whole Jewish problem. Most native Americans thrown into contact with the impoverished, unkempt throngs from the ghettos of eastern Europe viewed them with distaste.[24] Many German-American Jews, appalled at the outlandish looks and ways of the newcomers, feared that their own reputation was suffering from the popular habit of judging all Jews as alike. As early as 1872 a popular magazine article by a German-American Jew begged the public not to judge all Jews by the "ignorant . . . bigoted, and vicious" Poles and Russians who clustered around Chatham Street and East Broadway.[25] Although such statements were obviously drenched in prejudice, one cannot dismiss them as wholly without foundation. Certainly the new immigration accentuated the aura of foreignness that still clung to American images of the Jew. Moreover, this mass migration involved the Jews prominently in the multiple ethnic conflicts that arose along with the increasing volume and diversity of the whole immigrant influx.

23. "Issue and Sale of Bonds," *House Reports*, 53 Cong., 3 Sess., No. 1824, p. 3; James A. Barnes, *John G. Carlisle: Financial Statesman* (New York, 1931), 390–91, 397; *Review of Reviews*, XI (March, 1895), 261; *Jewish Messenger*, LXXVIII (July 12, 1895), 4.

24. John Higham, *Strangers in the Land: Patterns of American Nativism, 1860–1925* (New Brunswick, 1955), 66–67. See also *Allgemeine Zeitung des Judenthums* (Berlin), LV (October 9, 1891), appendix, p. 4.

25. W. M. Rosenblatt, "The Jews: What They Are Coming To," *Galaxy*, XIII (January, 1872), 47–48; *23rd Annual Convention of District Grand Lodge No. 6, I.O.B.B.*, 1891, appendix, p. 19. See also Zosa Szajkowski, "The Attitude of American Jews to East European Jewish Immigration (1881–1893)," *Publications of the American Jewish Historical Society*, XL (March, 1951), 222–32.

Whatever may be the exact weight of these various factors in shaping feeling about the Jews, the role that the victim plays in any ethnic friction explains only part of the hostility he meets. An appreciation of the ambiguity of ethnic stereotypes and of the objective dimension in group conflict may prevent simplification or sentimentality; but these approaches may leave the controlling factors in the larger social context entirely unexplored. Here a third rule of procedure suggests itself. To identify the critical elements in a conflict situation requires a consistently comparative approach. In other words, the status of American Jewry in a given era needs to be related to the experience of other American ethnic groups in the same period, to the Jewish experience in other periods of American history, and to the concurrent fate of Jews in other countries.

At the lowest and most immediate level of comparison, it is evident that many immigrant groups underwent attack in late-nineteenth-century America, though in varying ways and degrees.[26] Here it is sufficient to say that the Jews met neither as much hostility nor as much tolerance as certain other minorities. Although rapid social advancement apparently exposed and sensitized many Jews to more social discrimination than other European groups felt, in other respects they fared somewhat better. They did not fall victim to as much violence as did the Italians, and there was no organized anti-Semitic movement comparable to the anti-Catholic American Protective Association. Still, the Jews did constitute one of the prominent ethnic targets in the 1880's and 1890's. Certainly they did not share the relative exemption from nativist attack that the Scandinavians, for example, enjoyed. Comparisons of this kind indicate that the Jew experienced neither the unusual disadvantage which the New Deal interpretation implied nor the warm acceptance sometimes suggested by the neoliberal view.[27] Moreover, such comparisons

26. Higham, *Strangers in the Land*, 26–27, 66–67, 92–94.
27. Handlin, "American Views of the Jew," 326–29, compares the Jewish stereotype with other ethnic stereotypes but asserts that *none* of them reflected a deprecatory attitude. The truth would seem to be rather that *all* of them involved unflattering elements, but in different degrees. The further contention that Jews accepted the comic caricature of themselves (though in fact many Jews indignantly rejected it) points to a fact of minority psychology, not to the absence of hostility.

call attention to a fact of utmost significance—that anti-Semitism formed an integral part of a larger, more complex upswing of antiforeign feeling.

But perhaps a broader comparison in point of time and space may help to explain the link between anti-Semitism and the other ethnic tensions that arose along with it in late-nineteenth-century America. A general look backward across the whole development of political anti-Semitism in the United States and western Europe during the last hundred years discloses three periods of special intensity. On both sides of the Atlantic ideological agitation against Jews rose and fell more or less simultaneously. It reached a first crest in the late 1880's and 1890's, a second in the years immediately after the First World War, and a third in the 1930's. The first period saw the emergence of Adolf Stoecker in Germany, Édouard Drumont in France, and a movement against Jewish immigration in England. The second, from 1919 to 1923, brought the international circulation of the notorious *Protocols*, an outbreak of anti-Semitic journalism in England, the emergence of the National Socialist party in Germany and the assassination of Walter Rathenau and, in America, the crusades of Henry Ford and the Ku Klux Klan. The climax, here and in Germany, came in the thirties. In the intervals between these periods two breathing spells occurred. Anti-Semitism made no significant advances in America or western Europe in the early years of the twentieth century; and again in the mid-twenties the agitation declined.[28] The vast difference of intensity between America and some European countries should not obscure a common rhythm.

If, then, ideological anti-Semitism has ebbed and flowed on an international level, one cannot find the decisive forces that activated it by a merely internal examination of American traditions, circumstances, or habits of mind. Interpretation must pivot upon general developments in western civilization—developments that repeatedly inflamed or dampened anti-Semitism on both sides of the Atlantic at roughly the same time.

28. The downswing in the early twentieth century is treated in Hannah Arendt, *The Origins of Totalitarianism* (New York, 1951), 50–53, and Paul W. Massing, *Rehearsal for Destruction: A Study of Political Anti-Semitism in Imperial Germany* (New York, 1949), 113–48. On the 1920's see Sachar, *Sufferance Is the Badge*, 23–33, 256–57, 322, 351–53.

Here the economic interpretation—if broadly construed and stripped of the polemical character it had in New Deal historiography—offers a still valid insight. Certainly the cyclical rhythm of political anti-Semitism has depended upon factors that were partly economic. Each of the periods of anti-Semitic agitation was one of depression in both America and western Europe. Yet not of depression alone. In each case, economic distress functioned as one element in a complex of social and economic dislocations within the western nations. The years from 1873 to 1896 unleashed severe class conflicts and a general unrest that revived during the postwar disorganization after 1918 and reached a culmination in the 1930's. There was good cause to believe that the whole social system was somehow being undermined. The tensions relaxed in the early twentieth century as the achievements of imperialism and social democracy made themselves felt. Again, in the mid-1920's a growing stability revived confidence in the existing social order.

But social and economic frustrations did not stir up ethnic frictions automatically. The recurrent pattern of social and economic strain was accompanied by a persistent ideological disturbance. Each of the crisis periods produced a powerful display of nationalism, and it was the blindly cohesive energy of nationalism that channeled internal discontents into agitation against foreign influences. Consequently anti-Semitism in the modern world has reached maximum intensity as an integral component of movements aimed at defending the nation from various perils originating beyond its frontiers.

With these considerations in mind, the ethnic scene in America in the late nineteenth century becomes more intelligible. It was a time of mass strikes, widening social chasms, unstable prices, and a degree of economic hardship unfamiliar in earlier American history. On the same scene a strong upsurge of nationalism expressed itself in jingoist outbursts against England and other countries, proliferation of patriotic societies, a powerful tariff agitation, and the birth of a movement for immigration restriction that increased by leaps and bounds. In broad outline, both the social situation and the nationalist response paralleled the contemporary experience of western Europe. In such a likely context for anti-Semitism, the Jews of America were fortunate to have suffered as little as they did. The relative mildness of American, as compared to European, anti-Semitism must be attributed not only to the more tolerant traditions of the United States but also to the presence within the country of a great variety of ethnic targets. Since the fire of American nationalists was scattered among many adversaries, no one minority group bore the brunt of the attack. Hatred of Catholics, of Chinese, of the new immigration as a whole, and above all a diffuse nativist hostility to the whole immigrant influx overshadowed specifically anti-Jewish agitation. Nevertheless, a good deal of distinctively anti-Semitic sentiment also emerged. Significantly, it was strongest in those sectors of the population where a particularly explosive combination of social discontent and nationalistic aggression prevailed.

Three groups in late-nineteenth-century America harbored anti-Jewish feelings that went beyond mere social discrimination: some of the agrarian radicals caught up in the Populist movement; certain patrician intellectuals in the East, such as Henry and Brooks Adams and Henry Cabot Lodge; and many of the poorest classes in urban centers. Different as they were, each of these groups found itself at a special disadvantage in the turmoil of an industrial age—the poor because it exploited them, the patricians because it displaced them. Thus Henry Adams, whose anti-Semitism lacked the democratic restraints that qualified the thinking of the Populists, agreed with them in identifying the Jew with the menace of plutocracy. To judge from his published letters, it was only in the late 1880's, after a sense of the powerlessness of his own aristocratic class had settled upon him, that Adams began to see the Jew as the supreme expression of a commercial, bourgeois society. The depression of the nineties put matters in a still worse light for both of the Adams brothers. The economic collapse indicated to them the approach of a general social catastrophe, and the Jew loomed as both the symbol of a materialistic society and an agent of its destruction. In "a society of Jews and brokers," Henry Adams wrote in 1893, "I have no place." He looked forward to a complete smash-up. "Then, perhaps, men of our kind might have some chance of being honorably killed in battle."[29] It is worth adding that the Adamses were not the only upper-class intellectuals who felt this way. The same patrician pessimism underlay the anti-Semitic outbursts in Vance Thompson's elegantly bohemian magazine, *M'lle New York*.[30]

Beside a common resentment against a business culture, the patrician and the plebeian anti-Semite shared a similar kind of belligerent nationalism. Both had a touch of the jingo spirit and longed for a militant assertion of American power. There is evidence that jingoism arose mostly from the underdog elements in American society—notably from the urban lower classes who read the yellow press and from the southern and western Democrats and Populists who chafed under the stodgy respectability of Cleveland and McKinley.[31] Nevertheless, some of the most ardent jingoes belonged to the patrician elite, and they were capable of talking much like the mob about the need for reviving patriotism and about the pernicious influence of the "international Jew" over the American government. Henry Adams might not always concur with Brooks's avid pursuit of war and empire, but they agreed that America would somehow have to strike off the chains of Europe if it would free itself from Shylock's grasp.[32]

The jingoism of the Populists deserves special mention, for it suggests that their anti-Semitic rhetoric did not come from a radical impulse as much as from a nationalist one. The great enemy of the agrarian forces in the 1890's was an international mechanism, the gold standard; bimetallism, on the other hand, would constitute a strictly American policy. Radical bimetallists

29. Worthington C. Ford, ed., *Letters of Henry Adams*, 2 vols. (Boston, 1938), I, 388–89; II, 33–35, 98, 111; Thornton Anderson, *Brooks Adams: Constructive Conservative* (Ithaca, 1951), 60. Barbara M. Solomon, *Ancestors and Immigrants: A Changing New England Tradition* (Cambridge, Mass., 1956), 32–42, works out more carefully and extensively the same general point that has been made here about Henry Adams.

30. *M'lle New York*, I (November–December, 1895), n.p., and II (November, 1898), 2. See also Henry James, *The American Scene* (New York, 1907), 131, 138–39.

31. Richard Hofstadter, "Manifest Destiny and the Philippines," in Daniel Aaron, ed., *America in Crisis* (New York, 1952), 177–82.

32. Harold Dean Cater, ed., *Henry Adams and His Friends: A Collection of Unpublished Letters* (Boston, 1947), 391; Anderson, *Brooks Adams*, 73. See also *M'lle New York*, I (September, 1895), 2.

believed that the gold standard had been foisted on the United States by an international conspiracy centering in England, for was not England the leading champion of gold, as well as America's traditional adversary? Consequently the Populists and Bryan Democrats lost no opportunity to vent their Anglophobic spleen. Often they expressed the belief that war with England was essential to American economic independence. The Jew entered the picture—when he did—as the financial agent of British world power. The agrarians attacked English influence far more frequently than Jewish influence; and when they turned upon Shylock also, they associated him closely with John Bull.[33]

A third group in which anti-Semitism took strong root deserves, though it has not received, at least as much emphasis as the other two. The underprivileged masses in the cities, if less articulate than either patrician or Populist, were more deeply engaged in ethnic conflict. It is doubtful if any rural radical with vague visions of a Rothschild conspiracy felt as fiercely as the "Workingman" who wrote to the New York *Sun* that the Jews would soon either completely control the government and economy or would all be dead. Nor did any rustic pamphleteer even approach the venom of a New York agitator who accused the Jews of controlling the currency, fixing public opinion, overthrowing governments, driving workingmen into useless strikes, and spreading typhus and cholera.[34] Here, too, social unrest intersected with nationalistic belligerence. But what made urban anti-Semitism especially striking and intense was the further circumstance that it arose primarily from people of recent immigrant background.

This circumstance should hardly occasion surprise. Certainly the pressures of a raw, industrial age bore especially harshly on the disorganized minorities pent up in city slums; and it is a sociological commonplace that the second-generation immigrant often developed rabidly chauvinistic tendencies in his longing for acceptance. These factors accentuated the ethnic rivalries within

33. See the Populist writings reviewed in Hofstadter, *Age of Reform*, 77–81; those cited in notes 17 and 18 above; and William M. Stewart, *Bondholders' Conspiracy to Demonetize Silver* (San Francisco, 1885), 3, 24–25. On agrarian warmongering see also Barnes, *Carlisle*, 264, 410.

34. New York *Sun*, March 24, 1895; Anon., *The Talmud-Jew: A True Exposure of the Doctrines and the Aims of Judaism* (New York, 1892), 5–6.

immigrant districts. Jostling against one another in intimate competition for living space, livelihood, and status, the immigrants found their adversaries close at hand, and the influence of an Old World heritage gave much of this friction an anti-Semitic character. Consequently the teeming Jewish districts that sprang up in the slums of the big cities were surrounded by other immigrant enclaves where anti-Semitic attitudes transplanted from Europe could thrive.

In this situation the Jews no longer had—as they did before the Civil War—the protection of a secure place within the cultural orbit of German-America; for American Jewry was losing its predominantly German complexion, and the Germans were drawing aloof from the Jews. Sometimes Jews complained that hostility toward them was strongest among the German element.[35] The complaint was perhaps exaggerated. But it is noteworthy that the most violently anti-Semitic pamphlet published in nineteenth-century America followed slavishly a classic German source; that a German importer sponsored the abortive American lecture tour of Hermann Ahlwardt, leading anti-Semitic agitator; and that a self-styled "American Anti-Semitic Association" appeared in Brooklyn around 1896 under the leadership of F. J. Gross, E. Aug. Lehuermann, and E. Findeisen.[36]

Yet it was not Germans but rather two eastern Europeans who played the role of pioneers in introducing to these shores the new anti-Semitic ideology that was burgeoning in the Old World. In 1882 Mme. Zénaïde Alexeïevna Ragozin, a Russian woman who had come to the United States a few years before and who had just recently been naturalized, published in the *Century Magazine* a vivid explanation of why the Russian peasants were massacring Jews. The outbreaks, she declared, did not arise from a spirit of intolerance. The Jews themselves had goaded the long-suffering populace into its "momentary frenzy"; for they constituted an

35. *Ha-maggid* (Lyck, Prussia), XXIX (January 29, 1885), 36; *Ha-tsefirah* (Warsaw), IX (May 2, 1882), 119; Jacob R. Marcus, "Index to Americana in Foreign Jewish Periodicals" (Typescript copy, American Jewish Historical Society), 27–28.

36. *Talmud-Jew;* New York *Tribune*, December 13, 1895, p. 1; *Congressional Record*, 54 Cong., 1 Sess., 5215.

imperium in imperio, secretly and systematically conspiring to engross the entire wealth of the country.[37]

Mme. Ragozin wrote too early to phrase the attack in terms of race. The dubious honor of inaugurating race-thinking anti-Semitism in America belongs to a middle-class Greek immigrant, Telemachus Timayenis. While establishing himself in New York City as a language teacher and tutor, Timayenis developed a varied literary career. He produced fifteen books altogether, including popular history, romantic novels, and three works on the "Jewish question." An unprincipled schemer, he evidently hoped to be the advance agent of an organized anti-Semitic movement. To that end he formed a publishing house and tried to launch a monthly magazine.[38] The first of his books in this vein, *The Original Mr. Jacobs: A Startling Exposé,* appeared in 1888, two years after Édouard Drumont opened the floodgates of French anti-Semitism. Timayenis simply copied Drumont's ideas. According to Timayenis and Drumont, European history reveals an elemental conflict between the noble Aryan and the plotting Jew; the latter intrigues incessantly to overthrow the Aryan order of things through financial monopoly on the one hand and revolution on the other.

These effusions are of interest because their systematic virulence surpasses anything that can be identified with a native American writer during the nineteenth century. Otherwise, however, the writings of immigrant anti-Semites of the time are not important, for none of them left any visible impression on American culture. Whereas Drumont created a sensation in France, his disciple in America fulminated in obscurity and neglect. If immigrant anti-Semitism consisted of nothing more than the writing of unread tracts, it would deserve little notice. In fact, however, the Jews also suffered directly at the hands of their fellow immigrants. In the urban slums of the late nineteenth century "Jew-baiting" became a daily occurrence.

37. Z. Ragozin, "Russian Jews and Gentiles," *Century Magazine,* XXIII (April, 1882), 905-20. The *Century* editors cautiously subtitled the article "From a Russian Point of View," half apologized for the "extremely mediaeval aspect" of the charges (p. 949), and hastened to publish a rebuttal by Emma Lazarus in the next issue.

38. Harold J. Jonas and Leonard A. Greenberg kindly made available to me their biographical and critical study of Timayenis.

Beginning, apparently, in the 1880's, the Jewish peddlers who swarmed through the poorer districts of the large cities were continually taunted, stoned, and otherwise manhandled by street gangs. Beard-pulling was one of the commonest forms of bedevilment,[39] but more serious assaults became increasingly frequent in the 1890's. Irish and German rowdies seem to have caused most of the trouble. In 1899 a united protest from fourteen Jewish societies in Brooklyn declared: "No Jew here can go on the street without exposing himself to the danger of being pitilessly beaten."[40] Appeals for police protection were generally futile. At the end of the century, therefore, eastern European Jews in Chicago, Brooklyn, Worcester, and Holyoke formed protective associations designed to prosecute offenders and arouse officials.[41]

The climactic incident occurred on New York's Lower East Side in 1902. The occasion was a solemn event in the history of the New York ghetto: the mass funeral of the leading figure in the Orthodox community, Rabbi Jacob Joseph. Thousands of mourners took part in the vast, formless procession that followed the coffin from synagogue to synagogue en route to the grave in Brooklyn. To reach the Grand Street ferry, the procession had to pass through the Irish district near the East River. The Irish resented the constant encroachment of the teeming Jewish colony upon their own shrinking domain,[42] and Jewish funeral parties had often been molested on the same route before. As the wailing throng surged past a big factory where many of the local Irish worked, the employees pelted the crowd with iron nuts and bolts. A riot ensued as the Jews threw back the missiles and tried to break into the building. Order was almost restored when the

39. Louis Wirth, *The Ghetto* (Chicago, 1928), 180–81; *American Hebrew*, LXV (May 19, 1899), 71.

40. *Die Welt* (Vienna), III (June 2, 1899), 8. Cf. the troubles that a Jewish storekeeper's daughter had in a Welsh mining town in Iowa in the 1890's. Edna Ferber, *A Peculiar Treasure* (New York, 1939), 40–42, 50.

41. *American Hebrew*, LXV (July 14 and August 18, 1899), 307, 482; New York *Tribune*, June 29, 1899, p. 11; *Die Welt*, III (March 24, 1899), 10; (August 11, 1899), 13.

42. Philip Cowen, *Memories of an American Jew* (New York, 1932), 289. On the ethnic geography of the East Side see *Reports of the Industrial Commission*, 19 vols. (Washington, D.C., 1901), XV, p. xlvi and maps facing p. 470.

arrival of two hundred police reserves made matters much worse.[43] The New York police force was predominantly Irish and had a reputation for brutal treatment of East Side Jews. Political rivalry had recently inflamed bad feelings; the Jews had rebelled en masse against Tammany Hall in the mayoralty election of 1901, in which police corruption was the main issue.[44] Accordingly, the police hurled themselves upon what remained of the funeral procession with abusive language and flailing clubs. All told, about two hundred were injured, mostly Jews, with most of the injuries brought on by the police.

Throughout this period of ethnic turbulence, one must remember that the genial and democratic norms of American life remained basically undisturbed. Although some of the hostile trends in the late nineteenth century were obviously creating serious difficulties for many Jews, none of those trends occupied as yet a prominent place on the larger American scene. The story of anti-Semitism in the Gilded Age is worth telling, however, if it suggests how the basic pattern of the more serious movements of political anti-Semitism in the 1920's and 1930's came into being. For those later movements, the Gilded Age set the stage and trained the cast. When conditions comparable to those of the 1890's recurred a generation later, the same groups in society led the way. Patrician anti-Semites then had the opportunity to formulate a racist immigration policy. In the Midwest the tradition of agrarian nationalism energized the anti-Jewish campaigns of a succession of inflationists and Anglophobes from Henry Ford to Father Coughlin. And in the cities the Bund and the Christian Front got their membership from people of immigrant background.

Yet these three groups remained, as they had been at the out-

---

43. Testimony given to the Mayor's investigating committee is summarized in *American Hebrew*, LXI (August 15–22, 1902), 355–56, 384, and the official report appears on pp. 497–98. See also New York *Tribune*, July 31, 1902, pp. 1, 3; New York *World*, July 31, 1902, pp. 1–2, and August 2, 1902, p. 4.

44. *American Hebrew*, LXI (August 15, 1902), 355–56; Charles Bernheimer, ed., *The Russian Jew in the United States* (Philadelphia, 1905), 257. The overwhelmingly Gaelic complexion of the New York police force is evident from the random lists of names in *Report of the Police Department of the City of New York*, 1900, pp. 48–56.

set, remote and incompatible allies, poles apart at the extremes of American society. For half a century the pattern endured, but it never congealed. Its components never overcame their own alienation from one another.

Chapter Six

The Rise of
Social Discrimination

During the post–Civil War decades, when a full-blown anti-Semitic ideology touched for the first time some of the margins of American society, a more tangible problem was also emerging. Jews began to meet rebuffs in places where they thought they belonged. Were the two phenomena—ideology and discrimination—causally related? It is tempting to think so. But apart from their origin in a common fund of stereotypes they actually had very little connection. In following the development of social discrimination against Jews, we shall discern again the peripheral character of ideological anti-Semitism in America. Only after 1913, in the context of a wider cultural anxiety, did ideological fantasies and discriminatory behavior significantly converge.

Our inquiry may well begin with the stereotypes, for stereotypes about Jews long antedated any problem in actual social relations. During the era before the Civil War Jews enjoyed almost complete social acceptance and freedom. On the eve of the German immigration that began in the late 1830's, they numbered less than 15,000 in a total American population of 15,000,000.[1] This tiny minority, descended largely from colonial settlers, dwelled in a few large trading centers. Engaged particu-

1. One observer estimated the American-Jewish population at 6,000 in 1826, another at 15,000 in 1840. *American Jewish Year Book, 1899–1900*, p. 283.

larly as foreign traders and as stock and money brokers, the Jews formed on the whole a well-to-do and well-established part of the merchant class. By all accounts they occupied a secure, stable, and untrammeled place in American society. There was no pattern of discrimination in the sense of exclusion from social and economic opportunities which qualified Jews sought. "In all the various intercourse of social life," concluded an American writer in 1833, "we know of no uncharitable barriers between Jews and Christians in our happy community."[2]

A distinction has to be drawn, however, between behavior and attitudes; the prevalence of good relations does not mean that American images of Jews were ever wholly favorable. Unfavorable attitudes about a whole ethnic group do not necessarily compromise our practical response to individuals. If the situation encourages a harmonious adjustment, the attitudes remain mild or impersonal. Thus, the image of Scotsmen as stiff-necked and penurious and the image of Englishmen as snobs have not handicapped members of either of these groups in America. Similarly, the Jews in early-nineteenth-century America got along very well with their non-Jewish neighbors although American conceptions of Jews in the abstract at no time lacked the unfavorable elements embedded in European tradition.

We have already noticed the complexity and ambivalence—the mixture of attraction and repulsion—in American images of Jews in the nineteenth century. What is equally remarkable is the curiously denatured, remote, even unreal quality that invested negative attitudes toward Jews for many decades. In typical Protestant homilies about the downfall of the Jews one finds no sting, no rancor, but only a melancholy warning: "The Jews— they are the moral Tadmor of the desert; the fallen columns of the temple of Jehovah; a people, in their dispersion, subjugation and ruin, every where calculated to call up the deepest remembrances, and the most affecting reflections."[3] Similarly, the

---

2. Joseph L. Blau and Salo W. Baron, eds., *The Jews of the United States, 1790–1840: A Documentary History,* 3 vols. (New York, 1963), III, 683; Morris U. Schappes, ed., *Documentary History of the Jews in the United States, 1654–1875* (New York, 1950), 142, 158, 226.

3. "The Present State of the Jews," *Western Monthly Review,* II (January, 1829), 437.

grossest medieval superstitions could survive in America without seeming to affect contemporary behavior in any way. When the New York *Herald* was trying to increase circulation by publishing sensational hoaxes, it once reported that Jewish fanatics had bled to death a Christian missionary in the Near East, ground up his bones, and mixed his blood with unleavened bread. There is no indication that the story aroused the slightest animosity, any more than the medieval English ballad, "The Jew's Daughter," which country people sang throughout American history. In that song an accusation of ritual murder, made against a Jewish woman in England seven hundred years earlier, still echoed faintly in the hills of Virginia as recently as 1933:

> And then she took a red white towel
> And tied it 'round his chin,
> And then she took a carving knife,
> And cut his little heart in, oh in,
> And cut his little heart in.

> "Oh, place a Bible at my head
> And a prayer book at my feet;
> And ever my playmate call for me
> Pray tell him that I am asleep, asleep,
> Pray tell him that I am asleep."[4]

Until the mid-nineteenth century the average American seemed to think of Jews primarily as ancient patriarchs in flowing robes, smelling of frankincense and myrrh, but biblical stereotypes faded into the background with the increasing secularization of society and the multiplication of personal contacts with real live Jews. The economic stereotype of the Jew as a businessman is more relevant to the onset of discrimination. It is worth noting, therefore, that the impression of Jews as aggressive businessmen had always been widespread in America, even in an age of biblical piety when most people had never seen a Jew. The same writers who emphasized the religious significance of God's ancient people often depicted the modern Jew as sunk in the love

4. Foster B. Gresham, "'The Jew's Daughter': An Example of Ballad Variation," in Leonard Dinnerstein and Mary Dale Palsson, eds., *Jews in the South* (Baton Rouge, La., 1973), 201–5; New York *Herald*, April 6, 1850, p. 1.

of gain.[5] Although praise of Jewish enterprise was more common in the early nineteenth century than jibes at Jewish avarice, the presence of the negative judgment, and the ease with which the positive judgment could pass over into it, suggest that anti-Semitism did not lie dormant because of a lack of appropriate attitudes.

What, then, kept the Shylock idea sufficiently mild and impersonal before the Civil War so that no pattern of social discrimination issued from it? Partly, of course, we must credit the countervailing strength of democratic and humanitarian ideas in a period when the United States welcomed European immigrants of every sort and condition. But a contrast between the early and the late nineteenth century suggests that certain objective conditions affected the reception of the Jews more directly and immediately than did the general state of public opinion. From a comparative point of view, we must look to the character of the Jewish community and to the structure of the society in which it lived.

As for the Jews themselves, they comprised in the early nineteenth century too small, too insignificant, and too well assimilated a group to seem a problem. Though often successful, they had occupied a relatively comfortable middle-class station for a long time. They offered no target for envy either because of numbers or because of any rapid group advancement. As late as 1860 an editorial in the New York *Journal of Commerce* summed up their situation succinctly: "In this city, and generally throughout this country, where their rights are never invaded, they live so quietly that unless one goes into their quarters, he seldom meets with them. Few of our citizens know them socially, and all are too willing to believe Shylock their true type."[6] In other words, a widely prevalent stereotype remained abstract and inoperative.

With the arrival of a sizable German-Jewish immigration in

5. Hannah Adams, *The History of the Jews* (London, 1818), 544–45; *A Course of Lectures on the Jews* (Philadelphia, 1840), 193; American Sunday-School Union, *The Jew, at Home and Abroad* (Philadelphia, 1845), 12; Sarah S. Baker, *The Jewish Twins* (New York, 1860), 33 and passim; J. H. Ingraham, *The Gipsy of the Highlands: or, The Jew and the Heir* (Boston, 1843).

6. Schappes, *Documentary History*, 402.

the 1840's, this stable situation began to change. In the worst section of New York the immigrants opened squalid secondhand shops, hardly more than cowsheds, their little windows broken and patched with old newspapers. Commenting on these shops, a popular description of the sights of New York in 1849 referred casually to the typical proprietor's hooked nose, "which betrays the Israelite as the human kite, formed to be feared, hated and despised, yet to prey upon mankind."[7] Many of the newcomers spread rapidly throughout the country, making their way usually as peddlers. Concurrently, the incidence of disparaging comment seems to have increased. According to Rudolf Glanz, caricatures of Jewish peddlers in popular plays, songs, and stories tended more to display dirtiness and dishonesty from the late 1850's on;[8] and two decades later a distinguished rabbi, in the earliest thoughtful study of the problem, traced the beginnings of anti-Jewish feeling in America to the coming of the German Jews in the 1840's.[9] Some of the peddlers met warm and gracious receptions on their rural circuits. Also, many Americans had not yet learned to distinguish Jews from other German immigrants.[10] Yet gradually the growth of the Jewish population brought it more and more to public attention, and not all of the attention was favorable.

While the relative invisibility of the early American-Jewish community protected it from discrimination, the peculiar strength of the American social order also militated against restrictive social barriers. Stability is not a characteristic we ordinarily associate with nineteenth-century America; it was under-

7. George G. Foster, *New York by Gas-light* (New York, 1850), 58-59.
8. Rudolf Glanz, "Notes on Early Jewish Peddling in America," *Jewish Social Studies*, VII (1945), 131-33.
9. Gustav Gottheil, "The Position of the Jews in America," *North American Review*, CXXVI (1878), 305-6. Confirming this view, the Jewish press in the 1850's reported anti-Jewish diatribes that were harsher than one would expect a couple of decades earlier. See, e.g., *The Asmonean*, V (1852), 195, and *The Occident and American Jewish Advocate*, XIII (1855), 123-32.
10. Joshua Trachtenberg, *Consider the Years: The Story of the Jewish Community of Easton, 1752-1942* (Easton, Pa., 1944), 118-19; Schappes, *Documentary History*, 310-11. On peddlers see Oscar S. Straus, *Under Four Administrations* (New York, 1917), 6, and Adolph Kraus, *Reminiscences and Comments* (Chicago, 1925), 13, 21.

going such enormous expansion and economic growth that it gave an appearance of pervasive flux and change. Nevertheless, during the first half of the nineteenth century mobility and democracy did not disrupt the basic system of social stratification. Wide differences of wealth persisted and may even have increased, but they were obscured by the general belief that a substantial equality of opportunity was at last being realized. A conviction that America was becoming an open society of self-made men even justified great disparities of status, so long as those disparities did not seem rigidly fixed. Thus, substantial privilege for some coexisted fairly easily with extensive opportunity for the many because the public ethos discouraged sharp, overt definitions of rank. Anxiety was diffused and not easily focused on any group in the local community. Men rose and fell individually without straining the underlying structure of group relationships.[11]

The only instance so far reported of anti-Semitic discrimination in the ante-bellum period is the kind of exception that helps to prove the rule. In contrast to the generally porous, flexible pattern of civilian life, the United States Navy was a distinctly graded society in which habits of snobbery and even of cruelty strengthened the principle of hierarchy. Uriah P. Levy, a fourth- or fifth-generation American, enlisted in the Navy in 1812 after serving in the merchant marine. During a long and stormy career, he rose from the ranks to become the commanding officer of a squadron. Imperious and headstrong, resented by regularly commissioned officers for his swift ascent from the ranks, he was repeatedly court-martialed for his scrappiness. Often his Jewishness added to his troubles; many fellow officers snubbed him at mess and deeply resented serving with a "damned Jew."[12] Levy's personal difficulties in the stratified world of the Navy fore-

11. This interpretation draws especially on Edward Pessen, *Riches, Class, and Power Before the Civil War* (Lexington, Mass., 1973), Stephan Thernstrom, *The Other Bostonians: Poverty and Progress in the American Metropolis, 1880-1970* (Cambridge, Mass., 1973) 256-60, and Alexis de Tocqueville, *Democracy in America*, 2 vols. (New York, 1835-1840), II.

12. Abram Kanof, "Uriah Phillips Levy: The Story of a Pugnacious Commodore," *Publication of the American Jewish Historical Society*, XXXIX (1949-1950), 8, 24-30, 51-52.

shadowed the later Jewish problem that developed when America
as a whole became more status conscious.

II

The Civil War inspired a mild flurry of ideological anti-Semitism,
which brought upon the Jews occasional accusations of disloyalty. These subsided when hostilities ended, without having
affected the habitual intercourse of Jews with their neighbors.[13]
A pattern of discrimination began to take root only in the 1870's,
as the prewar situation decisively changed. Now a new, more
anxious status consciousness was altering the simpler lineaments
of the early republic; and American Jewry was becoming a very
different community from what it had been in the 1830's. The
changes within Jewish life and in the society around it acted
together to generate anti-Semitic restrictions.

By 1877, German and some Polish immigration had swelled the
Jewish population of the United States to a quarter of a million.
The immigrants and their families by that time vastly outnumbered the descendants of the older Jewish population. The newcomers had settled and adopted mercantile roles in every state, so
that Jews became visible almost everywhere. Also, a major
concentration developed for the first time. About one-fifth of
American Jewry now lived in New York City.[14] The fact is
important because the first restricted social facilities catered
largely to a New York clientele.

Moreover, by the 1870's a remarkable proportion of the Jewish
immigrants who had arrived in the forties and fifties was prosper-
ing mightily. Proportionately speaking, in no other immigrant
group have so many men ever risen so rapidly from rags to riches.
The first-generation millionaires included the manufacturer Philip
Heidelbach, the bankers Joseph Seligman, Lewis Seasongood, and

13. Bertram Wallace Korn, *American Jewry and the Civil War* (Philadelphia, 1951), 121–88; Schappes, *Documentary History*, 466.

14. *American Jewish Year Book, 1918–1919*, p. 32. For other statistics see
ibid., *1945–1946*, p. 644, and Nathan Glazer, "Social Characteristics of American Jews, 1654–1954," *American Jewish Year Book, 1955*, p. 9.

Solomon Loeb, the railroad magnates Emanuel and Mayer Lehman, and a good many more. The general body of American Jews participated in the same upward thrust. A survey of 10,000 Jewish families in 1890 showed that 7,000 of them had servants.[15] As a group, this extraordinary generation evidently outdistanced old-stock Americans as well as other immigrants. Comparing career patterns of native and foreign-born Bostonians in the late nineteenth century, Stephan Thernstrom has found that a considerably larger percentage of Jews than of Yankees attained white-collar status.[16]

Yet the Jewish immigrants derived largely from poor villages and humble, uneducated families.[17] In America they acquired money much more rapidly than culture. The intellectual drive and distinction so prominent in American-Jewish life today arose only in the next generation, after the coming of the east Europeans. In the middle of the nineteenth century there was no American-Jewish literature, and the only Jewish periodical with intellectual pretensions, *Israels Herold*, expired after three months from public indifference.[18] As late as 1881 a Jewish newspaper, discussing card-playing, complained that American Jewry "reads very little and plays very much."[19]

Not only were most Jews more or less uncultivated, but also there is considerable evidence that many were loud, ostentatious, and pushing. Both Jews and friendly non-Jewish observers confessed something of the kind. The San Francisco *Hebrew* affirmed that the Jews' offensiveness of manner would disappear before long. Other Jews grieved that the conduct of some of their people brought obloquy upon all. One admitted that the body of rich Jews had mounted too rapidly to the top of the

15. Isaac Markens, *The Hebrews in America* (New York, 1888), 139–73; Glazer, "Social Characteristics," 10.

16. Thernstrom, *Other Bostonians*, 123, 132, 150–51.

17. Bernard D. Weinryb, "The German Jewish Immigrants to America (A Critical Evaluation)," in Eric Hirshler, ed., *Jews from Germany in the United States* (New York, 1955), 116–18.

18. Bertram Wallace Korn, *Eventful Years and Experiences: Studies in Nineteenth Century American Jewish History* (Cincinnati, 1954), 31–34, 45. See also Hirshler, *Jews from Germany*, 142–43.

19. Rudolf Glanz, *Jews in Relation to the Cultural Milieu of the Germans in America up to the Eighteen Eighties* (New York, 1947), 44.

commercial ladder. Anna Laurens Dawes's generally warm and sympathetic book attributed to "the German Jew"

> the half education and the little breeding of the small trader. He adds to this the shrewdness of his nation and the self-assertion which has grown out of the long certainty that he is despised. When such a man becomes very rich in a country where riches are made into a golden calf and worshipped as in America . . . he naturally assumes the manners of the peacock, and receives the usual dislike of that bird among his fellows.[20]

One of the best contemporary studies noted that European manners in general were less restrained than those of English and American society. While Americans increasingly emulated the cold reserve practiced in England, a German (whether Jew or Christian) did not think he was intruding when he attempted to open a conversation with strangers.[21]

Thus a new stereotype, superimposed on the Shylock image, took form after the Civil War. In cartoons and in a good deal of middle-class opinion, the Jew became identified as the quintessential parvenu—glittering with conspicuous and vulgar jewelry, lacking table manners, attracting attention by clamorous behavior, and always forcing his way into society that was above him.[22] To treat this stereotype entirely as a scapegoat for somebody else's psychological frustrations is to overemphasize the irrational sources of "prejudice" and to clothe the Jews in defensive innocence.[23] The parvenu stereotype held up a distorted

20. San Francisco *Hebrew*, March 30, 1894, p. 1; *American Hebrew*, Aug. 19, 1887, p. 19; *Jewish Messenger*, May 10, 1889, p. 5; Nina Morais, "Jewish Ostracism in America," *North American Review*, CXXXIII (1881), 270; Edwin J. Kuh, "The Social Disability of the Jew," *Atlantic Monthly*, CI (1908), 438; Anna Laurens Dawes, *The Modern Jew: His Present and Future* (Boston, 1884), 29–30.

21. Alice Hyneman Rhine, "Race Prejudice at Summer Resorts," *Forum*, III (1887), 527.

22. Ibid., p. 525. See also cartoon reprinted in John Higham, *Strangers in the Land* (New Brunswick, N.J., 1955), plate 1.

23. Before the 1930's sober and humane observers repeatedly took note of the core of reality behind the stereotype. See Bruno Lasker, *Jewish Experiences in America* (New York, 1930), 71, 97–98, on the Jews as "an aggressive minority"; Louis Golding, "Anti-Semitism," *Outlook*, CXLVIII (1928), 248–49; Ralph Philip Boas, "The Problem of American Judaism," *Atlantic Monthly*, CXIX (1917), 150.

mirror to the immigrants' foreignness and cultural limitations and above all to their strong competitive drive and remarkable social mobility.

Still, the American tradition of treating people as individuals (at least if they were of European descent) posed a substantial obstacle to the creation of a new group ostracism. If American society had kept its indistinct contours, group discriminations might not have accompanied the new stereotype, at least as quickly as they did. But during the Gilded Age a general struggle for place and privilege upset the equilibrium of urban life. A large part of the American middle class was becoming rich. From small-town women's clubs to Fifth Avenue drawing rooms, pomp and splendor enhanced the significance of money as a mark of distinction. At every level so many successful people clamored for admission to more prestigious circles that social climbing ceased to be a simple expectation; it became a genuine social problem. The problem had two aspects. While material acquisitions stimulated vast numbers to swift social advancement and the money standard seemed to qualify them for it, the new industrial economy also made the gap between rich and poor more visible and more frightening. There is little convincing evidence that the distribution of income among American whites was actually becoming more unequal in the late nineteenth century. Many feared that was happening; their confidence in the social order was accordingly shaken. But the objective basis of their distress was probably an increased affluence, which reduced the share of wealth controlled by entrenched elites and produced an undignified scramble for status.[24] Thus, a hectic social competition resulted from greater opportunities for getting ahead as well as greater fears of falling behind.

In order to protect recently acquired gains from latecomers, social climbers had to sharpen the informal lines of status that had

24. On these changes there are helpful perspectives in Arthur M. Schlesinger, *Learning How to Behave* (New York, 1947); Dixon Wecter, *The Saga of American Society* (New York, 1947); Mrs. John King Van Rensselaer, *The Social Ladder* (New York, 1924); Richard Weiss, *The American Myth of Success: From Horatio Alger to Norman Vincent Peale* (New York, 1969), 97–101; and especially Frederic C. Jaher, "Nineteenth-Century Elites in Boston and New York," *Journal of Social History*, VI (Fall, 1972), 55–68.

functioned well enough in the ante-bellum period. With a defensiveness born of insecurity, they grasped at distinctions that were more than pecuniary, through an elaborate formalization of etiquette, the compilation of social registers, the acquisition of aristocratic European culture, and the cult of genealogy. These were all criteria that could not be met by money alone. The Jews symbolized the pecuniary vices and entered more prominently than any other ethnic group into the struggle for status. Practically, anti-Semitic discriminations offered another means of stabilizing the social ladder while, psychologically, a society vexed by its own assertiveness gave a general problem an ethnic focus.

There is no need to suppose, or evidence to show, that the pattern of discrimination began at the top of American society and spread downward. This view, once held by historians as different as Oscar Handlin and Carey McWilliams, assumed that discrimination grows as reactionary opinion-makers impose undemocratic values on the innocent masses.[25] Such an assumption appeals to our democratic instincts and serves to complete the circuit between ideology and mass behavior. If, however, my structural view is correct, discrimination can arise more or less simultaneously at every social level where a crush of applicants poses an acute problem of admission. Discrimination is less a game of follow-the-leader than one of limiting the followers. In fact, all the evidence indicates that insecure social climbers rather than relatively more secure patricians first resorted to this means of reducing competition. Several years before the Seligman incident at Saratoga captured headlines, a New York National Guard regiment put in operation a policy of excluding Jews.[26] In 1876, a hotel on the Jersey shore advertised in the New York *Tribune* that "Jews are not admitted." And by that time Jews were also beginning to have trouble at the Saratoga resorts.[27]

The highly publicized exclusion of Joseph Seligman, one of the leading American bankers, from the Grand Union Hotel in

25. Oscar Handlin, "The Acquisition of Political and Social Rights by the Jews of the United States," *American Jewish Year Book, 1955*, pp. 72, 74, and Carey McWilliams, *A Mask for Privilege* (Boston, 1948), 17–21.

26. Schappes, *Documentary History*, 559–60.

27. New York *Tribune*, June 1, 1876, p. 4; Hugh Bradley, *Such Was Saratoga* (New York, 1940), 188.

Saratoga in 1877 brought into the open a trend already under way. Yet even this event lacked the patrician overtones usually attributed to it. No longer the unrivaled summer capital of the United States, Saratoga in the seventies was steadily losing ground to Newport, Nahant, and Long Branch. Instead of a fortress of the best society, Saratoga was becoming a flashy resort of the *nouveaux riches*, where wealthy sportsmen mingled with prominent politicians, Wall Street tycoons, western copper kings, ladies of easy virtue, as well as a good many Jews. Moreover, the Grand Union was not quite the most fashionable establishment there, though it had made headway by entertaining President Grant in 1869.[28] The ban which the hotel imposed on Jews in 1877, in an obvious attempt to improve its social rating, reflected the exigencies of the parvenu spirit faced by uninhibited competition and uncertain rewards.

Saratoga soon became a battleground. Rather than knuckle under, Jews retaliated by buying several of the leading hotels. In a decade half the summer population was Jewish. Against this influx, non-Jewish establishments blatantly publicized a restrictive policy, even (it is said) setting up placards: "No Jews or Dogs Admitted Here." But the real battle was lost. Saratoga's decline as a center of social prestige continued.[29]

During the 1880's anti-Semitic discrimination spread like wild-fire through the vacation grounds of New York State and the Jersey shore. The problem was more acute at resorts than elsewhere, for no other institution combined such indiscriminate social mingling with such ardent social aspirations. Ten years after the Seligman incident, an acute reporter asserted that in the Catskills a nearly equal division had developed between resorts with an all-Jewish clientele and those that accepted only Christians. Significantly, she added that prejudice was most pronounced among patrons of cheap boardinghouses, where the charges ranged from five to ten dollars a week.[30]

28. The details of the Seligman incident are in Lee M. Friedman, *Jewish Pioneers and Patriots* (New York, 1943), 269–78, which exaggerates the eminence of Saratoga and of the Grand Union. Bradley, *Such Was Saratoga*, pp. 135–59, 187–88, sketches a fuller and more reliable background.

29. Bradley, *Such Was Saratoga*, 188; *Public Opinion*, III (1887), 441.

30. Rhine, "Race Prejudice," 524.

A dramatic but quite ineffective blow fell in 1879 near the center of American-Jewish life. Austin Corbin, the developer of Manhattan Beach, issued a public statement of his fervent wish that the Jews would go elsewhere. A new and booming resort, Manhattan Beach daily drew great throngs of New Yorkers of all sorts, races, and conditions. Corbin's huge Manhattan Beach Hotel had facilities for hundreds of daily commuters who munched their sandwiches and puffed happily on cheap cigars in the Grand Pavilion. Corbin hoped that his regular patrons, a "somewhat exclusive" type, would make Coney Island "the most fashionable and magnificent watering place in the world," but these fled before the swarm of transients. "We cannot," he declared bitterly, "bring the highest social element to Manhattan Beach if the Jews persist in coming."[31] Again discrimination was an instrument of social ambition; and again, as at Saratoga, the interdict failed to hold.

Aside from resorts, two other institutions showed discriminatory tendencies in the eighties. Certain eastern private schools, chiefly those for girls, began as a matter of policy to reject applications from Jewish children.[32] Meanwhile, social clubs in some of the big cities were blackballing proposed Jewish members. Mentioned as a common practice by a writer in 1881, this interdict often met considerable resistance as it spread during the nineties. A liberal minority kept a loophole open in the Columbia Club of New York by giving a place on the board of governors to a Jew. The University Club of Cincinnati was embarrassed by the resignation of a prominent Jewish member when another Jew was rejected.[33] New York's august Union League Club was rocked in 1893 by the majority's refusal to add Theodore Seligman to the few Jewish members of long standing, though he was the son of one of the club's founders. Although a number of socially

---

31. *Coney Island and the Jews* (New York, 1879); *Jewish Messenger,* Aug., 1, 1879, p. 2.

32. *Ha-Maggid,* XXIX (1884), 36; *American Hebrew,* April 4, 1890, p. 165. A good many instances of this kind of exclusion in the 1890's are indexed in Jacob R. Marcus, "Index to Americana in European Jewish Periodicals" (American Jewish Historical Society), 20, 24, 28.

33. Morais, "Jewish Ostracism," 270; *Selected Letters of George Edward Woodberry* (Cambridge, Mass., 1933), 27–28; Claris Edwin Silcox and Galen M. Fisher, *Catholics, Jews and Protestants* (New York, 1934), 78.

prominent members supported Seligman, an opposition led by "hustling young chaps" carried the day.[34]

By the end of the century Jewish penetration into the most elite circles in the East had become almost impossibly difficult. In fact, in the seventies and eighties Jews in New York, Rochester, Baltimore, Detroit, and other cities formed their own fashionable clubs.

III

If the exuberance of the Gilded Age diminished somewhat in the early twentieth century, wealth nonetheless remained conspicuous, social climbing continued apace, and discrimination steadily expanded. The pattern had been set, and now no one tried very hard to stem the widening consequences. Indeed, one important circumstance of the early twentieth century put the Jews at a greater disadvantage than before. This was the rise of the east European Jews. They had been pouring in great waves into the urban slums for some time, of course; but before 1900 the first generation had remained there, almost as isolated from the German Jews as from the older American population. Socially and economically, the east Europeans could not push upward as rapidly as the Germans had done; but by 1907 a few of the new immigrants were becoming rich as clothing manufacturers and real estate speculators, while many of the second generation were beginning to enter middle-class life.[35] Their advancement mitigated somewhat the otherwise sharp cleavage between the two Jewish communities in America.[36] But the partial integration of east Europeans into the Jewish middle class strengthened the surrounding walls of discrimination.

34. *Jewish Messenger*, April 21, 1893, p. 4. This affair caused much public comment not only because Seligman was evidently a cultivated gentleman but also because of the close historical association between the Union League and the Republican party.

35. This process is best portrayed in Abraham Cahan, *The Rise of David Levinsky* (New York, 1917), but see also Burton J. Hendrick, "The Great Jewish Invasion," *McClure's Magazine*, XXVIII (1907), 310–20.

36. Glazer, "Social Characteristics," 19. A continuing polarization, however, is extensively documented in Robert Rockaway, "Ethnic Conflict in an Urban Environment: the German and Russian Jew in Detroit, 1881–1914," *American Jewish Historical Quarterly*, LX (Dec. 1970), 133–50.

Because immigration became a general problem toward the end of the nineteenth century and because the east European Jews looked as bizarre and unkempt as any of the other immigrants, they aroused distaste among native Americans from the moment they landed. At first, public comment (abetted by assimilation-minded German Jews) often distinguished between the new and the older Jewish population to the latter's clear advantage.[37] But after 1900 the differentiation almost vanished from popular consciousness. Consequently, the nativistic feelings excited by the still-growing immigration from eastern Europe applied to American Jewry as a whole. Furthermore, the behavior of many of the newcomers who got ahead in the world confirmed the parvenu stereotype.[38] The descendants of their German predecessors were acquiring a more subdued gentility, but the very size of the east European influx overshadowed this evolution.

Accordingly, discrimination in summer resorts, clubs, and private schools increased during the years before the First World War. The Century Club in New York rejected the distinguished scientist Jacques Loeb because he was a Jew. At least in the higher degrees of Masonry, most lodges now kept out Jews, compelling them to form their own segregated chapters.[39] Some of the very best preparatory schools, such as Andover, Exeter, and Hotchkiss, are said to have put no artificial obstacles in the way of Jewish applicants; but most schools established very small Jewish quotas. One well-known private school which resolutely refused to discriminate lost practically all its Christian clientele because it attracted too many Jews. Then Jewish parents would no longer send their children there because the school had become too Jewish. So it was ruined and had to be shut up.[40]

37. New York *Tribune*, June 28, 1882, p. 4; *Allgemeine Zeitung des Judenthums*, October 9, 1891, appendix, p. 4; *Reports of the Industrial Commission* (Washington, D.C., 1901), XV, 194–95 and passim.

38. On this point see the realistic picture of a Catskill resort in Cahan's *The Rise of David Levinsky*.

39. *American Jewish Year Book, 1914–1915*, p. 141; Sydney Reid, " 'Because You're a Jew,' " *Independent*, LXV (1908), 1212.

40. Professor Richard J. H. Gottheil writing for the London *Jewish Chronicle* and reprinted in *American Citizen*, I (1912), 146–47. See also Norman Hapgood, "Jews and College Life" and "Schools, Colleges and Jews," *Harper's Weekly*, LXII (1916), 53, 77.

A similar trend affected summer resorts with equal or greater severity. Thrown into resorts of their own, the Jews converted Far Rockaway and Arverne, as well as parts of the Catskills, into almost exclusively Jewish settlements in the summertime. Long Branch, New Jersey, lost its former grandeur and became largely Jewish.[41] The classic example was nearby Lakewood, a new and luxurious winter resort. In the 1890's the leading hotel had turned away Nathan Straus, whereupon he promptly built next to it a hotel, *twice as large*, for Jews only. In a few years other Lakewood hotels sold out to Jewish operators, and kosher establishments multiplied on all sides.[42] The town became a Jewish enclave.

Also, we now find the first evidence of segregation at work in the summering places of the Midwest and Far West. The Chicago *Tribune* published its first resort advertisements specifying "Christian" or "Gentile" clientele in 1913; the frequency of such notices increased steadily thereafter. About the same time a Minnesota hotelkeeper told B'nai B'rith that he cared little whether he entertained Jews or non-Jews, but the latter would abandon a place when the Jews appeared in any number. "This, he stated, was an equally desirable condition, except for the fact that Jewish people were much more likely to desert a summer resort en masse and go to another, whither the finger of fashion pointed, than was the case with non-Jews, and that he would then have an empty hotel on his hands."[43]

The problem was circular. The more desperately the Jews sought to escape from confinement and move up the social ladder, the more panic-stricken others became at the possibility of being "invaded." The irony was that the difficulties flowed from the acceleration of a process which ultimately held the whole society together. The free movement of individuals across

41. Gottheil in *American Citizen*, I, 146.

42. William Nelson, *The New Jersey Coast in Three Centuries* (New York, 1902), II, 32; Konrad Bercovici, "The Greatest Jewish City in the World," *Nation*, CXVII (1923), 261.

43. *B'nai B'rith News*, November, 1914, p. 1; A. L. Severson, "Nationality and Religious Preferences as Reflected in Newspaper Advertisements," *American Journal of Sociology*, XLIV (1939), 545.

social boundaries maintained the cohesion of the United States—
yet also threatened it.

The resort problem became so acute that some Jews at last
sought the protection of public law. The American Jewish Committee put pressure on the New York legislature to enact a civil
rights bill forbidding places of public accommodation from
advertising their unwillingness to admit anyone because of race,
creed, or color. Violations were to be punished as misdemeanors.
Governor William Sulzer signed the bill into law in 1913. In the
next few years, with the aid of the Anti-Defamation League of
B'nai B'rith, similar measures were enacted in several other
states.[44] These long-forgotten laws form one of the small beginnings of the twentieth-century movement to outlaw discrimination.

Two further types of discrimination appeared in the prewar
years. The social life of many eastern private colleges fell in line,
as the sons and daughters of east European Jews enrolled in large
numbers and quickly demonstrated their intellectual prowess. As
early as 1901, the College of the City of New York was "practically filled" with Jewish students, and in 1908 they comprised 8.5
per cent of the male students in seventy-seven collegiate institutions.[45] They arrived at a bad time. An all-absorbing, extracur-
ricular life of sport and snobbery was overrunning the campuses
at the turn of the century, making hard study and good grades
unfashionable and creating an intricate status system dominated
by the Ivy League.[46] After 1900 few Jews were elected to the
Princeton clubs or to the fraternities at Yale and elsewhere. The
literary and gymnastic societies at Columbia kept Jews out
entirely, and at Harvard one of the best college dormitories
suffered a serious decline in reputation because a good number of
Jews lived there.[47] As a result, Jewish students gradually formed

44. American Jewish Committee, "Seventh Annual Report, 1914," pp. 30–
31 (Louis Marshall Papers, Box B, in Archives of the American Jewish Committee); Kraus, *Reminiscences*, 228.

45. Industrial Commission, *Reports*, XV, 478; Glazer, "Social Characteristics," 15; Alexander Francis, *Americans: An Impression* (New York, 1909),
187.

46. Ernest Earnest, *Academic Procession* (Indianapolis, 1953), 204–36.

47. Ibid., 216; N. Hapgood, "Jews and College Life," *Harper's Weekly*,
LXII, 53–55; *American Citizen*, I, 147.

their own fraternities, the first appearing at Columbia in 1898. Some of the same feeling infected college faculties. By 1910, there were complaints that few Jews could gain entry or advancement in academic circles.[48] In the years just before the war, a few colleges began to limit Jewish enrollment, but on the whole restrictions operated only in the unofficial areas of social intercourse. In all respects the western state universities preserved a freer atmosphere than eastern institutions, while southern schools showed very little anti-Semitism at all.[49]

A second advance in the pattern of discrimination during the period from 1900 to the First World War affected American-Jewish life far more generally and profoundly than could any campus snobbery. While the second generation of east European Jews was heading toward college, their parents were moving out of the original enclaves of immigrant settlement. Before 1900 in the major American cities east European Jews had lived in dense inner-city neighborhoods, interspersed with other nationalities but clinging gratefully to a bit of stability. Thereafter, pulled by ambition and pushed by the pressure of new arrivals crowding in from overseas, many of them moved out to cleaner, less poverty-stricken neighborhoods. The outpouring set off conflict and attempts at restriction all along the urban frontier.

The antipathy the east Europeans met was not totally unprecedented. The German Jews who preceded them in the eighties and nineties sometimes had a chilly reception. Property values allegedly declined in some of the fashionable districts of Boston in the 1880's after wealthy Jews bought houses there. In Cincinnati the entry of German Jews into the upper-class Hilltop neighborhoods stirred some resentment. Walnut Hills became known as

---

48. Alvin E. Duer, ed., *Baird's Manual: American College Fraternities* (Menasha, Wisc., 1940); Charles S. Bernheimer, "Prejudice Against Jews in the United States," *Independent*, LXV (1908), 110; Francis, *Americans*, 84–85. In the nineteenth century the church connection of most private colleges had stood in the way of hiring Jewish teachers, but I am not aware that they faced obstacles in the secular university until the twentieth century. See W. Stull Holt, ed., *Historical Scholarship in the United States, 1876–1901, as Revealed in the Correspondence of Herbert Baxter Adams* (Baltimore, 1938), 70.

49. *American Citizen*, I, 147; Hapgood, "Jews and College Life," 54–55, 77. Cf. Reid, " 'Because You're a Jew,' " 1212.

New Jerusalem, and some of its Protestant residents escaped to the temporarily more exclusive environs of Avondale. But in fact Walnut Hills retained a preponderance of old-stock Americans while accommodating German and Irish newcomers as well.[50] Reports of residential discrimination before 1900 are scant, for nineteenth-century American cities were not highly segregated. Neighborhoods tended to be heterogeneous, and in all but a few places Jews were too few in number to be felt as an intrusive element in established neighborhoods. At the end of the nineteenth and in the twentieth century, however, the larger cities became increasingly segregated by occupational function as well as ethnic background.[51] Concomitantly the Jewish population swelled—from less than one million in 1897 to three and a third million in 1917—and became more concentrated in the larger cities. Whether the families who moved out of the slums were fleeing from a ghetto or simply in search of more room and air, they found themselves caught up in a struggle for turf.

Already at the turn of the century a great stream of humanity was crossing from the Lower East Side of New York into Williamsburg, Greenpoint, and Brownsville. Other Brooklyn residents took so unkindly to the newcomers that the latter established a Jewish Protective Association in 1899 to spur civil action against Jew-beating rowdies.[52] Another sizable colony formed in Harlem. As it expanded, many a landlord in the area hung out a "to-let" sign bearing the warning, "No Jews."[53]

About the same time Boston Jewry broke out of the tenement

50. Kermit Vanderbilt, "Howells Among the Brahmins: Why 'the Bottom Dropped Out' During *The Rise of Silas Lapham*," *New England Quarterly*, XXXV (September, 1962), 302; Zane Miller, *Boss Cox's Cincinnati: Urban Politics in the Progressive Era* (New York, 1968), 47–48.

51. Sam Bass Warner, Jr., *The Private City: Philadelphia During Three Periods of Its Growth* (Philadelphia, 1968), 169–76; Sam Bass Warner, Jr. and Colin B. Burke, "Cultural Change and the Ghetto," *Journal of Contemporary History*, IV (October, 1969), 173–87; Howard P. Chudacoff, "A New Look at Ethnic Neighborhoods: Residential Dispersion and the Concept of Visibility in a Medium-Sized City," *Journal of American History*, LX (June, 1973), 76–93.

52. Samuel Abelow, *History of Brooklyn Jewry* (Brooklyn, 1927), 11–13; New York *Tribune*, June 29, 1899, p. 11.

53. Industrial Commission, *Reports*, XV, xlvi; Bercovici, "Greatest Jewish City," 261.

districts around the harbor and pressed southward, with similar consequences. As the migration descended upon the middle-class suburbs of Dorchester and Roxbury, homeowners either fled or resorted to restrictive covenants. In Roxbury a mass meeting of Jews demanded more adequate police protection against hooligans. Real estate agents in both areas refused to rent apartments to Jews; and often their neighbors' unpleasant behavior forced Jews to vacate newly acquired homes.[54]

Meanwhile, the east European Jewish settlement in Minneapolis expanded from its primary base into the adjacent Oak Lake district, which had been snobbish and substantial. The thought of living near rag peddlers and junk dealers evoked bitter opposition. But after the first Jewish pioneers had passed the outer fringes, the whole district was rapidly taken over.[55] Elsewhere restrictive covenants effectively sealed off attractive areas. An English traveler reported in 1909 that anyone who bought property in the best residential districts of St. Louis and many other cities came under legal obligation not to sell or lease to boarding-house keepers or Jews.[56]

I V

Virtually the whole system of anti-Semitic discriminations was worked out by 1917. The most important new barriers to come into existence after that time applied to relationships that were primarily economic (business activity, employment) rather than social and that lie therefore outside the range of this chapter. On the whole, the decade of the 1920's witnessed a consolidation of existing exclusionist practices, although some notable additions

54. Francis Russell, "The Coming of the Jews," *Antioch Review*, XV (1955), 21–22; *American Hebrew*, August 12, 1910, p. 374; *American Jewish Year Book, 1913–1914*, p. 244.

55. Albert I. Gordon, *Jews in Transition* (Minneapolis, 1949), 27–28, 30, 46.

56. Francis, *Americans*, 85. On Jewish residential mobility during this period see also P. F. Cressey, "Population Succession in Chicago: 1898–1930," *American Journal of Sociology*, XLIV (1938), 67–68, and Charles Reznikoff, "New Haven: The Jewish Community," *Commentary*, IV (1947), 470–71.

occurred, and a decline began in one or two fields toward the end of the decade.

In the early twenties discrimination of all kinds gained an extra incentive from the aggressively conformist nationalism that came out of the First World War. For the first time an ideological note sounded in the rhetoric of discrimination. Popular writers criticized the Jews for maintaining a seclusive solidarity instead of becoming "American first"; restricted communities advertised themselves as composed of "fine upstanding American Families";[57] and in the Midwest the Ku Klux Klan widened the cleavage in many places.[58] Yet this agitation, insofar as it affected segregation, did little more than accentuate established patterns.

Against every obstacle, the Jews continued to prove themselves the most mobile of American ethnic groups. The main force now beating against the walls of discrimination consisted of a second, and even a third, generation. Many of them, determined to prove they *were* "American first," were fleeing more or less consciously from their Jewish heritage and identity.[59] Some, of course, gained at least a conditional acceptance; but the rebuffs that others met were all the more painful because of the social distance they had put between themselves and their immigrant fathers.

In smaller cities, such as Newburyport, Jews found their way into all sections of town in spite of a great variety of obstacles.[60] In big cities, on the other hand, the separation apparently increased. Second-generation Jews poured out of the tenements of Manhattan into the apartment houses of the Bronx and Brooklyn.

57. Don C. Seitz, "Jews, Catholics, and Protestants," *Outlook*, CXLI (1925), 478–79; Herbert Adams Gibbons, "The Jewish Problem," *Century Magazine*, CII (1921), 792; John Jay Chapman to Louis Marshall, December 13, 1920, and clipping from Bronxville *Press*, March, 1925, in Marshall Papers, Box B (American Jewish Committee Archives).

58. Robert S. Lynd and Helen Merrell Lynd, *Middletown* (New York, 1929), 479, 481–84; Leonard Bloom, "The Jews of Buna," in *Jews in a Gentile World*, ed. Isaac Graeber and Stuart H. Brett (New York, 1942), 198–99.

59. Leo Srole, "Impact of Antisemitism," *Jewish Social Studies*, XVII (1955), 276; Samuel Koenig, "The Jews of Easterntown," *Jewish Review*, V (1948), 26, 29.

60. W. L. Warner and Leo Srole, *The Social Systems of American Ethnic Groups* (New Haven, 1945), 44–45, 307–9.

In Brooklyn the tide rolled south, engulfing Borough Park, Bensonhurst, and Coney Island—Corbin's old domain which now was more solidly Jewish than the Lower East Side of Manhattan had ever been.[61] At nearby Sea Gate, gentile exclusiveness made its last stand on the New York beaches, but one restrictive device after another failed to stem the Jewish influx. A parallel migration of non-Jews during the 1920's preempted most of the booming suburbs of Queens, although not without challenge; by the end of the decade Jews were contesting rental restrictions in Jackson Heights.[62] Other battlegrounds lay in Manhattan itself, where upper-class Jews flocked to Riverside Drive. As the Drive became "too Jewish," some of them, through real estate coups, scaled the dizzy social heights of Park Avenue.[63]

Suburbanization in the 1920's. popularized the country club. There the barriers held quite rigidly, though an occasional "pet Jew" might be accepted. Reluctantly, Jewish suburbanites organized their own country clubs, whereupon one of the leading associations of such clubs ruled that Jewish clubs would be admitted to associate membership only.[64]

Social discrimination reached a climax in the quota systems adopted by colleges and medical schools. Following precedents earlier established in the private schools and in campus social life, many college administrations set limits on Jewish admissions. This, the only major extension in the pattern of discrimination during the twenties, came with a rush soon after the war; and the critical factor was the clamorous pressure of postwar youth on the facilities of higher education. General college enrollments spurted so rapidly that the whole prestige system built up in earlier years seemed threatened by democratization, and second-generation Jews (who, unlike the Catholics, had no colleges of

61. An elaborate survey of Jewish population movements in New York City between 1916 and 1925, made by the Bureau of Jewish Social Research, was reported in the *New York Times*, March 18, 1928, sec. X, p. 12.

62. W. Schack, "Conquest of Sea Gate," *Menorah Journal*, XVIII (1930), 54; *New York Times*, February 2, 1927, p. 4; Heywood Broun and George Britt, *Christians Only: A Study in Prejudice* (New York, 1931), 256.

63. Ibid., 258–63; Bercovici, "Greatest Jewish City," 260–61.

64. Silcox and Fisher, *Catholics, Jews and Protestants*, 78; Leo M. Franklin, "Jews in Michigan," *Michigan History Magazine*, XXIII (1939), 89.

their own) stood out more and more as the most numerous and successful ethnic minority invading the campuses.

The first big interdict descended at Columbia University and the University Heights branch of New York University. On these little cultural islands in the urban sea, the proportion of Jewish students rose to 40 per cent or more. Fearful of losing entirely their Ivy League atmosphere, the administrations cut Jewish registration sharply by instituting "psychological" and "character" tests.[65] At Harvard College, where Jewish enrollment had reached about 20 per cent, President Lowell in 1922 made the *faux pas* of openly recommending what other institutions were doing covertly. In a series of stormy meetings the faculty first approved and later rescinded Lowell's graceless proposal. But a quiet and discreet application of differential standards on the entrance examinations partially accomplished the administration's objective.[66] Smaller colleges, perhaps more rigidly than some of the large ones, elaborated their application questionnaires, required a photograph of the candidate, and enforced a geographical distribution. On the other hand, some of the big private institutions in urban centers, such as Pennsylvania, Chicago, and Fordham, held out against the discriminatory trend. That the situation was far from desperate is indicated by the fact that in the twenties there was no flight of northern Jews to the unrestricted state universities of the lower South and the trans-Mississippi West; Jewish enrollments there remained very slight.[67]

Much more formidable were the barriers thrown up around the medical schools. Quotas spread throughout the country and became increasingly severe as the decade advanced. Hundreds of Jews applied to foreign medical schools; thousands more, defeated, turned to dentistry or pharmacy. The best comparative statistics are for graduates of C.C.N.Y. Among non-Jewish

65. "May Jews Go to College?" *Nation*, CXIV (1922), 708; Broun and Britt, *Christians Only*, 74–75, 106–10; Ralph Philip Boas, "Who Shall Go to College?" *Atlantic Monthly*, CXXX (1922), 444–48.

66. Harris Berlock, "Curtain on the Harvard Question," *Zeta Beta Tau Quarterly*, VII (May, 1923), 3–5; Russell, "Coming of the Jews," 23 footnote. See also "The Jews and the Colleges," *World's Work*, XLIV (1922), 351–52.

67. Broun and Britt, *Christians Only*, 72–123.

graduates who applied to medical schools, the proportion accepted varied between 70 and 80 per cent during the period from 1927 through 1930. Among the Jewish applicants from C.C.N.Y., the number accepted some place or other declined steadily from 50 per cent to 20 per cent.[68]

The acuteness of the problem derived from economic—not just social—competition in a difficult supply-demand situation. As a result of the reforms that transformed American medical schools after 1910, medical education was severely limited by costs greatly in excess of student fees. By contrast, the law schools did not discriminate, for they operated at a profit and could expand with enrollment demands. Yet the traffic jam was also a function of a rush of second-generation Jews toward a profession where they could escape stereotypic identification as businessmen, operate as individuals, and exercise fully their keen intellectual capacities. Even in the face of heavy restrictions, Jews constituted about 18 per cent of American medical students at the end of the decade.[69]

While these new areas of discrimination developed, an older interdict showed some signs of weakening. Segregation at resort hotels began to diminish in the 1920's. Whether the new civil rights laws played a real part is hard to say. In the states without them resort owners still flaunted such slogans as, "Altitude 1,860 ft. Too high for Jews." Where the laws applied, they at least compelled subtlety.[70] But a forceful deterrent to discrimination did materialize in the form of the automobile. Many of the settled, all-season guests of yesteryear took to the road. Now vacation areas teemed with hotels and cabins catering to tourists who stopped for a short time only. These establishments could not afford to be as arbitrary, and did not need to be as socially conscious, as the older type.[71] They accepted the passing throng. Here was mobility with a vengeance.

Wherever the summer resort still seemed to confer prestige on

68. Ibid., 145.

69. Ibid., 150, 162. The earliest discussion I have found of the problem of quotas in medical schools is in Louis I. Newman, *A Jewish University in America?* (New York, 1923), 11.

70. *American Hebrew*, March 30, 1923, pp. 645, 670.

71. Broun and Britt, *Christians Only*, 266.

those who frequented it, a problem still existed. But for many that institution now had a more purely recreational value, and access to it correspondingly widened. In other areas of American life, the struggle for status continued unabated. And discrimination reflected, as it had for fifty years, a conjunction of two factors: the insecure inequalities of a middle-class society in which men striving for distinction feared inundation; and the urgent pressure which the Jews, as an exceptionally ambitious immigrant people, put upon some of the more crowded rungs of the social ladder.

V

No part of the country seems to have escaped entirely the status panic that caused discrimination. Even the South, historically the section least inclined to ostracize Jews, was not completely unaffected. In the nineteenth century Jews belonged to the most fashionable city club in Richmond; by the 1940's it and other leading Richmond clubs excluded them. In New Orleans, one of the very best cities for Jews, they no longer received invitations to the Mardi Gras balls, though a Jew had been the first king of the Mardi Gras in 1872.[72]

Within such broad chronological uniformities, however, anti-Semitic discrimination has varied greatly from place to place. All the evidence for the period under review agrees that it generally affected small towns less than cities of perhaps 10,000 population or more; that it influenced the trans-Mississippi West less than the East or older Middle West; and that it touched the South least of all. A closer look at some of the sharpest contrasts between localities should help to test the causal pattern evident on the national level. Although we may not know enough about the total social structure of various cities and sections to see the whole picture, at least the more obvious differences in Jewish-gentile relations should be illuminating.

72. David and Adele Bernstein, "Slow Revolution in Richmond, Va.," *Commentary*, VIII (1949), 542; Julian B. Feibelman, *A Social and Economic Study of the New Orleans Jewish Community* (Philadelphia, 1941), 133-35.

Certainly the striking southern situation offers one key; contrasts between northern cities provide another. Three medium-sized cities that took form at about the same time present especially salient differences: Minneapolis, St. Paul, and San Francisco. By 1920, the Jews of Minneapolis lay under a singularly complete ostracism. It was perhaps the only city in the land that shut out Jews from the service clubs (Rotary, Kiwanis, and Lions), to say nothing of the local realty board and the numerous civic welfare boards.[73] Across the river, the twin city of St. Paul behaved somewhat more decently. Jews could at least belong to the local service clubs and the Automobile Club. San Francisco presented the other extreme. There, acceptance of Jews extended very widely in elite social organizations, civic activities, and even residential patterns.[74] Thus discrimination has been strong in Minneapolis, moderate in St. Paul, and weak in San Francisco, as in the whole South. Yet all three cities had concentrated Jewish districts produced by recent immigration, and the ratio of Jews to the total population in 1930 was highest in San Francisco (6.5 per cent) and lowest in Minneapolis (3.5 per cent).[75]

What differentiated these cities from one another? What, on the other hand, did such obviously unlike places as San Francisco and the South have in common? Separate studies have advanced a good many reasons for the peculiar situation in each of these localities, but only a few of the alleged explanations withstand comparative analysis. For example, in the case of Minneapolis attention is sometimes given to the anti-Semitic influence of religious fundamentalism emanating from the Baptists' Northwestern Bible Institute. Yet Baptist fundamentalism has certainly been stronger in the South than in Minneapolis. A close observer of southern Jewish life argues that the most complete social integra-

73. Charles I. Cooper, "The Jews of Minneapolis and Their Christian Neighbors," *Jewish Social Studies*, VIII (1946), 32–33; Selden Menefee, *Assignment: U.S.A.* (New York, 1943), 101–2.

74. Carey McWilliams, "Minneapolis: The Curious Twin," *Common Ground*, VII (1946), 61–64; Earl Raab, " 'There's No City Like San Francisco,' " *Commentary*, X (1950), 369–71.

75. Sophia M. Robison, ed., *Jewish Population Studies* (New York, 1943), 152–82. On St. Paul see also Calvin Schmidt, *Social Saga of Two Cities* (Minneapolis, 1937), and *Universal Jewish Encyclopedia*, IX, 315.

tion and civic acceptance have been attained in the small towns of the South, where the Jew still figures as "the heir, guardian, and living embodiment of the Old Testament tradition."[76] It is reasonable to conclude that religious ideology was not the critical factor in either situation.

If we examine the areas of low discrimination, two circumstances stand out. Both the South and San Francisco fought for decades to uphold white supremacy in the face of a colored race, the Negro in one, the Oriental in the other. For a long time this overriding preoccupation bound all white men together as partners and equals. By the time other ethnic issues intruded, the Jews had become more fully integrated in the local culture than anywhere else.[77] As late as 1916, the leading anti-Japanese organization in San Francisco, the Native Sons of the Golden West, held a mass meeting to raise funds for persecuted European Jews. The Grand President of the Native Sons, forgetting for the moment the Oriental issue, asked San Francisco to "say to all mankind that there exists in this world one spot at least where every one worthy is entitled to citizenship, and where every citizen is within the pale."[78]

A second, and undoubtedly more important, factor in the two areas was the relatively stable character of the local Jewish communities. Outstanding Jews achieved a notable and highly respected place in both public and private life before the status rivalries of the late nineteenth century crystallized. In early San Francisco Jewish mayors, judges, financiers, and merchants helped to construct the basic institutions of the city. In the antebellum South widely scattered Jewish merchants partly made up for the lack of a native merchant class. In both areas assimilation proceeded even to the point of extensive intermarriage. Later immigrations did not come with disruptive force. An old-line, patrician leadership maintained rapport with the non-Jewish elite while gradually absorbing the newcomers. The proportion of Jews to the total population did not vary much from decade to

76. Cooper, "Jews of Minneapolis," 34–36; Harry L. Golden, *Jewish Roots in the Carolinas* (Greensboro, N.C., 1955), 56.

77. On the South see C. Bezalel Sherman, "Charleston, S.C., 1750–1950," *Jewish Frontier*, XVIII (1951), 14–16, and Golden, *Jewish Roots*, 47–48.

78. *Grizzly Bear*, March, 1916, p. 3.

decade.[79] Consequently, the social climbing of Jews never stood out sharply or took on any special significance.

A dramatically different situation obtained in Minneapolis. There the early German Jews did not lay an adequate foundation for the integration of later immigration. The first Jewish settlers arrived fifteen or twenty years after Minneapolis took shape in the 1850's, and they never acquired a position of any importance in civic life. Then Russian and Rumanian Jewish ghettos materialized swiftly in a section abutting directly on an upper-middle-class neighborhood. A head-on collision ensued. In neighboring St. Paul, where relations were better, the Jews established themselves earlier in the history of the city, developed a wealthier and more influential Jewish community before 1900, and presumably experienced a more even rate of growth.[80]

In summary, each of our test cases shows a direct correlation between discrimination and the degree to which the growth of the local Jewish community disturbed the existing social structure. But one must beware of an explanation so elastic that it embraces an endless range of ethnic conflicts. Did not other European minorities who flooded into the cities of America along with the Jews disturb the social structure also? Was their fate any different?

No one who has looked beneath the surface of the American scene will doubt that discrimination of some kind and degree has affected other European groups in America aside from Jews. The Italians and Irish, especially, come to mind. Social discrimination against these groups, however, has attracted little scholarly notice. In the present state of knowledge the best one can do is to compare stereotypes. We must remember, of course, that stereotypes may not have any significant behavioral consequences. Unfavorable attitudes need not produce discriminatory acts. Nevertheless, a study of attitudes has at least a suggestive value for the present theme. Insofar as attitudes reflect reality, they may help us to

79. Raab, " 'There's No City Like San Francisco,' " 370–72, 376. On the South, in addition to references already cited, see Charles Reznikoff and U. Z. Engelman, *The Jews of Charleston* (Philadelphia, 1950), 186–88, 193–97, 235–37.

80. *Jewish Encyclopedia* (1904), VIII, 599–600; McWilliams, "Minneapolis," 63–64.

understand how the Jewish situation differed from that of other immigrant groups.

Ordinarily, except, that is, during periods of political or economic crisis, Americans have rated immigrant groups according to their approximation to the cultural and racial norms of American society. Orientals, being more conspicuously remote in culture and race than any European group, have fared worse than any. At the opposite end of the spectrum, the British and Anglo-Canadian peoples have hardly seemed foreigners at all; a sense of cultural identity even exempted them from the Anglophobia that was widespread in nineteenth-century America. The image of southern and eastern Europeans, on the other hand, excited strong dislike long before a mass migration from those regions began.[81]

In the case of nearly every immigrant group, unfavorable judgments have softened as the forces of assimilation have reduced the cultural gap. Thus, American opinion of the Germans rose steadily from a low point in the 1850's to a high point in 1913, plunged disastrously during the political crisis of the war, and then quickly rebounded. The Irish, too, at one time so unpopular that they constituted a separate caste in American society, have gradually risen in reputation during the last eighty years in spite of recurrent waves of nativism. This improvement has derived not only from a growing tolerance of Catholicism but also from increasing social differentiation among the Irish and their integration into an overall American culture. Indeed, the assimilation of the Irish has undoubtedly been a large factor in the decline of anti-Catholic feelings. Similarly, antipathy toward southern and eastern Europeans has greatly diminished since the 1920's.

What about the Jews? Their experience, during the period under review, was different. Whereas other European groups generally gained respect as assimilation improved their status, the Jews reaped more and more dislike as they bettered themselves. The more avidly they reached out for acceptance and participation in American life, the more their reputation seemed to suffer. Moreover, this contrast in the trend of sentiment corresponded

81. Higham, *Strangers in the Land,* 24-25, 65-66.

to a basic difference in ethnic stereotypes. Ordinarily, old-stock Americans have felt at least equal and usually superior to the ethnic minorities in their midst. Only during periods of crisis, when beset by a sharp sense of danger, have Americans imagined such groups as the Germans or the Irish to be qualitatively more vigorous and potent than themselves. Normally, unfavorable stereotypes have stressed the ethnic's inferiority—his incapacities which are thought to drag down or hold back American society. Jews, however, have commonly left the opposite impression of equal or superior capacity. Unfavorable stereotypes have pictured an overbearing Jewish ability to gain advantage in American life. Only one other important immigrant group—the Japanese—has normally been disliked for its strength rather than its weakness.[82]

The stereotype of Jewish power becomes, of course, grossly unreal in the context of ideological anti-Semitism. But the difference between the Jewish stereotype and the stereotypes of other European immigrant groups may roughly reflect a real cultural contrast. The other groups with backgrounds markedly different from the American have progressed relatively slowly in the United States. The social expectations of the first and even the second generations have characteristically been modest; often a peasant's fatalism and a peasant's habit of deference to superiors have curbed their desires, so that critics have thought of them as inert, backward, etc. But the relative slowness of assimilative mobility has protected many immigrant peoples from painful rebuffs. Probably only a limited proportion of nineteenth-century Irishmen wanted to belong to native American groups, just as the Italians in Burlington, Vermont, in the 1930's did not want to move into a neighborhood where the people were "too classy to sit out on their porches."[83] The aspirations of these nationalities have been economic (and sometimes political) long before they sought an equivalent social status. Consequently, the

82. Chester Rowell, "Chinese and Japanese Immigrants—A Comparison," *Annals of the American Academy of Political and Social Science*, XXXIV (1909), 223–30; Carey McWilliams, *Prejudice: Japanese-Americans* (Boston, 1944), passim.
83. Elin Anderson, *We Americans: A Study of Cleavage in an American City* (Cambridge, Mass., 1937), 43.

barrier they felt and struggled against was economic discrimination. It is significant that the bulk of the available evidence on discrimination against non-Jewish European immigrants concerns occupational restrictions. The nineteenth-century newspaper advertisements warning "No Irish Need Apply" referred to jobs, not to membership in clubs.[84]

The Jews, on the other hand, met little economic discrimination before 1910 or so, for they did not enter labor markets crowded with other applicants. They encountered social discrimination much earlier, and the reason seems clear. Compared to other groups with a background markedly different from the American, they progressed rapidly in the United States, and their social aspirations kept pace with their economic advance. They wanted the full privileges and opportunities of the middle-class society into which, unlike the other major immigrant groups, they moved en masse. Perhaps we are now in a position to understand why social discrimination against Jews but not against other European peoples has long seemed a problem worth writing about: our sense of injustice is most easily stirred when people are denied something they passionately want.

VI

If the discussion so far has been persuasive, it should suggest that virtually the entire story of social discrimination in the United States can be explained and understood without reference to ideological factors. This does not mean, of course, that ideology has not elsewhere played a major role in Jewish-gentile relationships. Nor should we conclude that the myths of anti-Semitism are of no importance if they do not determine the behavior of the host society. Ideological anti-Semitism may serve ulterior purposes without materially damaging its victims. It may supply the

84. Oscar Handlin, *Boston's Immigrants* (Cambridge, Mass., 1941), 67. See also Severson, "Nationality and Religious Preferences," 540–50, and references to discrimination in Higham, *Strangers in the Land*. On the difficulties of a rising Irish middle class in the 1890's, however, see Thomas Beer, *The Mauve Decade* (New York, 1926), 156–65.

rationale for an agitator seeking power; it may give a certain stimulus to general policies such as immigration restriction or isolationism; or it may simply provide an inconsequential outlet for general social frustrations and aggressions. Furthermore, ideological campaigns may have psychological effects on Jews without destroying their status in the community. Many Jews may depend on the cries of the ideologist in order to maintain a defensive posture and to nourish a sense of separateness. In America, anti-Semitic ideologies have worked in all of these ways, but they have not determined the range of social opportunity.

Among the ideologies commonly held guilty of fomenting anti-Jewish discriminations, the oldest is Christianity. Whatever the role of early Christianity, in the nineteenth and twentieth centuries it probably elicited more sympathy for Jews than hostility. In both respects—and they tend to cancel one another—the influence of Christianity since the late nineteenth century has been blunted by secularization and by the secular nature of most of the involvements between Christians and Jews. Discrimination has been aimed at the social and economic Jew, not at Judaism. It is true that survey researchers in the mid-1960's, on setting out to investigate the religious sources of anti-Jewish attitudes, found what they were looking for. They found it particularly among poorly educated people and in the more orthodox denominations. Apparently, traditional Christian dogmas still encouraged some to be critical of Jews. This inquiry reminds us of the persistence of a substratum of opinion that may not appear in the secular press. But there was a certain unreality about the study. It did not probe nonreligious sources of the attitudes under examination. It was not concerned at all with the religious sources of philo-Semitism.[85] Moreover, the findings seem in flat contradiction to the behavioral studies that tell us that small-town Jews in the

85. Charles Y. Glock and Rodney Stark, *Christian Beliefs and Anti-Semitism* (New York, 1966) was sponsored by the Anti-Defamation League of B'nai B'rith. An intensive study of Lutherans, replicating the research of Glock and Stark but subjecting it to more elaborate analysis, controverts their findings. See Merton P. Strommen et al., *A Study of Generations* (Minneapolis, 1972), 203–12, 216.

Bible Belt have generally enjoyed a close identification with their local community.[86]

The one significant Christian attack on the Jew came from the Ku Klux Klan in the 1920's. Based as it was on an aggressive antiurban fundamentalism, the Klan activated the old folk myths about Jews as Christ-killers and carnal sinners. Temporarily, some Jewish merchants suffered boycotts, and a certain amount of social cleavage may have lingered in some Klan areas. But in many such areas, particularly in the South, anti-Semitic discrimination remained slight compared to other regions, such as New England, where the Klan was very weak. In the South, moreover, the Klan was considerably less anti-Semitic than in the North: behavioral patterns inhibited ideology. What there was of anti-Semitism in the southern Klans was discharged against the shadowy, imaginary Jew who lived far away in the big cities. Klansmen felt distinctly uncomfortable at picking on the Jews whom they had known as good neighbors all their lives. The Klan's boycotts of Jewish merchants usually failed abysmally.[87]

More commonly, students of anti-Semitism have located the heart of the modern Jewish problem in a second ideology: racism. Here too, differences between America and Europe have not been clearly enough appreciated. Except in the 1930's, American racists rarely singled out the Jew as the exclusive or even as the major object of attack. Traditional American racism manifested itself as the exclusion of dark-skinned people from any possibility of equal social status in white society. It simply did not apply to Jews, except as a basis of identification with other whites. In 1851 a frontier newspaper editor wrote: "In vain have nations and sects hurled anathemas against . . . the Jew. . . . He belonged to a superior race. . . . He was a WHITE man— he was of the God-appointed, ruling, progressive race of humanity, for such all nature, all experience, all the philosophy of facts, and the attestations of religion, prove the white race to

86. Dinnerstein and Palsson, *Jews in the South*, should be supplemented with Golden, *Jewish Roots;* Omer C. Stewart, "Rural Anti-Semitism," *Frontier*, II (August, 1951), 14–16; Eugene Schoenfeld, "Small-Town Jews' Integration into Their Communities," *Rural Sociology*, XXXV (June, 1970), 175–90.

87. Information from former Klan leader. See also Samuel Taylor Moore, "Consequences of the Klan," *Independent*, CXIII (1924), 534.

be."[88] This traditional racism changed in the late nineteenth and early twentieth century, as an elaborate ideology extended its proscriptions to southern and eastern European immigrants. The new racism was intensely anti-Semitic, but not in a distinctive or exclusive sense. Parallel racist doctrines in France and Germany rested on a primary distinction between Aryans and Jews; but American racists differentiated principally between Anglo-Saxons or Nordics and every other variety of human being, Jews along with the rest. Thus racism does not particularly illuminate the special difficulties they faced.

The most significant ideological attack on American Jewry has focused not on religion or on race but rather on political subversion. The international Jew, half banker and half Bolshevik, is seen as conspiring to seize control of the nation. This belief, foreshadowed during the Civil War and partially emergent in the 1890's, really crystallized around the time of the First World War. It should perhaps be called anti-Semitic nationalism, for it immolated the Jew on the altar of national loyalty. If any pattern of ideas activated discrimination, surely the nationalist theme must have done so.

Yet an examination of the life history of anti-Semitic nationalism shows no close correlation with the incidence of social discrimination. Both the ideological attack and discrimination obviously received an initial impulse from the rise of Jewish immigration in the latter decades of the nineteenth century. Also, when most intense, as in the early 1920's, the ideological agitation undoubtedly sharpened the edge of discrimination. Otherwise, however, the two forms of hostility took separate and even divergent courses. Whereas discrimination steadily increased from the 1870's to the 1920's, anti-Semitic nationalism rose and fell cyclically. It reached a minor peak in the 1890's, dropped out of sight for about a decade, climbed again during the period of the First World War to a new climax in the early twenties, and then faded away for a second time.[89] Also, the two hostilities had their strongest impact in different places. Like religious prejudice, the nationalist ferment to which Tom Watson, the Dearborn *Independent*, and the Ku Klux Klan contributed, was most

88. Minnesota *Democrat*, quoted in *Asmonean*, IV (1851), 36.
89. Ch. 7 above; Higham, *Strangers in the Land*, 92–94, 160, 277–86, 327.

widespread and in many ways most intense in the small-town culture of the South and West, where local Jews were usually not regarded as foreigners or outsiders. Discrimination, a product of status rivalries in an urban middle class, rested on foundations much more tangible than the specters that sometimes haunted the rural imagination.

Our inquiry into the origins and rise of social discrimination is now complete; but that is hardly the end of the matter. The course of the argument has led into a labyrinth of distinctions: between different kinds of stereotypes, between stereotypes and discrimination, between varieties of discrimination, between diverse ideologies, and finally between ideology and action. The usefulness of these distinctions for specific analytic purposes should not obscure the complexity of the experience they dissect. Seen as a whole, its various dimensions interacting with one another, American anti-Semitism may have a larger meaning than its separate facets reveal. A dramatic event that occurred in Georgia in 1913 illustrates the incompleteness of our exposition thus far.

Leo Frank had recently arrived from the North to take charge of a pencil factory in the booming city of Atlanta. A thirteen-year-old girl from the country who worked in the plant was found bestially murdered in the basement. The principal evidence against Frank was the accusation of a black employee who claimed to have helped dispose of the body. Contrary to the usual southern tendency to blame the black man in such a situation, public opinion and the prosecution fixed on Frank as the culprit. Years later a local clergyman remembered feeling, when the police arrested the night watchman, "this one old Negro would be poor atonement for the life of this innocent girl. But, when on the next day, the police arrested a Jew, and a Yankee Jew at that, all of the inborn prejudice against Jews rose up in a feeling of satisfaction, that here would be a victim worthy to pay for the crime."[90] Convicted amid a positive frenzy of indignation, Frank was spared from execution by the governor of the state, who

90. Leonard Dinnerstein, *The Leo Frank Case* (New York, 1968), 33. In addition to this standard study see Charles and Louise Samuels, *Night Fell on Georgia* (New York, 1956).

commuted his sentence to life imprisonment. A mob then snatched him from prison and hanged him in the woods.

The Frank case was an exceptional incident, but it deserves note because it does not fit neatly in any of the categories that help explain particular types of anti-Semitism. The hatred of Frank was profoundly charged with class and status feeling. It was permeated with religious images of the Jew as a corrupter and despoiler of the innocent. It was intensified by a quasi-political determination to thwart the wealthy northern Jews who carried Frank's case to the Supreme Court. It was connected in some way with the rampant racism of the period. Yet the terrible passions that claimed Leo Frank seemed to have at their heart something more than a mere combination of these impulses. To understand the Frank case, and to appreciate the intensity anti-Semitism sometimes reached in the era from 1913 to 1945, we shall have to look more broadly at American culture.

Chapter Seven

Anti-Semitism and American Culture

There is a startling contrast between the neglect of anti-Semitism by American historians and the intense fascination it has had for social psychologists and sociologists. Beginning in the 1930's and continuing into the early 1960's, social researchers probed and measured and hypothesized endlessly about the causes of anti-Semitism and the characteristics of the anti-Semite. A bibliography published in 1961 listed scores of research studies. The most imposing of these works, *The Authoritarian Personality*, was acclaimed as "an epoch-making event in social science." Another critic hailed it as "one of the seminal volumes of our time."[1] It assigned to anti-Semitism an extraordinary importance by arguing that critical attitudes toward Jews reveal a basic personality type that threatens the survival of democratic society. Anti-Semitism in this view is not just a serious problem in human relations; it is the very archetype of prejudice, the model through which all the hatreds and all the intolerance that besiege modern man can be exposed. An appreciation of the appeal this set of ideas acquired after the Second World War will help us to round

1. Melvin M. Tumin, *An Inventory and Appraisal of Research on American Anti-Semitism* (New York, 1961), 10; Martin Jay, *The Dialectical Imagination: A History of the Frankfurt School and the Institute of Social Research, 1923-1950* (London, 1963), 250; T. W. Adorno et al., *The Authoritarian Personality* (New York, 1950).

out an assessment of the strength and the vicissitudes of anti-Semitism in America.

Two premises supplied crucial underpinnings to *The Authoritarian Personality*. First, the authors postulated the emergence of a new type of personality which largely explains modern anti-Semitism and which reveals itself most nakedly in attitudes toward Jews. Second, they attributed to the authoritarian personality a rigid, punitive psychic life—associated with conservative views on political, economic and moral issues—which endangers all deviant groups. Modern anti-Semitism, therefore, is inseparable from a generic need to hate.

In hindsight the *succès d'estime* of this ponderous, pretentious, often confusing book seems grossly disproportionate to its scientific merit. As events have demonstrated, the whole theory was rooted in the special conditions of a particular era, and the era was closing even before the book appeared. The fixation on anti-Semitism as the prototypic prejudice, and its identification with an authoritarian personality, reflected, of course, the traumatic impact of Hitlerism on the consciousness of the western world. Until the 1930's American social scientists had paid little more attention to anti-Semitism than had historians. When social scientists had taken notice, they duly pointed out the specifically American circumstances which both limited and conditioned negative feelings toward Jews.[2] In the 1930's and 1940's, however, the holocaust in Germany threw a blazing light on every sort of bigotry. The destruction of the European Jews now appeared as the extreme case of a repressive rage that might overtake any or all of America's varied minorities.

On a more personal level, anti-Semitism was also given a special significance by the anxieties of a generation of American Jews who accomplished after the war an extraordinary ascent in the academic world. In other words, *The Authoritarian Personality* focused on the kind of prejudice to which young American social scientists were themselves most sensitive. Yet the vogue the book enjoyed in American colleges and universities ironically demonstrated the collapse there of the kind of prejudice it

2. Bruno Lasker, ed., *Jewish Experience in America: Suggestions for the Study of Jewish Relations with Non-Jews* (New York, 1930).

scrutinized so intently. The exceptional importance postwar social scientists attached to anti-Semitism fitted European circumstances better than American.

Nevertheless, the theory of the unitary character of prejudice did rest on some foundations in modern American experience. Before the twentieth century ethnic, racial, and religious animosities in America were so diverse that no single concept encompassed them. "Prejudice" was defined as a prepossession *for or against* anything, formed without due examination of the facts. No one supposed that it might be reified. No one assumed that it referred distinctively to negative judgments of minorities and therefore connoted a certain kind of exclusionist mentality.[8] In the early twentieth century, however, the generalized syndrome the authors of *The Authoritarian Personality* described did in fact emerge, with profound consequences for all minority groups. Under the pressure of an immense, heterogeneous immigration, together with other social dislocations, hostility toward various ethnic, religious, and political minorities coalesced around the time of the First World War. The result was a sweeping rejection of all groups deviating from a conservative, Protestant, northern European pattern. The lynching of Leo Frank, which seems so grotesque if viewed only in the light of previous Jewish experience in the South, becomes more comprehensible as a sign of a new mobilization of defensive emotions: a fear of everything strange, polyglot, and impure.

The discovery that a broad-spectrumed fear was abroad in the land did not wait for the publication of *The Authoritarian Personality*. Liberal intellectuals denounced ethnocentrism and race thinking with mounting horror throughout the interwar period. Social psychologists in the 1930's published a number of studies showing that nationalism, imperialism, anti-Negro prejudice, and

3. The current definition of prejudice as "an irrational attitude of hostility directed against an individual, a group, a race, or their supposed characteristics" apparently did not get into dictionaries until the early 1960's. It is absent from the *Oxford English Dictionary*, from the second edition of *Webster's New International Dictionary* (1934), and from *Webster's New Collegiate Dictionary* (1960). It appears in *Webster's Seventh New Collegiate Dictionary* (1963).

economic conservatism were interrelated.[4] Thus the conceptual framework of *The Authoritarian Personality* accorded with a received body of academic opinion, which in turn reflected fairly accurately a real constellation of emotions in American society.

Though real enough for a time, the constellation proved unstable. No one in the 1940's could know that it was already breaking up. Not until the 1960's, after a generation of dizzying changes, was it unmistakably clear that ethnic hostilities had again splintered. As a general fear of minorities subsided, the specific antipathies it had exacerbated seemed less threatening. Anti-Semitism was one of those. Accordingly, the history of American attitudes toward Jews falls into three stages. In the first stage Jews developed a distinctive relationship to American society and a distinctive image. Toward the end of that period, in the late nineteenth century, the image deteriorated, but it remained idiosyncratic. In the second stage anti-Semitism, without losing its special features, was much inflamed by interfusion with a pervasive cultural anxiety. In the third stage, since 1945, the generalized anxiety significantly declined; and so did the distinctive anti-Semitism inherited from an earlier era.

II

The extraordinary freedom and acceptance Jews enjoyed in early America was primarily a consequence of the unobstructed sway of a capitalistic way of life.[5] The presence of great religious and ethnic diversity in the Anglo-American colonies was also important, for it meant that Jews did not stand out as a solitary body of nonconformists. But the diversity was itself a consequence of reliance on voluntary, competitive enterprise to create a new society. In Europe Jews depended on royal protection, which

4. Gardner Murphy, L. B. Murphy, and Theodore Newcomb, *Experimental Social Psychology* (New York, 1937), 889–1046; David Krech and Richard S. Crutchfield, *Theory and Problems of Social Psychology* (New York, 1948), 487.

5. Ellis Rivkin, "A Decisive Pattern in American Jewish History," *Essays in American Jewish History* (Publications of the American Jewish Archives, IV, Cincinnati, 1958), 28–34.

gave them a corporate identity marked out by laws and charters. There they occupied a distinct, confined sphere of life. In America royal authority was remote and ineffective. No one who paid his own passage had a separate legal status. Only a few Jews appeared on the North American mainland in the seventeenth century, perhaps 250 in all. They were not numerous enough to be either threatening or indispensable. As merchants they performed an essential function, but in no way an exclusive or unique one. They fitted inconspicuously into expansive societies, the denizens of which were engrossed in the profitable exploitation of natural resources rather than the retention of traditional privileges and prescriptions.

At first Jews encountered sporadic restrictions on their right to vote and to engage in certain kinds of trade. These restrictions were mere vestiges. Like other efforts to transplant medieval controls to the American wilderness, they tended to wither away. In the eighteenth century Jews became assimilated into Anglo-American society to a remarkable degree. Well-to-do Jews joined the same clubs patronized by their Christian peers, subscribed to the same private libraries, attended the same dancing assemblies, sent their children to the same schools. Jewish merchants accepted Christian apprentices, inherited property from Christian friends, and not infrequently married Christian women. Full political rights lagged somewhat behind social integration. Religious tests for public office lingered in a few states into the early nineteenth century. The tests, however, were not distinctively anti-Jewish, and in any case they survived only where the absence of an active Jewish community left them unchallenged and inconsequential.[6]

Supporting these favorable circumstances was a general compatibility between Jewish and American values. In addition to the special affinity New England Puritans felt for ancient Israel, nearly all American Protestants by the nineteenth century believed that religious liberty was a cornerstone of national identity. The great threat to a free society emanated from despotic

6. Jacob R. Marcus, *The Colonial American Jew, 1492–1776*, 3 vols. (Detroit, 1970), III, 1123–1235; Salo Wittmayer Baron, *Steeled by Adversity: Essays and Addresses on American Jewish Life* (Philadelphia, 1971), 80–98.

hierarchies. The Jews heartily agreed. A depoliticized people, they had no central institutions, only independent congregations. They shared with American Protestants similar memories of the coercions of centralized, ecclesiastical authority. Burned into their consciousness were similar images of the Pope, the Inquisition, the Middle Ages. Naturally the Jews embraced America's voluntaristic, pluralistic pattern. It should not surprise us that anxious American nationalists in the middle of the nineteenth century focused their hatred on two authoritarian religions— Mormonism and Catholicism—while acclaiming the Jews' loyalty to American institutions.[7]

If a predilection for localized liberty united Jews and Protestants in the religious sphere, another important link bound together their economic habits. As an ethnic group, Jews have traditionally emphasized the materialistic, competitive values of business life that are so deeply ingrained in American culture. The prestige America confers on the businessman—the man of thrift, enterprise, and rational calculation—has ordinarily encompassed the Jew. "Wherever there is a chance for enterprise and energy the Jew is to be found," declared an editorial in the Philadelphia *Evening Telegraph* in 1872. "He brings into every community wealth and qualities which materially assist to strengthen and consolidate its polity. . . . No other element in the community is so orderly."[8]

Nowhere does this deference appear more vividly than in the immense respect Americans felt for the house of Rothschild during a great part of the nineteenth century. Aware as we are of the anti-Semitic potentialities of the Rothschild stereotype, we may find it hard to credit how cheerfully rank-and-file Americans once attributed vast power to that family. In 1856, a Know-Nothing newspaper, patronized largely by lower-class readers, concluded a worshipful sketch of "The Money Kings" with the statement that the Rothschild family "for forty years past has

7. Eugene Lawrence, "The Jews and Their Persecutors," *Harper's Weekly*, XLIX (1874), 79-92; David B. Davis, "Some Ideological Functions of Prejudice in Ante-Bellum America," *American Quarterly*, XV (1963), 115-25.

8. Morris U. Schappes, ed., *Documentary History of the Jews in the United States, 1654-1875* (New York, 1950), 557-58.

controlled the destinies of our century more than any other power." Similarly, the conservative editor of *Harper's Monthly*, in the course of praising the Jews, wrote quite casually that Rothschild was "the most powerful man in the world." Rudolf Glanz has perceptively attributed the mythic scale of the Rothschild legend to a "need to express the essence of capitalism in one great human example, that was, moreover, no individual fortune doomed to extinction, but a family undertaking, continuing from generation to generation."[9]

Still, the symbiosis in values was not complete. There was a fissure in American economic morality: a cleft where ideological anti-Semitism, when it crossed the Atlantic, could lay its charges. While the American value system celebrated the businessman as provider, community builder, and industrious trader, it was more uncertain about the merits of bankers and creditors. Americans always put an exceptionally high premium on productivity—on the work of the hand and the machine in mastering the wilderness, creating abundance, and achieving industrial efficiency. Many American heroes, from Benjamin Franklin to Charles A. Lindbergh, have been skilled in making things; few have been idolized for manipulating intangibles like money or ideas.

One of the major traditions of social thought in America, a tradition historians have usually called "agrarian," fixed on the speculative dealer in paper credits and privileges as the corrupter of the simple virtues of a republic. Transplanted in the eighteenth century from England to America, this body of ideas was a reaction against the whole system of centralized patronage, power and corruption associated with the growth of banks and public credit. An ideology of protest and opposition against an entrenched elite, agrarianism idealized the virtuous independence of the small freeholder; but its appeal has by no means been limited to farmers. Agrarians drew a fundamental distinction between the "producing classes" and unproductive speculators and monopolists. The former group comprised the industrious

9. New York *Dispatch*, November 23, 1856, p. 1; "Editor's Easy Chair," *Harper's Monthly*, XVII (1858), 267–68; Rudolf Glanz, "The Rothschild Legend in America," *Jewish Social Studies*, XIX (1957), 5. See also "The Jews—A Cursory Glance at Their Past and Present Status," *De Bow's Review*, V (1868), 694–700.

makers of things; the latter the parasitic makers of money.[10] The producing classes made up, in Andrew Jackson's telling phrase, the "bone and sinew of the country." The others were an idle, conspiratorial few. From Jefferson through Jackson to Thorstein Veblen, this tradition shaped the native American criticism of capitalism and economic inequality.

As we have already noticed, ideological anti-Semitism in America concentrated on economic rather than religious themes, on Shylock rather than Judas. In an intense form, it conjured up secret intrigues to gain control of the money supply and wreck the financial system. A milder version depicted the Jews as parasites, living by their wits on the hard work of others. This was exactly the image many Americans already had of a class of idle rich in their midst. Thus, in identifying the Jew as unproductive, anti-Semitism tapped an authentic vein of indigenous social criticism. "The Hebrew immigrants rarely lay hand to basic production," wrote the midwestern sociologist E. A. Ross. "In tilling the soil, in food growing, in extracting minerals, in building, construction and transportation they have little part. Sometimes they direct these operations, often they finance them, but even in direst poverty they contrive to avoid hard muscular labor."[11]

The charge of nonproductivity figured prominently in the earliest faint foreshadowing of ideological anti-Semitism that I have discovered in American sources. In 1820 the editor of the famous news magazine, *Niles' Weekly Register,* discussed the need to eliminate officeholding restrictions from the Maryland constitution. Wondering why the Jews in most countries were denied some part of the rights of other men, he concluded:

There must be some moral cause to produce this effect. In general, their interests do not appear identified with those of

10. J. G. A. Pocock, *Politics, Language and Time: Essays on Political Thought and History* (New York, 1971), 80–147; Marvin Meyers, *The Jacksonian Persuasion: Politics and Belief* (New York, 1960), 15–22; Carl N. Degler, "The Locofocos: Urban 'Agrarians,' " *Journal of Economic History,* XVI (1956), 322–33; Irwin Unger, *The Greenback Era: A Social and Political History of American Finance, 1865–1879* (Princeton, 1964), 29–33, 195–212.

11. Edward A. Ross, *The Old World in the New* (New York, 1914), 146.

the communities in which they live, though there are some honorable exceptions to this remark. But they will not sit down and labor like other people—they create nothing and are mere consumers. They will not cultivate the earth, nor work at mechanical trades, preferring to live by their wit in dealing, and acting as if they had a home no where. . . . But all this has nothing to do with their rights as men. . . .[12]

What *Niles' Register* said so tranquilly, with so noticeable an absence of fear, could become a cry of alarm after immigration made Jews more numerous and visible in the United States. But this happened only in moments of crisis, when war or depression sharpened resentment at the speculator and the profiteer. The first instance of something approaching explicit ideological anti-Semitism occurred during the Civil War, when Jews were accused of exploiting the war effort and occasionally of trying to destroy the national credit. A second and more considerable manifestation took place during the socioeconomic crisis of the 1890's, a time of searing depression, intense class resentments, and widespread fears of an end to individual opportunity.

On both occasions anti-Semitism drew on European ideas and stereotypes, but a more direct source of rhetoric and attitudes was the American agrarian tradition. Native American complaints about Jewish economic-political influence in the late nineteenth century typically rested on the old producer ethic. Deeply troubled by the soft materialism of an urban civilization, anti-Semites looked back nostalgically—as agrarians had always done—to a time when no idle exploiters lived in corrupting luxury. Having little understanding of the problem of industrial overproduction, they attributed society's troubles primarily to the lords of finance. Like other American agrarians, the anti-Semites felt a special animus against banks, moneylenders, and bond-holders. In this sense, for example, Brooks Adams was a kind of agrarian, not only in his inflationary schemes but even more in his social theory. The history of the nineteenth century, as Adams read it, turned not on the Marxian theme of capital versus labor but

12. *Niles' Weekly Register*, VII (October 21, 1820), 114.

rather on the agrarian lament—the bankers had triumphed over a preceding regime of "the producers."[13]

The link between ideological anti-Semitism and a nostalgic, agrarian turn of mind may be tested by comparing Brooks and Henry Adams with one of Henry's closest friends, John Hay. The epitome of eastern upper-class snobbery, Hay was chockfull of racial and class biases. But he never felt threatened by Jews, and as Secretary of State he did much to please them. To Hay, Henry Adams's anti-Semitism was preposterous. Adams is "clean daft," Hay commented privately. "The Jews are all the press, all the cabinets, all the gods and all weather. I was amazed to see so sensible a man so wild." The critical difference between the two friends centered in Hay's unqualified enthusiasm for industrial and financial capitalism. Adams, yearning to be back in the eighteenth century, complained bitterly of "the total irremediable, radical rottenness of our whole social, industrial, financial and political system." Hay, on the other hand, had not a trace of nostalgia. He busied himself with running the system and defending it at every turn.[14]

Still, the limits of ideological anti-Semitism must be further narrowed. Not only was it checked by the dominant business culture, but among the discontented the overwhelming majority remained unaffected. In view of the dark forebodings that saturated agrarian thought—in view especially of its proneness to a conspiratorial interpretation of events—why did so few agrarians attack the Jews? Perhaps it was partly because the true agrarian mind clung to environmentalism. Following their eighteenth-century prophets, Jefferson and Paine, agrarians located the danger to republics in bad institutions and false doctrines, not in the nature of men. Most nineteenth-century Americans who responded to the agrarian indictment felt that political reforms could reverse the increasing corruption of American life. In contrast, the few anti-Semites apparently had a sourer view of human

13. Brooks Adams, *The Law of Civilization and Decay* (New York, 1955), 257–82.
14. Kenton J. Clymer, "Anti-Semitism in the Late Nineteenth-Century: The Case of John Hay," *American Jewish Historical Quarterly*, LX (1971), 344–54. For Henry Adams see Edward N. Saveth, *American Historians and European Immigrants, 1875–1925* (New York, 1948), 74.

gullibility and a more cataclysmic vision of the future. An early instance was *The Quaker City* (1843), a phantasmagoric novel by the radical Jacksonian, George Lippard. Its anti-Semitism, embodied in an utterly duplicitous hunchback named Gabriel Von Gelt who could literally smell gold, was a very minor theme. But anti-Semitism was part of Lippard's nightmarish picture of the total depravity of urban society, from the ruination of which the only escape was back to nature. Fifty years later the few Populists who gave vent to anti-Semitic diatribes were also extravagantly susceptible to fears of a breakdown of the whole civilized order.[15] At a moment when Ignatius Donnelly was assailed by doubts that civilization could survive, he imagined a world ruled by Jewish oligarchs. Tom Watson turned to anti-Semitism only after his hopes for a new alignment of parties had been defeated. Brooks Adams's rage at the Jews accompanied his formulation of a pessimistic philosophy of history. Among critics of the power of money in American society, anti-Semitism was a symptom of despair.

III

In the nineteenth century anti-Semitism was on the whole a special problem, a problem only for Jews. Its early manifestations produced shock and dismay among traditional liberals, for discrimination against Jews was immediately identified as "altogether un-Christian and un-American." Leaders of opinion branded it as "forever irreconcilable with the genius of American institutions."[16] But it was seen as an aberration of democracy, rather than a fundamental danger to democracy. Every minority group had enemies. Although a few great liberals like Wendell

15. Frederic Cople Jaher, *Doubters and Dissenters: Cataclysmic Thought in America, 1885–1918* (New York, 1964), 104–28; Alexander Saxton, "*Caesar's Column:* The Dialogue of Utopia and Catastrophe," *American Quarterly*, XIX (1967), 224–38.

16. *Appleton's Annual Cyclopaedia,* 1890, p. 466; S. B. Brittan, *A Plea for the Jews: The Crusade Against Israel Is War on Christianity and Democracy* (New York, 1879), 4; Alice Hyneman Rhine, "Race Prejudice at Summer Resorts," *Forum*, III (1887), 524.

Phillips championed nearly all minorities, ethnic tensions were relatively discrete. The hysteria over foreign radicals in the late 1790's did not touch foreign Catholics.[17] The Know-Nothing movement of the 1850's concentrated its fire on Catholics, ignored Jews, and attracted many northerners who sympathized with the plight of blacks.[18] The anti-Chinese movement in California seems to have helped the Irish feel at home there. A strong upsurge of anti-Catholicism in the Midwest during the 1890's contained not a trace of the anti-Semitism concurrently developing in other sections; and neither agitation touched the blacks, whose situation in the North had temporarily stabilized.[19] Neither Jews nor others could see a single, antidemocratic mentality at work in these various ethnic conflicts. Under the circumstances it is not surprising to find Jews often aligned with Anglo-Americans against another minority, such as the Irish or the blacks.[20]

In the early twentieth century the generalized prejudice that has fascinated modern social psychologists crystallized. Jews now found themselves part of a motley array of outsiders, confronting an ever more fearful majority. Among many white Protestants, a host of tensions and frustrations came together to produce a broadly exclusionist spirit, which proponents sometimes labeled "100 per cent Americanism." It expressed a mounting determination to repress and repel.

So far as Jews were concerned, the roar that came out of Georgia against Leo Frank in 1913 announced the new situation.

17. Note, for example, the genial attitude of Federalist Boston toward Bishop John Lefebvre de Cheverus at this time. Frances S. Childs, *French Refugee Life in the United States, 1790–1800* (Baltimore, 1940), 41, 199.

18. Oscar Handlin, *Boston's Immigrants* (Cambridge, Mass., 1959), 201–4; Leonard Pitt, "The Beginnings of Nativism in California," *Pacific Historical Review*, XXX (1961), 36–37; Mary R. Coolidge, *Chinese Immigration* (New York, 1909), 40, 64–67.

19. Donald L. Kinzer, *An Episode in Anti-Catholicism: The American Protective Association* (Seattle, 1964), 47, 90; Gilbert Osofsky, *Harlem: The Making of a Ghetto: Negro New York, 1890–1930* (New York, 1966), 36–37.

20. Robert Ernst, *Immigrant Life in New York City, 1825–1863* (New York, 1949), 167–68; Bertram Wallace Korn, *Eventful Years and Experiences: Studies in Nineteenth Century American Jewish History* (Cincinnati, 1954), 58–73; *Jewish Messenger*, LXXVIII (November 22, 1895), 4.

A rising crime rate and anxiety over law and order, an increasing rigidity and punitiveness in racial discipline, an embattled defense of sexual purity, a baffled rage at industrial oppression—these were some of the emotions that swirled around the courtroom in Atlanta. Above all, Leo Frank was hated as an outsider, who focused the multiple fears the new prejudice brought together. Frank was not a southerner. He was a northern Jew, whom northern newspapers, national Jewish leaders, and cultivated opinion in general defended so strenuously that Georgia's country people knew they were indeed beleaguered. In the most fundamental sense he was seen as a deviant—the term "pervert" was constantly used—who incarnated all the alien forces that threatened the traditional culture.[21]

To explain in detail how and why a generalized prejudice came into being is beyond the scope of this essay, but three factors may be briefly mentioned. First, the strains of a largely unregulated industrial capitalism produced more insecurity than most people could tolerate. Secondly, the idealistic beliefs of an earlier day yielded to a biologistic racial determinism, which both reflected and intensified the sense of insecurity. The new racist ideology heightened feelings of vulnerability because it made cherished values and institutions depend on biological purity rather than their own intrinsic merits. Finally, a sweeping ethnocentrism was aroused in the early twentieth century by the sheer scale and variety of immigration. The great problem was not just the Jews but outsiders of all kinds, alien in blood and faith and heritage. The United States was becoming so heterogeneous that every social problem could be interpreted in terms of ethnic subversion. The "100 per cent Americans" tried desperately to impose unity and social stability by asserting against all intrusive groups their own sense of possession and preeminence in the land of their fathers.

The 1920's was probably the high point of 100 per cent Americanism. The forces of prejudice played across Catholics, Jews, blacks, Japanese, southern Europeans, and Bolsheviks. The Ku Klux Klan embodied this convergence of antiminority feelings,

21. Leonard Dinnerstein, *The Leo Frank Case* (New York, 1968), 90-106, 118, 134; John Higham, *Strangers in the Land: Patterns of American Nativism, 1860–1925* (New Brunswick, N.J., 1955), 185–86, 204–12.

providing a single outlet for every racial and religious hatred and every defensive anxiety that festered among the nation's white Protestant majority. Instead of concentrating on a single adversary, the Klan proposed to "restore" the supremacy of the "old stock" and thus to purify America of moral and racial pollution. In this milieu anti-Semitism became part of a multifaceted, exclusionist movement. Its distinctive features nevertheless persisted. A generic prejudice did not dissolve the separate antagonisms in American culture, but enriched and interconnected them. Anti-Semitism changed less in character than in intensity and pervasiveness.

Accordingly the upheavals of war and depression complicated and strengthened the anti-Semitic ideology without altering its central theme in any essential way. At its core still was agrarian disillusion—a frustrated longing for the imagined innocence of a Jeffersonian world. To the image of the Jew as a money power was added, after 1918, an image of the Jew as Bolshevik; and both kinds of economic subversion became linked with fears of biological pollution. But the chief spokesmen of ideological anti-Semitism remained, as in the nineteenth century, people who subscribed to the old producer ethic, which divided society into the industrious many and the idle few, the indigenous people and the parasitic conspirators who were stealing their heritage. In 1920 Henry Ford launched against the "international Jew" the most sustained anti-Semitic campaign the United States had yet seen. It was undertaken at a time when Ford had already stepped forth as a crusader against "the money changers of Wall Street," and Ford put his attack on Jews in the context of a global struggle between "creative Industry" and "international Finance." Although Ford's newspaper, the Dearborn *Independent*, accused Jews of every imaginable conspiracy against the American people, the moral center of his indictment was squarely in the agrarian tradition. "Jew financiers are not building anything," Ford told an interviewer. Indeed, they had organized the labor unions in order "to interrupt work."[22]

22. "The International Jew: The World's Problem," *The Dearborn Independent*, May 22, 1920, pp. 1–3; Seymour M. Lipset and Earl Raab, *The Politics of Unreason: Right-Wing Extremism in America, 1790–1970* (New York, 1970), 135–38.

It is also pertinent that Ford's popularity centered in the small towns and the countryside of the upper Middle West, which is where Father Coughlin's anti-Semitic tirades received their widest approval a decade later. The Reverend Charles E. Coughlin became the most influential anti-Semitic agitator in the 1930's, as Ford was in the 1920's. Like Ford, Coughlin turned his fire on the Jews only after fixing on international bankers as the despoilers of America.[23] In the late thirties Coughlin took on a fascist coloration, as he aligned himself with Hitler and Mussolini in foreign and domestic policies, but his movement was nonetheless rooted in American soil.

In some quarters of the high culture the same ideological susceptibilities operated. Ezra Pound, for example, moved into anti-Semitism on a path almost identical with Father Coughlin's. Pound too began a career of political agitation as a monetary crank, convinced that gold and "usury" were at the root of the country's troubles. In Pound's case the agrarian origins of this theme seem especially clear, for Pound's intellectual cosmopolitanism was mixed with a deep personal identification with the early American republic. Born in Idaho and convinced that a man should "stand unabashed in the face of the largest national luminaries," Pound once told an American official, "I do not think I have ever abandoned the frontier." He was intensely proud of his grandfather, an agrarian Congressman who fought for monetary reform in the 1870's, and Pound's own monetary pamphlets consistently harked back to the true faith of Thomas Jefferson. "We were diddled out of the heritage Jackson and Van Buren left us," Pound wrote in 1933, when he was still blaming the financiers in general. "The real power just oozed away from the electorate. The de facto government became secret. . . . The people grovelled under Wilson and Harding, then came the nitwit and the fat-face."[24] Yet a fixation on Jews, which Pound as

23. Charles J. Tull, *Father Coughlin and the New Deal* (Syracuse, 1965), 10–12, 21, 35, 193–238; Lipset and Raab, *Politics of Unreason*, 175. On Ford's popularity see *Literary Digest*, LXXVII (June 30, 1923), 5–7; Allan Nevins and Frank Ernest Hill, *Ford: Expansion and Challenge, 1915–1933* (New York, 1957), 315.

24. Ezra Pound, *Jefferson and/or Mussolini* (New York, 1936), 97. See also Noel Stock, *Poet in Exile: Ezra Pound* (Manchester, Eng., 1964), 143–219.

well as Coughlin revealed about 1938, did not overtake Pound until he despaired of the democratic process and concluded that only an authoritarian regime could stand up against the international bankers.

The agrarian lament echoed more gently, but unmistakably, in some of the novelists who came out of the Middle West before and after the first World War and who could never forget "the fresh green breast" of a world they had lost. Willa Cather's *The Professor's House* (1925) was one of the most delicate and haunting statements of the contrast between the moral purity of an older America and the corruption of the present. On one level the book offered a comparison between two young men who wooed the professor's daughter. Tom Outland, a son of pioneers, understood the nobility of selfless, creative work and the intrinsic beauty and dignity of nature. Louie Marcellus, a cosmopolitan Jew, understood how to make money from what the other produced. The first young man is seen only in flashbacks. He died before the book opens, and the Jew has taken possession of the professor's daughter. The antithesis between the two men, like the larger antithesis between past and present, is symbolized by a gift each has made to the young woman. Tom Outland gave her a "dull silver" bracelet he found in his explorations of a vanished Indian civilization. Louie Marcellus presented her with a showy gold necklace. The professor's daughter (America?) wears the gold about her throat. The silver, which might have encircled her hand, lies forgotten in a drawer, for she has no understanding of its craftsmanship and history.[25]

These symbols convey some of the agonies of a part of American culture that was dying in the period between the two world wars while another subculture was coming rapidly forward. In the last chapter we observed in the 1920's a sharpening of social discrimination against Jews, particularly through quota systems in educational institutions. This hardening resistance, we can now understand, was not only a function of social competition. It was also part of a wider conflict of cultures. Jews, as a result of their intellectual energy and economic resources, constituted an advance guard of the newer peoples who had no feeling for the

25. James Schroeter, "Willa Cather and the Professor's House," *Yale Review*, LIV (1965), 494–512.

traditions of rural America, and the newcomers were beginning to demand a fair share of the country's heritage.

On top of everything else, competition for jobs exacerbated the struggle. Until the twentieth century Jews had not sought the white-collar jobs that were in general demand. The eastern European immigrants were petty tradesmen or workingmen, employed in a largely Jewish environment. But they wanted their children to get out of the factories. By the eve of the First World War great numbers of Jewish high-school graduates, the immigrants' sons and daughters, were looking for jobs as clerks, stenographers, and secretaries in non-Jewish firms. Their widespread debarment from such openings came to light in 1916, when Jacob Schiff resigned from the board of directors of a large employment agency because its mercantile branch discouraged Jewish applicants.[26]

Economic discrimination peaked during the Great Depression. Colleges rarely hired Jewish faculty; private schools virtually never. One study showed that Catholic colleges, with 3 per cent of their faculties Jewish, were considerably more receptive than non-Catholic institutions. Even the Jewish-owned *New York Times* accepted help-wanted advertisements specifying "Christians only." Other newspapers ran ads asking explicitly for Anglo-Saxons. In New York it was generally understood that a Jew stood no chance of getting a white-collar job if a non-Jewish applicant was available. This led to painful subterfuges. Some girls wore crosses. Some job candidates changed their names. Some joined a church in order to be able to withstand the inquiries of vigilant personnel managers.[27]

On the other hand, Jews made striking advances in labor markets where discrimination was ineffective or inoperative. Public employment was one of these. The spread of a civil service

26. Cyrus Adler, *Jacob Schiff: His Life and Letters*, 2 vols. (New York, 1928), I, 363; A. L. Severson, "Nationality and Religious Preferences as Reflected in Newspaper Advertisements," *American Journal of Sociology*, XLIV (1939), 540–42.

27. J. X. Cohen, *Jews, Jobs, and Discrimination: A Report on Jewish Non-Employment* (American Jewish Congress, 1945), 16–17, 20–21; J. X. Cohen, *Towards Fair Play for Jewish Workers: Third Report on Jewish Non-Employment* (American Jewish Congress, 1938), 2–3, 18.

system based on competitive examinations enabled bright young second-generation Jews to get municipal and federal jobs more easily than private ones. As early as 1914 it was said that Jews were driving the Irish out of the city jobs in New York; in the public school system Jewish women already outnumbered the female teachers of any other ethnic background.[28] Throughout the interwar period Jews continued to gain under the merit system. Ultimately the great majority of school principals in New York City were Jewish. In the 1930's the New Deal attracted large numbers of idealistic young Jews to Washington, where they gave an added thrust to welfare agencies and to legal work. These economic and social gains help to explain the envy of the Roosevelt-haters, who sneered at the "Jew Deal," and the alarming belligerence displayed by Irish and Negro rabble-rousers on the streets of New York during the late 1930's.

IV

Intense anti-Semitic agitation in the late thirties was more than counterbalanced by the rise of the broadest, most powerful movement for ethnic democracy in American history. Its beginnings may be traced to a rebellion among intellectuals against the scientific racism and the generalized prejudice of the 1920's. But the movement acquired momentum only when the New Deal, the new industrial unions, and the public schools became its vehicles. Without having intended to do so, the New Deal united the aggrieved minorities. It provided a means by which intellectuals could combine with the racially excluded and the economically underprivileged against a common enemy: the conservative bigot, the 100 per cent American.

Nevertheless, in the early years of the Second World War, there were ominous signs of an upswing in prejudice. The entire Japanese-American population of the West Coast was interned. "Zoot suit" outbreaks against Mexican-Americans hit Los Angeles; appalling race riots scarred Detroit and New York.

28. Ross, *Old World in the New*, 148; Baron, *Steeled by Adversity*, 54.

Nearly a quarter of the respondents to a 1944 poll named the Jews as a threat to America.[29] Only as the war drew to a close, and the full horrors of the Nazi concentration camps spilled out to an aghast world, did a decisive change of direction occur. The change was dramatized by President Truman's notable address supporting the historic 1947 report of his Committee on Civil Rights. Government, as Truman defined its role, would be more than a neutral umpire of human rights. It would promote affirmative efforts to achieve equality.[30]

During the Truman administration (1945–1953) the movement against racial and religious prejudice advanced on every front. A guilt-stricken society repudiated its previous treatment of the Japanese. Initiatives from the President and the Supreme Court desegregated the armed forces and public facilities in the District of Columbia, outlawed segregation in interstate commerce, defended the rights of religious minorities, shattered quota systems in higher education, and made restrictive covenants unenforceable. In the decade beginning in 1945, ten states and more than thirty cities created fair employment practices commissions.[31] The fear of communism lingered, but lost a specifically ethnic coloration. Anti-Catholic agitation virtually disappeared. In the South, Catholic parochial schools took a lead in racial desegregation; yet a close observer of southern life noted in 1955 that an anti-Catholic pronouncement on an editorial page of a southern newspaper, or even in the "open forum" columns, had become "absolutely unthinkable."[32]

Within this broad realignment of social forces, the decline of anti-Semitism was especially striking because Jews were so prominent in the liberal coalition and so vulnerable to counterattack. Jewish names and faces turned up again and again in postwar trials and allegations about Communist spies in the

29. Charles Herbert Stember et al., *Jews in the Mind of America* (New York, 1966), 127–29.

30. Donald R. McCoy and Richard T. Ruetten, *Quest and Response: Minority Rights and the Truman Administration* (Lawrence, Kans., 1973), 99–101.

31. Will Maslow, "The Uses of Law in the Struggle for Equality" (mimeographed, National Community Relations Advisory Council, 1954), 3.

32. *The Carolina Israelite*, September–October, 1955, p. 13.

United States. In behalf of the new state of Israel Jews brought intense pressure to bear on American foreign policy, and during the debate over the Six-Day War a Jew represented the United States in the United Nations. Moreover, northern Jews threw themselves into the Negro civil rights drive with what their southern brethren—remembering Leo Frank—regarded as a suicidal disregard of the danger of an anti-Semitic backlash. None of these provocations checked the precipitous decline of every variety of anti-Semitism. By 1962 only one per cent of the respondents in an opinion poll named the Jews as a threat to America. Only 3 per cent said they would dislike having a Jewish family move in next door. Even major shifts of population no longer inspired anything like the old dread of invasion. An intensive study in the early 1960's of an upper-middle-class suburb in the Middle West, which was attracting a sizable influx of Jewish newcomers, showed a broad spirit of Jewish-gentile cooperation. Almost half the non-Jews said they did not care how many Jews lived in their neighborhood.[33] By 1965 the issue of anti-Semitism had become so trivial that the *American Jewish Year Book* for the first time in its long history dropped the section chronicling that subject and replaced it with a section entitled "Civil Rights and Intergroup Tensions."

This remarkable change—so totally unforeseen by the social science of the 1940's and 1950's—has flowed from reciprocal developments in American culture and in the nature of the American-Jewish community. Still in some sense a capitalist society, America has continued to esteem individual enterprise and material success. The countervailing tradition of agrarian dissent, on the other hand, has collapsed. The integration of rural America into an urbanized national culture has largely dissipated the old suspicion of the city as a place of alien intrigue. Americans still have little love for their cities, but no longer regard

33. Stember, *Jews in the Mind of America*, 96, 128, 268; Benjamin B. Ringer, *The Edge of Friendliness: A Study of Jewish-Gentile Relations* (New York, 1967). Some of these findings are contested in Gertrude J. Selznick and Stephen Steinberg, *The Tenacity of Prejudice* (New York, 1969). Some of the limitations of the latter study have been pointed out in Lucy Dawidowicz, "Can Anti-Semitism Be Measured?" *Commentary*, L (July, 1970), 36–43.

them as un-American. Moreover, the agrarian distinction between "producing classes" and the idle rich has lost both its conceptual framework and its moral relevance. Instead of visualizing the mass of people as independent producers, modern culture defines them as dependent consumers. The agrarian ethic put a premium on the independence that could be attained by living simply and avoiding entanglement in debts. It rested on an ascetic disapproval of luxury and worldly pleasure. Modern culture, however, has undermined puritanical attitudes toward worldly enjoyment, as it has dissolved the old fears of financial dependence. A consumption ethic, in short, has superseded a production ethic. As this transition went forward swiftly in the 1940's and 1950's, the cultural distance closed between Jews, who had always appreciated pleasure, and other Americans. Jewish entertainers (Danny Kaye, Barbra Streisand), Jewish novelists (Saul Bellow, Philip Roth), and Jewish literary critics (Alfred Kazin, Leslie Fiedler) became leading disseminators of an urban morality which gave a new emphasis to hedonism, intellectuality, and anxiety.[34]

While American culture became more receptive to Jews, they in turn were becoming more fully Americanized. By the 1950's about three-quarters of American Jews were native-born, and most of these were at least third-generation Americans. The overbearing manners of the aggressive, insecure huckster had faded. The huge evacuation of the slums was over; so was the flight from working-class jobs. The center of gravity in postwar Jewish life shifted to the suburbs, where settlement was frequently more dispersed than it had been in the central cities. The suburban Jews made and spent their money in much the same way as their gentile neighbors. Whereas the older Jewish middle class was concentrated in independent businesses, the third generation passed into corporate bureaucracies and college faculties in large numbers. This in turn encouraged an increasing migration from the northeastern centers of Jewish population to areas without strong Jewish communities. In spite of strenuous efforts by Jewish defense agencies to keep the issue of anti-Semitism

34. I am indebted to some comments on this subject by Lawrence Fuchs in a book review in *American Historical Review*, LXXIII (1968), 941.

alive, it was elbowed aside in the early 1960's by an opposite worry: intermarriage, total assimilation, the loss of a Jewish identity. In little more than a generation the image of the Jew as the quintessential alien was virtually obliterated. Instead, some critics now saw the Jew as "a quintessential middle class American secularist . . . saturated with the emerging hedonistic ethos of the mass consumption, mass culture society."[35]

Clearly, this transformation could not have come about if the broad-spectrum prejudice of the early twentieth century had persisted. Before a reintegration of Jewish and American culture could take place, the stresses that produced the exclusionist mentality had to relax. Chief among those stresses was mass immigration. Its termination in the 1920's made possible, on the one hand, the rapid Americanization of the Jewish community and, on the other, the breakup of 100 per cent Americanism. As the great wave of immigration subsided and the immense heterogeneity of early-twentieth-century America diminished, the rigid perception of all deviating groups as impure and corruptive tended to dissolve.

For Jews the new situation created unexpected perplexities. Success and civic honor were sweet indeed. But for many the price of that success was a certain loss of moral engagement. The struggles of the era from 1933 to 1964 had united all the minorities against a common enemy, and Jews could take a justifiable pride in being in the very forefront of the coalition. By the mid-sixties the common enemy was becoming hard to find. As he withdrew the coalition weakened. Ethnic tensions became once more relatively discrete. The disintegration of generic prejudice, which taught Jews to think of themselves as a racial minority allied with blacks, revealed the painful distance between the two.

35. Irving Greenberg, "Adventure in Freedom or Escape from Freedom? Jewish·Identity in America," *American Jewish Historical Quarterly,* LV (1965), 5–21; Judd L. Teller, *Strangers and Natives: The Evolution of the American Jew from 1921 to the Present* (New York, 1968), 219–34.

Chapter Eight

Integrating America: The Problem of Assimilation

To speak of assimilation as a problem in nineteenth-century America is, in an important sense, to indulge in anachronism. That is because nineteenth-century Americans seemed for the most part curiously undaunted by, and generally insensitive to, the numerous and sometimes tragic divisions in their society along racial and ethnic lines. Leaving aside some significant exceptions, the boundaries between groups with different origins and distinct cultures caused little concern. Assimilation was either taken for granted or viewed as inconceivable. For European peoples it was thought to be the natural, almost inevitable outcome of life in America. For other races assimilation was believed to be largely unattainable and therefore not a source of concern. Only at the end of the century did ethnic mixing arouse a sustained and urgent sense of danger. Only then did large numbers of white Americans come to fear that assimilation was *not* occurring among major European groups and that it was going too far among other minorities, notably blacks, Orientals, and Jews.

This acute consciousness of assimilation as a problem marked a great crisis in ethnic relations. Extending from the 1890's to the 1920's, the crisis persisted until a new ethnic pattern came into being. The objects of this chapter are, first, to describe the ethnocultural system of the nineteenth century in a way that may help us to understand more fully the ensuing crisis, and second, to glimpse within that crisis the origins of a new system of ethnic relations that has unfolded in subsequent decades.

Before considering assimilation as a newly perceived problem at the end of the nineteenth century, it will be necessary to give some account of assimilation as a process in earlier decades. Here we may note in passing that the blending, merging, and incorporation of peoples has occurred on many levels in the United States, not just on the level of nation-building that historians and politicians ordinarily have in mind when they speak of assimilation. Surely the most impressive instances of assimilation in American history are to be found in the formation of racial or national minorities from more particularistic antecedents. The African slaves imported into the English colonies in the late seventeenth and eighteenth centuries were a medley of peoples, differing widely in appearance, traditions, and language. In their own minds they belonged to distinct tribes, not to a race. Their English masters threw them together quite indiscriminately, however, and gave them a single, inclusive name: Negroes. Accordingly, the plantations of the colonial South functioned as a remarkable melting pot, in which distinctions between Mandigoes, Ibos, Angolans, and other African peoples were largely obliterated.[1] Partly because the English ascribed a common identity to them, and partly because certain common themes in west African cultures facilitated their amalgamation in spite of disparate languages and customs,[2] the Afro-Americans gradually became a single people in spite of enormous differences in their circumstances and their exposure to Anglo-American influences.

Although the slaves present the most striking example, a similar process of assimilation entered into the making of major European ethnic groups as well. Most of the peasants and villagers who came to the United States in the nineteenth century brought with them very little sense of having belonged to a nation. At first they thought of themselves as the people of a particular local area—a village or at most a province. They were not Germans

---

1. Gerald Mullin, *Flight and Rebellion: Slave Resistance in Eighteenth-Century Virginia* (New York, 1972), 34–82; Ira Berlin, "Time, Space, and the Evolution of Afro-American Society on British Mainland North America," *American Historical Review*, LXXXV (1980), 66–77.

2. Lawrence W. Levine, *Black Culture and Black Consciousness: Afro-American Folk Thought from Slavery to Freedom* (New York, 1977), 4–30.

but Wurttembergers, Saxons, and Westphalians; not Italians but Neapolitans, Sicilians, Calabrians, and Genoese; not Chinese, but members of particular districts and clans.[3] Speedily in most cases, slowly in a few, these localized attachments were submerged within the wider identities we know today: identities that demonstrate both the special bond a common language provides and the special respect Americans have accorded to the principle of nationality as a basis of social identification.

When we turn from this very successful, intermediate level of assimilation, which Victor Greene has called "ethnicization,"[4] and consider the higher level on which an overarching American consciousness has formed, we find a more confusing and complicated situation. An enormous amount of inter-ethnic assimilation did in fact occur in the experience of individuals. Even while the emerging ethnic groups of nineteenth-century America were crystallizing, each of them was losing highly mobile families who cast off the old ways and the old identity, became in speech and manners indistinguishable from the native white population, and gradually faded into it. In the South, for example, many German Jews in the nineteenth century were so fully accepted into the white society that their descendants ceased to be Jewish. Meanwhile, in the North, miscegenation and mobility made possible a continual, silent passing of light-skinned Negroes across the color line. According to a black physician in 1844, at least six of his former classmates at the New York African Free School were then living as whites.[5]

Even more important, entire ethnic groups lost much of their distinctiveness in the course of time. In upper New York State the asperities between the old Dutch settlers and incoming

3. Jonathan D. Sarna, "From Immigrants to Ethnics: Toward a New Theory of 'Ethnicization,'" *Ethnicity*, V (1978), 370–78.

4. Victor Greene, *For God and Country: The Rise of Polish and Lithuanian Ethnic Consciousness in America* (Madison, Wis., 1975), 3–10.

5. Harry L. Golden, *Jewish Roots in the Carolinas: A Pattern of American Philo-Semitism* (Greensboro, N.C., 1955), 25–27; Ray Stannard Baker, *Following the Colour Line: American Negro Citizenship in the Progressive Era* (New York, 1908), 162–73; Carter G. Woodson, ed., *The Mind of the Negro as Reflected in Letters Written during the Crisis, 1800–1860* (New York, 1969), 273.

Yankees from New England gradually softened. By the 1820's the descendants of the French Huguenots in New Rochelle and elsewhere retained little more than their names to mark their origin.[6] By the end of the nineteenth century the Irish Catholics, though still keenly distrusted in New England, were elsewhere sufficiently accepted and well established so that comic magazines no longer felt free to portray them as drunken louts with the faces of gorillas.[7] In the twentieth century the crumbling of the great German-American community is the most familiar and spectacular case of collective assimilation. In some degree a multi-ethnic melting pot indubitably *has* worked—but so imperfectly, so inconsistently, so incompletely! It worked, but it did not prevail. Whereas virtually all of the local or tribal identities that the people of this country brought with them from other lands have been obliterated, every one of the racial and national groupings that was created in America has stubbornly persisted. It is not an outright failure of assimilation that needs to be understood in comprehending nineteenth-century America, but rather the peculiar contradictions the process of assimilation displayed.

The most obvious of these contradictions was between theory and reality. The theory of assimilation, as formulated by Hector St. Jean de Crèvecoeur in the Revolutionary era, seemed to allow for no exceptions. "Here individuals of all nations are melted into a new race of men," this wandering Frenchman declared.[8] The Revolutionary belief that America offered a new start for mankind acquired, from Christian and classical sources, rich millennial overtones. Listen, for example, to Herman Melville's musings as he watched German emigrants boarding ships for America:

> We are not a nation, so much as a world. . . . Our ancestry
> is lost in the Universal paternity; and Caesar and Alfred,
> St. Paul and Luther, and Homer and Shakespeare are as

6. James Fenimore Cooper, *Notions of the Americans*, 2 vols. (New York, 1828), I, 87, 305–6.

7. John Higham, *Strangers in the Land: Patterns of American Nativism, 1860–1925* (New Brunswick, N.J., 1955), 86.

8. Moses Rischin, ed., *Immigration and the American Tradition* (Indianapolis, Ind., 1976), 26.

much ours as Washington, who is as much the world's as our own. We are the heirs of all time, and with all nations we divide our inheritance. On this Western Hemisphere all tribes and peoples are forming into one federated whole; and there is a future which shall see the estranged children of Adam restored as to the old hearthstone in Eden.[9]

More prosaically, Oliver Wendell Holmes described his compatriots as "the Romans of the modern world—the great assimilating people." This was not enough for George Bancroft, the first great historian of the United States, who declared: "Our country stands . . . as the realisation of the unity of the [human] race."[10]

In actuality, of course, white Americans had no intention of translating a national myth into a literal command. Even the most radical abolitionists shrank from the accusation that they were promoting an amalgamation of races.[11] Yet some kinds of assimilation did bridge the chasm between blacks and whites; and the relations of both blacks and whites with other minorities varied enormously. What needs to be explained is not a simple opposition between theory and practice but rather a baffling mix of inconsistencies.

Consider, for instance, how white Americans behaved and felt a century ago toward the Indian tribes. United States Indian policies, as one Commissioner of Indian Affairs confessed, were "hopelessly illogical." In some situations expediency dictated a resort to warfare; in others it produced a mixture of subsidies and neglect. In still other situations the federal government pursued a conscientious (though often misguided) program of

---

9. Philip Rahv, ed., *Discovery of Europe: The Story of American Experience in the Old World* (Boston, 1947), 137–38.

10. Holmes quoted in Merle Curti, *The Growth of American Thought*, 3d ed. (New York, 1964), 225; Bancroft quoted in Daniel J. Boorstin, *The Americans: The National Experience* (New York, 1965), 371.

11. Theodore Tilton, *The Negro: A Speech at Cooper Institute* (New York, 1863), reprinted in *The Burden of Race: A Documentary History of Negro-White Relations in America*, ed. Gilbert Osofsky (New York, 1967), 102–3.

assimilation.[12] Private attitudes ranged from a special respect for Indians to outright contempt. Throughout the nineteenth century the Currier and Ives prints, which often treated blacks condescendingly, never demeaned or ridiculed Indians. They appeared always as dignified human beings with a legitimate life of their own. Similarly it was not uncommon in the southern states for upper class whites of both sexes proudly to claim descent from Indian ancestors.[13] Yet middle-class tourists at the same time were sneering at the Indians they saw at transcontinental railroad stops; and a leading historian in the 1870's urged his readers to appreciate the fascination their forebears had had with Indians, although "To us, of course, the American Indian is no longer a mysterious or even an interesting personage—he is simply a fierce dull biped standing in our way."[14]

Education is another sphere in which paradox and contradiction abounded. Americans characteristically viewed the common school as the one instrumentality essential for molding a common citizenry, education of the young being the only organized effort the nation needed to make to promote assimilation. Yet many public schools also served contrary objectives that had more to do with maintaining segregation or preserving minority cultures. In some parts of the country control of the local schools gave ethnic minorities substantial protection from the dominant culture. In rural areas of the Middle West where Germans predominated heavily, some public schools were taught mainly or even entirely in the German language—a practice that aroused little notice or objection before the 1890's.[15]

12. Francis P. Prucha, ed., *Documents of United States Indian Policy* (Lincoln, Neb., 1975), 138.

13. Morton Cronin, "Currier and Ives: A Content Analysis," *American Quarterly*, IV (1952), 329–330; Edward A. Freeman, *Some Impressions of the United States* (New York, 1883), 150; Theodore Roosevelt to Henry Fairfield Osborn, December 21, 1908, in *Letters of Theodore Roosevelt*, ed. Elting Morison et al. (Cambridge, Mass., 1951–54), VI, 1434.

14. *Harper's Weekly*, October 24, 1874, p. 880; Moses Coit Tyler, *A History of American Literature*, 2 vols. (New York, 1878), I, 10.

15. Heinz Kloss, "German-American Language Maintenance Efforts," in Joshua Fishman et al., *Language Loyalty in the United States* (The Hague, 1966), 232–36. See also Selwyn Troen, *The Public and the Schools: Shaping the St. Louis System, 1838–1920* (Columbia, Mo., 1975), 55–78.

In other parts of the country assimilation through education was vigorously supported as a national goal but severely qualified in local practice. Nowhere was public education stronger, or zeal for social integration greater, than in New England. During the post–Civil War decades New England educators and reformers threw themselves into campaigns to inculcate the ex-slaves of the South, the Indians of the Great Plains, and the Chinese of California with the knowledge and the values they would need to become effective participants in a free society.[16] At the same time, however, these New Englanders showed scant interest in assimilating the French Canadians—contemptuously described as "the Chinese of the Eastern States"—who were pouring into their own towns and cities. Like the Chinese, the French resisted the culture and society they encountered in the United States and did not send their children to public schools. The Yankees, no doubt glad to have the schools to themselves, allowed their own school-attendance laws to go unenforced.[17]

The examples I have chosen have in common a feature that is central to the contradictions in nineteenth-century America. In responding to Indians and in formulating educational strategies, white Americans showed particularly receptive attitudes toward people who were distant in time or in space from themselves: people whose disembodied remoteness made them suitably abstract objects of an abstract faith in assimilation. Toward outsiders who crowded into one's immediate environment—like the French Canadians in New England and the Indians who asked for handouts at railway stations—a greater distrust or resistance was manifested. Some of this difference between sympathy at a distance and repulsion on closer contact may be inescapably and perennially human, but the glaring contrasts we find in nineteenth-

16. James M. McPherson, *The Abolitionist Legacy: From Reconstruction to the NAACP* (Princeton, N.J., 1976); Gunther Barth, *Bitter Strength: A History of the Chinese in the United States, 1850–1870* (Cambridge, Mass., 1964), 157–73.

17. Iris Podea, "Quebec to 'Little Canada': The Coming of the French Canadians to New England in the Nineteenth Century," *New England Quarterly*, XXIII (1950), 370–72; Massachusetts Bureau of Statistics of Labor, *Twelfth Annual Report, 1881*, 469–70.

century America owe their salience to a distinctive combination in American culture of jealous localism and universalistic beliefs.

By localism I mean both a condition and an attitude. I mean a condition of decentralization, enabling towns and other local districts to be largely autonomous communities. I mean also a reinforcing attitude that such autonomy is the key to liberty. The settlements from which the United States emerged shared nothing more than an animus against remote, consolidated power. Scattered over 1,300 miles of the Atlantic coast, the English colonies in the eighteenth century were separated from one another to a degree hard to imagine today. Few people travelled from one province to another. Little news passed between them. Most colonists also felt remote from their own provincial capitals. While colonial assemblies continually chipped away at the power of royal governors and London officials, within each colony districts that were relatively distant from the centers of trade felt a similar distrust for the more cosmopolitan towns. In every colony the revolutionary impulse sprang from a profound suspicion of consolidated power.[18] No wonder it took well over a decade before the patriots of 1776 could bring themselves to create a national government, and then only with great difficulty and reluctance.

Once established, the new government merely stabilized and perpetuated the traditional dispersal of power. As late as 1831, to serve a population of thirteen million people who were spreading rapidly over a territory of 1,750,000 square miles, the United States government employed just 11,491 civilians. Only 666 of them resided in the raw little capital on the banks of the Potomac.[19] The rest were scattered across the country and beyond—a few in customs houses and embassies while nearly all the others operated the tiny post offices of which contemporary genre painters have given us many charming glimpses. It would not be unfair to say that the United States government in the nine-

18. Robert Kelley, *The Cultural Pattern in American Politics: The First Century* (New York, 1979), 31–80.

19. U.S. Bureau of the Census, *Historical Statistics of the United States, Colonial Times to 1970* (Washington, D.C., 1976), 428, 1103.

teenth century consisted during peacetime mostly of post offices, and to conclude with Robert Wiebe that America was "a society without a core."[20]

The point was made more colorfully by Henry James:

> No State, in the European sense of the word, and indeed barely a specific national name. No sovereign, no court, no personal loyalty, no aristocracy, no church, no clergy, no army, no diplomatic service, no country gentlemen, no palaces, no castles, nor manors, nor old country houses, nor parsonages, nor thatched cottages, nor ivied ruins; no cathedrals, nor abbeys, nor little Norman churches; no great universities nor public schools—no Oxford, nor Eton, nor Harrow; no literature, no novels, no museums, no pictures, no political society. . . .[21]

By putting first among America's shortcomings the absence of a state "in the European sense of the word," James's litany suggests that this was the most embracing of the symbols of legitimacy, the most fundamental of the structures of authority, that he missed. A society lacking that kind of state might have to do without all of the rest.[22] Such was the situation of the American republic. Very scantily endowed with the outward trappings of power and social connection, it had almost no visible means of instilling allegiance. There was a flag and a Capitol, but no capital city in a European sense. Even the Capitol building was, at the

20. Robert H. Wiebe, *The Search of Order, 1877–1920* (New York, 1967), 12.

21. Quoted in Stanley M. Elkins, *Slavery: A Problem in American Institutional and Intellectual Life* (Chicago, 1959), 143. I am indebted to Elkins's discussion here of American institutions.

22. James's view was anticipated by Hegel, who observed that a true state appears "only after a distinction of classes has arisen, when wealth and poverty become extreme." In the absence of such pressure the state as a fundamental mode of expressing human solidarity has not developed. America remains, Hegel continued, an aggregation of individuals, whose government is "merely something external for the protection of property." Shlomo Avineri, *Hegel's Theory of the Modern State* (Cambridge, 1972), 135, 236–37.

time of the Civil War, still undergoing major alterations. The flag was not yet fully defined.[23] The only really imposing memorial in the country, the Washington Monument, was not completed until 1885.

Nevertheless, this almost disembodied state lived as an idea—resonant, compelling, and universally espoused. The Americans depended on an ideology—a set of abstract principles—to hold their country together. Although nationalism everywhere in the nineteenth century acquired an ideological thrust, it seems unlikely that any other country defined itself so preeminently as a community of belief, a nation gathered around a creed.[24] Americans who lived or traveled in Europe sometimes regretted the relative abstractness of American patriotism. To Nathaniel Hawthorne it seemed "as cold and hard . . . as the steel spring that puts in motion a powerful machinery," and he contrasted it with the human warmth and rich concreteness of an Englishman's sense of nationality.[25] Yet the nonspecific and therefore universal aspect of American nationalism served a loose-knit, heterogeneous society well. A national ideology enabled Americans to do without—and even told them why they did not need—the unitary state, the imposing monuments, and the dense social fabric that James observed in Europe.

We are now in a position to understand how the localization of power in nineteenth-century America allowed innumerable separations to flourish within a matrix of national unity. First, decentralization encouraged ethnic groups to act differently in different contexts. As a result none of them—neither the powerful nor the weak—could present a united front against the rest of society. The dominant segment of the population was of course severely handicapped, in defining an exclusive identity or main-

23. Boorstin, *The Americans: The National Experience*, 373–75. On the lack of a capital see James Bryce, *The American Commonwealth*, 2 vols. (London, 1891), II, 660–66.

24. John Higham, "Hanging Together: Divergent Unities in American History," *Journal of American History*, LXI (1974), 10–19.

25. *Our Old Home: A Series of English Sketches* (The Centenary Edition of the Works of Nathaniel Hawthorne, 1970), V, 325. Henry James, Sr., grasped the same difference, without Hawthorne's ambivalence, in *The Social Significance of Our Institutions* (Boston, 1861), 28.

taining an exclusive preeminence, by the absence of a centralized state and its accouterments. Who were these Anglo-Americans, to call them by a name that always sounded slightly foreign or presumptuous? There was little to mark them as anything but a miscellany of regional and local types—southerners and northerners, easterners and westerners, rural and urban folk—all intensely conscious of their differences from one another. Similarly, ethnic minorities in the United States could not close ranks in stubborn resistance to assimilation because they did not, as in Europe, confront a centralized state controlled by others. At most, ethnic groups might hope to gain preponderance in particular localities; when that happened, decentralized power came easily into their hands.[26] The system worked for them, and elicited their allegiance.

Secondly, decentralization fostered a scattering of population. This enabled local ethnic clusters to keep a certain distance from one another, particularly where economic competition could be acute. For a homogeneous people to have sprung from America's diversities, extensive interaction would have been required between the subordinate groups in addition to the contacts each might have with the dominant majority. It is true that minorities could not escape some involvement with one another, but the attention historians have given to spectacular incidents of conflict like the New York Draft Riots of 1863 has made us overlook the great extent to which ethnic groups in the nineteenth century kept out of one another's way. Moving west, European immigrants avoided areas where blacks were concentrated. At the same time the presence of huge immigrant populations in northern cities discouraged the northward migration of blacks.[27] The principle of mutual avoidance also influenced the distribution of German and Irish immigrants, the former settling in the Middle West and the latter in the Northeast. Where large concentrations of both groups materialized, as in Detroit and Milwaukee, they clustered

26. Compare the American situation with the relation between core and periphery in other countries, as described in Michael Hechter, *Internal Colonialism: The Celtic Fringe in British National Development, 1536–1966* (Berkeley, Calif., 1975), 4–27.

27. Brinley Thomas, *Migration and Economic Growth: A Study of Great Britain and the Atlantic Economy*, rev. ed. (Cambridge, Mass., 1973), 130–33.

in widely separated divisions of the city.[28] Thus, in a decentralized society mutual avoidance checked both conflict and assimilation.

The conditions that limited conflict between ethnic groups while promoting differences within each group were admirably suited to an ideological definition of America as a whole. A single canopy of beliefs made an otherwise loose-knit society of dissociated towns and neighborhoods comprehensible. Violations of the ideological norms could usually be understood as pragmatic adjustments to local realities rather than fundamental contradictions. Public schools could segregate minorities or preserve their cultures, depending on the particular ethnic accommodation in each locality, while all of them taught the same promises of the American ideology.

In addition to these disparities between a national ideology and localized institutions, there was also a deep fracture in the substance of the ideology itself. Any fully developed ideology provides its believers with a collective image of themselves, and in this respect the American ideology was profoundly split. On the one hand, nineteenth-century Americans conceived of themselves —in the images I have already quoted from Melville and Bancroft—as a cosmopolitan and unbounded people. On the other hand, the overwhelming majority were white Protestants, whose culture and religion permeated American institutions. On this second and more parochial level of consciousness white Protestants regarded the United States as a white man's country and as a Protestant country, and so had no special name for themselves because they *were* the Americans and all others were outsiders, though the same people on another level of consciousness took pride in the United States as an open and free society resting on universal, self-evident principles rather than any exclusive origins, a society dedicated to the separation of church and state and the

28. Olivier Zunz, *The Changing Face of Inequality: Urbanization, Industrial Development, and Immigrants in Detroit, 1880–1920* (Chicago, 1982), 50–59; Kathleen Conzen, *Immigrant Milwaukee, 1836–1860: Accommodation and Community in a Frontier City* (Cambridge, Mass., 1976), 126–53. See also Rowland Berthoff, "The Social Order of the Anthracite Region, 1825–1902," *Pennsylvania Magazine of History and Biography*, LXXXIX (1965), 266–70.

elimination of all barriers to mobility and opportunity, a society of individuals rather than groups.

A capacity to entertain both of these sets of beliefs, applying them selectively to different situations and avoiding any ultimate reckoning by all manner of equivocation, evasion, and compromise—that capacity to minimize, ignore, and defuse the contradictions—was essential to the stability of American society in the nineteenth century. The one serious attempt to resolve an elemental contradiction tore the nation apart in 1861.

I may run a risk here of overstating the contradictions in nineteenth-century American culture. In principle at least the exclusionary image of a white Protestant nation could be reconciled with the eclectic image of a universal homeland by identifying the former with the past and the latter with the future and then projecting as the nation's destiny a gradual enlargement of one into the other. Idealists did just that. They depicted a "United States of the United Races," an unfinished nation that was creating a composite people on a sturdy Anglo-Saxon base.[29] Over the very long run, this synthesizing vision has expressed a basic truth. It is a truth of historical continuity: a reminder that the American identity has proved capable of enormous extension partly because it never required a drastic transformation. From its narrowest Anglo-Protestant beginnings, the new society carried an evangelical and messianic outreach, which made possible its eventual conversion into a heterogeneous and cosmopolitan republic.

In spite of this undeniable continuity between the relatively restrictive national consciousness that goes back to our Puritan origins and the more embracing national consciousness we usually attribute to the Enlightenment, the tensions between the two in daily life and in the ways people thought about themselves were profound. A host of ambiguities and divisions in nineteenth-century culture arranged themselves around these opposing visions of a national community. There was endless uncertainty

29. *The National Era*, September 15, 1853, p. 146; Thomas Wentworth Higginson, "Americanism in Literature," in *Oxford Book of American Essays*, ed. Brander Matthews (New York, 1914), 218; Gilbert Osofsky, "Wendell Phillips and the Quest for a New American National Identity," *Canadian Review of Studies in Nationalism*, I (1973), 15-46.

over the attributes an American should have as a legal category, a social type, and a moral ideal.

The difficult legal questions were about citizenship. Who was eligible? In keeping with the cosmopolitan idea of nationality, Americans rejected the English presumption that people belong immutably and naturally to a political community, as they do to a family. One became an American by subscribing to the principles of republican government. Thus membership in the new nation derived from individual choice; and the newcomer, casting off the encumbrances of his past, served as the model of American citizenship. Since the logic of these assumptions worked against discriminations in terms of origin or previous condition, free blacks claimed the full rights of citizenship. Some states grudgingly recognized the claim. Others from the outset restricted citizenship to whites, and so did the federal government. After the Civil War compelled the extension of citizenship to people of African descent, confusion continued over the status of other nonwhites and over the privileges and immunities that citizenship should guarantee. The United States never had in the nineteenth century a single standard of membership in a national community.[30]

Nor had it a literature that was concrete and unambiguous in interpreting national character. In contrast to their generalized rhetoric about national purposes and institutions, American writers rarely attempted specific descriptions of an American people or a national type. When Henry James dared in 1877 to define the American type, he produced an extraordinary melange of contrarieties. The American, as he appeared in the opening pages of the novel by that name, had straight brown hair, brown complexion, aquiline nose, cold grey eyes, flat jaw, and above all a "typical vagueness" of expression, a "blankness which is not simplicity, that look of being committed to nothing in particular

---

30. James H. Kettner, *The Development of American Citizenship, 1608–1870* (Chapel Hill, N.C., 1978). See also James M. Banner's comments on this fine study in *Reviews in American History*, VIII (1980), 23–24, and Arthur Mann's summary of continuing uncertainties in *The One and the Many: Reflections on the American Identity* (Chicago, 1979), 88–93. On further contradictions in American culture see Michael G. Kammen, *People of Paradox: An Inquiry Concerning the Origins of American Civilization* (New York, 1972).

. . . so characteristic of many American faces."[31] Notice that James's American combines the grey eyes that used to suggest a man of destiny with other features that are typically Indian; yet his vague expression is not what we expect either of an Indian or of a man of destiny. What an eclectic image!

Significantly, Christopher Newman's character was a compound of opposites. He was, according to James, both frigid and friendly, both frank and cautious, both shrewd and credulous, both positive and skeptical, both confident and shy. His eye "was full of contradictory suggestions. . . . You could find in it almost anything you looked for." Such was the ambiguous figure who, James assures us, "filled out the national mould [with] almost ideal completeness."

At the same time, a reader can hardly miss in Christopher Newman the qualities associated with a white-Protestant and specifically English heritage: above all, a simple consciousness of preeminence and rightful possession.

Of all the complexities Christopher Newman projected, none are more intriguing than those imbedded in his moral values. Like Huckleberry Finn, Newman was tolerant, open-minded, easygoing, and shrewd. A maker of washtubs, he belonged to an eminently practical world. On the other hand, Newman also revealed an unconditioned goodness that James called innocence and others described as purity. Here again Newman resembled Huck Finn and Deerslayer as well. Each of these mythic figures in American literature harmoniously united purity with practicality. But was that not because an opposition between purity and practicality was so fundamental to the contradictions in American life?

A practical turn of mind—fertile in expedients, adaptive to circumstance, skilled in collaboration and compromise—has long been regarded as characteristically American. According to Frederick Jackson Turner it arose on the frontier. Others have traced it to the ethos of unimpeded capitalism. Still others attribute the American pragmatic temper to the interactions

31. Henry James, *The American* (Boston, 1877), 6–8. See James W. Tuttleton, *The Novel of Manners in America* (New York, 1974), 14–27, 58–85.

among a heterogeneous population under conditions of mobility and freedom. Whatever its social roots, this open and flexible mentality infused the ideas and institutions of America's "moderate" Enlightenment. Through Franklin and Jefferson a system of thought designed to allay religious strife became the means of tolerating and eventually legitimizing conflict and variety of every sort.[32] Enshrined in the lives and words of the Founding Fathers, pragmatic values have provided a common standard for a polyglot society.

The tolerant, practical attitudes that relaxed and enlarged the boundaries of an extended national identity clashed with another moral tradition that sometimes stiffened an exclusive American identity. A yearning for purity has always been a central feature of the Puritan mentality. A burning zeal to purify the church, the community, and the self inspired the earliest New England settlements. A religion based on a sharp separation between the elect and the damned, Puritanism induced a horror of contamination; and it assigned major importance to expunging "all manner of *Uncleanness.*"[33] For Puritans and their spiritual descendants, purity meant both a deliverance from evil and the attainment of unity. It meant keeping distinct the categories of creation while maintaining absolute conformity to a single moral standard.

These impulses survived the breakup of a more complex Puritan culture and were carried down into the nineteenth century by evangelical Protestantism. The quest for purity was not always defensive in the nineteenth century, but it did sustain among white Protestant Americans the old Puritan vision of an elect

32. The practical tendencies in the Enlightenment are discussed, from different points of view, in Peter Gay, *The Enlightenment: An Interpretation, Vol. II: The Science of Freedom* (New York, 1969), and Henry F. May, *The Enlightenment in America* (New York, 1976).

33. Quoted in Ronald A. Bosco, "Lectures at the Pillory: The Early American Execution Sermon," *American Quarterly*, XXX (1978), 156. More broadly, see Philip Greven, *The Protestant Temperament: Patterns of Child-Rearing, Religious Experience, and the Self in Early America* (New York, 1977), 141–48, and Mary Douglas, *Purity and Danger: An Analysis of Concepts of Pollution and Taboo* (New York, 1966), 53–54. There are some stimulating comments on the theme of contamination in Christopher Lasch, *The World of Nations: Reflections on American History, Politics, and Culture* (New York, 1973), 13–15.

nation: God's chosen people, summoned like their biblical ancestors to struggle against enemies without and corruption within.[34] In this struggle they would need to close ranks against an evil world.

How nineteenth-century Americans dealt with opposing injunctions to be practical and to be pure is too large and unexplored a subject to take up here in a serious way; but it may be suggested that this basic contradiction touched not only the problem of national identity but also other vital social relationships. One major strategy for coping with the contradiction, especially in the late nineteenth century, was to narrow the idea of purity, focussing it chiefly on the private world of home and family. In that context purity meant freedom from irregular sexual indulgence; it implied a sanctification of womanhood.[35] The identification of purity with private life and with women seems to have permitted an almost free reign of practicality in the public world of work, politics, and men.[36] This segregation of the two moralities was heavily underlined in popular fiction and the theatre. On the stage and in the sentimental novel practical choices were never allowed to compromise a sacred sphere in which spotless virtue always triumphed over unmitigated evil.[37]

By assigning to purity a separate and private sphere of influence, nineteenth-century Americans may have checked the impulse to purify the entire national community, but the separation of spheres was always imperfect. Throughout the nineteenth century a hunger for purity more or less constantly threatened the worldly compromises and the double standards that structured Victorian society. Americans still wanted to think of themselves as innocent and to perceive their history as a redemptive quest.

34. Sacvan Bercovitch, *The American Jeremiad* (Madison, Wis., 1978).

35. James Hastings, ed., *Encyclopedia of Religion and Ethics*, 13 vols. (New York, 1908–1929), X, 455, 515–16. See also David J. Pivar, *Purity Crusade: Sexual Morality and Social Control, 1868–1900* (Westport, Conn., 1973).

36. For an interesting discussion of this disjunction see Edward Morse Shepard, "Dishonor in American Public Life," in *Representative Phi Beta Kappa Orations*, ed. Clark S. Northup (New York, 1927), II, 216–17.

37. David Grimsted, *Melodrama Unveiled: American Theatre and Culture, 1800–1850* (Chicago, 1968), 204–48.

Only by elaborate compartmentalization, much compromise, and a certain measure of hypocrisy could they value purity while practicing it only in limited and special ways.

Let us return now to our main concern with assimilation. I have suggested that nineteenth-century Americans developed no consistent theory of how they should behave. The decentralization of society and the disjunction of values and traditons made every alternative feasible and no one policy authoritative. Issues could not crystallize; discontents could not converge. The ethnic crises of the 1850's present a major exception, but still a partial one. In all essential respects the antebellum pattern survived until the 1890's. Then a general and prolonged upheaval in ethnic relations, lasting from the nineties into the 1920's, marked the breakdown of that pattern and the beginning of a new social order.

The clearest indication of a fundamental change at the end of the nineteenth century was the interlinking of racial and religious tensions that had formerly been discrete. During the 1850's, for example, the Know-Nothing movement had been unable to formulate a national program. In the North Know-Nothings focussed almost exclusively on foreign Catholics as the subversive element in American society. Southerners, living in dread of slave conspiracies and of abolitionists, were completely unresponsive to the Catholic issue. Californians, preoccupied with the problem of the Chinese, cared nothing about the phobias of the South or the fears of the Northeast; and the indifference was reciprocated. In contrast, the ethnic hostilities that developed around the beginning of the twentieth century acquired a more generalized character. One fed into another. Southern whites became aroused for the first time about Catholics, Jews, and immigrants. Midwesterners and Far Westerners started to think of themselves as defenders of an America beleaguered on all sides. A sweeping rejection of all outsiders—of everyone who deviated from a conservative, Protestant, northern European pattern— gave a new, comprehensively ethnocentric meaning to the term "prejudice."[38]

38. See above, pp. 154–56, 163–65.

What was happening? In brief, the conditions that had sustained the intricate segmentation of the nineteenth century no longer prevailed. The local community lost much of its cherished autonomy, leaving Americans feeling increasingly vulnerable to the intrusion of outsiders. At the same time that the separateness of groups and localities diminished, the wall of separation between opposing values in American minds gave way as well.

The first of these two changes, the shift away from localism, is the more obvious and familiar. Recent interpretations of the political, economic, and cultural turmoil of the 1890's have highlighted, as the critical change in American life at that time, a new awareness of interdependence.[39] Under the inroads of industrialism, bureaucracy, and specialized knowledge, the self-sufficiency of the "island communities" was irretrievably passing. As national organizations crisscrossed an increasingly crowded terrain, more and more of the American people became integrated into economic networks and status hierarchies that drastically reduced the significance of the local arena. On the international level also the world contracted alarmingly, and the entanglements of interdependence multiplied. Wherever one looked, the state was becoming a palpable reality. All this could be enormously stimulating to Americans who were ready and eager to move outward into a larger, less provincial milieu. It could also be very threatening. Either way, a consciousness of racial, national, and ethnic differences dramatically intensified.

The tightening mesh of interdependence goes far to explain why the internal disjunctions within nineteenth-century culture also broke down. The willingness of Americans to live with a divided heritage and an ambiguous national identity declined. A demand for consistency and sincerity—for an end to lies, deception and hypocrisy—swept through the tangled underbrush of American opinion in the first two decades of the twentieth century. Baffled by the obscure, complex forces that filled the

39. Thomas L. Haskell, *The Emergence of Professional Social Science: The American Social Science Association and the Nineteenth-Century Crisis of Authority* (Urbana, Ill., 1977), 14–17, 27–47. I am also indebted to Robert H. Wiebe, *The Segmented Society: An Historical Preface to the Meaning of America* (New York, 1975).

modern world, millions of Americans cried out for light in dark places, for simplicity and wholeness, and finally for purification of the entire society.[40] This was one of the meanings of Progressivism.

It was a sure instinct for cultural definition that inspired Lewis Mumford to call the 1870's and 1880's the Brown Decades.[41] The period that ended with the Chicago World's Fair of 1893 seemed, from a point of view located in the early twentieth century, as dingy in physical appearance as in moral hue. The dazzling luminescence of the White City—as the Chicago Exposition was popularly known—heralded an era of light. American cities glowed at night as never before. White, symbolizing purity and unity, became the essential color of the exterior of government buildings and the interior of hospitals. Windows were enlarged and domestic interiors swept clean of clutter.[42] Campaigns against disease, dirt, darkness, ignorance, "tainted" money, and moral pollution formed a continuous sequence of public endeavor. The zeal of progressives for "clean-ups," which were understood to be simultaneously physical, moral, and social, suggests how a passionate desire to recreate a homogeneous society could evolve into the exclusionary spirit of the Ku Klux Klan. The old American passion for purity burst the compromises and constraints of the Victorian Age.

Historians have conventionally interpreted the repressive waves of nativism and racism from 1890 to 1924 in more concrete terms. They have emphasized class antagonisms, economic dislocations, and Darwinian ideas.[43] All of these were present. Yet the phe-

40. Although writing with other questions in mind, Paul Boyer gives some of the evidence in *Urban Masses and Moral Order in America, 1820–1920* (Cambridge, Mass., 1978), 252–63.

41. Lewis Mumford, *The Brown Decades: A Study of the Arts in America, 1865–1895* (New York, 1931).

42. David T. Day, "Light: The Civilizer," *American Magazine*, LXI (1906), 658–64; Frederick S. Lamb, "Civic Treatment of Color," *Municipal Affairs*, II (1898), 114–19; Edward S. Martin, "Manhattan Lights," *Harper's Monthly Magazine*, CXIV (1907), 359–67; Edward Bok, *The Americanization of Edward Bok* (New York, 1922), 238–45, 251–53.

43. My own book, *Strangers in the Land*, in this respect has much in common with C. Vann Woodward, *Origins of the New South, 1877–1913* (Baton Rouge, La., 1951).

nomena to be explained transcend these categories. We have to ask why the period from the nineties through the First World War witnessed both a systematic campaign to humiliate and ostracize blacks and a sweeping drive for immigration restriction. These campaigns did not correlate with any sustained economic crisis. Rather, they went along with the triumph of prohibition, the criminalization of prostitution, an intense concern about personal hygiene, pure foods and drugs, public sanitation, and infectious diseases, and a national effort to wipe out corruption of every sort.

The great evil native white Americans associated with blacks in this era was essentially identical to what they discerned in immigrants. The evil in both cases was pollution: politically, through the sale of votes; socially, through the spread of crime, disease, and immorality; racially, through contamination of the very body of the nation.[44] In the racism of the early twentieth century the critical factor was surely not its scientific rationale, to which most people paid little attention, but rather a new feeling of defilement through contact with what was dark and unclean. The ultimate defilement was that of rape, since it directly violated "purity of blood," and the Southern white woman's quite unprecedented fear of rape in the early twentieth century had a more generalized parallel in the growing belief that alien peoples were polluting the bloodstream of the nation. Both of these anxieties interlinked with the prohibition movement, which came alive in the South only when whites became convinced that cheap whiskey was responsible for turning blacks into ravenous beasts.[45] The polluter had been himself polluted.

44. Woodward, *Origins*, pp. 326–27, reports that the primary reason given at the time for Negro disfranchisement was repugnance for corrupt elections. On crime and immorality see George M. Fredrickson, *The Black Image in the White Mind: The Debate on Afro-American Character and Destiny, 1817–1914* (New York, 1971), 258–82. On blacks as a source of pollution see also *Literary Digest*, LV (September 22, 1917), 34.

45. "The Psychology of the Race Question," *The Independent*, LV (1903), 1939–1940; John Corrigan, "The Prohibition Wave in the South," *American Monthly Review of Reviews*, XXXVI (1907), 328–34; John T. Graves, "The Fight Against Alcohol," *Cosmopolitan Magazine*, XLV (June, 1908), 88–89; P. H. Whaley, "Some Aspects of Prohibition in the South," *Collier's Weekly*, L (May 31, 1913), 32.

Thus a broad movement for purification offered a way of overcoming the contradictions in American life and making the hegemony of the white-Protestant culture impregnable. But this was not the only path toward a more consistent society, and ultimately it was not the path Americans chose. Progressivism also had a humanistic side, rooted in the ideology of equal rights and congenial to the cosmopolitan idea of nationality. This side of Progressivism showed itself in the cooperative ethic of the settlement houses and the civil-rights initiatives of the newly formed National Association for the Advancement of Colored Peoples. The purity crusades of the early twentieth century therefore widened the old rift in the American ideology instead of closing it. The compartmentalization of differences gave way to bitter ideological conflict. In politics the conflict led to a mobilization of minorities on an unprecedented scale. In thought and culture the boldest spokesmen for an inclusive Americanism were driven to new positions that would be labelled pluralism and modernism.

What I have in mind especially is the emergence in the early twentieth century of a number of young cultural rebels, like Randolph Bourne and Hutchins Hapgood, for whom any ethnic identity—any distinct group allegiance—had become an encumbrance. Provincialism of all kinds was the enemy.[46] The point to be emphasized is that both sides, both cosmopolitans and puritans, had rejected the Victorian compromise. Both were in revolt against equivocation and complexity. Critical thought, from the "Muckrakers" onward, concentrated fiercely on exposing sham and pretence. The characteristic hypocrisies, dualisms and double standards of the nineteenth century became intolerable both to those who would revitalize and those who would radicalize the traditional culture. A passion for exposés, for unmasking underlying realities—the very assumption that reality is always hidden

---

46. David A. Hollinger, "Ethnic Diversity, Cosmopolitanism, and the Emergence of the American Liberal Intelligentsia," *American Quarterly*, XXVII (1975), 133-51.

—this became the leitmotif of intellectual life in the twentieth century.[47]

In sum the Progressive Era brought finally into the open the challenge that a divided heritage and an ambiguous, dualistic national identity posed to the American people. The problem of assimilation could no longer be evaded.

47. Richard Hofstadter, *The Age of Reform: From Bryan to F.D.R.* (New York, 1955), 196–200.

Chapter Nine

Ethnic Pluralism in Modern American Thought

For many years writers on American ethnic problems have invoked a vision of pluralism as an ideal all men of goodwill should cherish. Pluralism, we are told, will save us from a foolish belief in assimilation. But what pluralism means in a positive sense—even the extent to which it runs against an assimilationist philosophy—seldom appears. This chapter is a preliminary effort to examine the chronic indistinctness of the pluralist idea in ethnic relations. That idea has undergone major changes, and I believe it is today in acute need of rethinking. Whatever coherence the idea once had has been dissipated in the course of its popularization during the 1950's and 1960's. Traditional liberals continue to celebrate "our pluralistic society." Those radicals who pay heed to the theory of pluralism denounce it but have nothing to put in its place; and ethnic spokesmen, without much regard to either, pursue their own group interest in whatever ways seem expedient. I propose not to offer a solution to the present confusion, but to explain how it came about.

If my inquiry is not itself to become mired in the confusion it examines, it will have to focus steadily on the problem of intellectual coherence. Several years ago Professor Philip Gleason complained of the mind-boggling ambiguities in the current discussion of a "new pluralism," and since then the situation has become a good deal worse. Seeking unity, former New York

Mayor Robert F. Wagner in the election of 1972 contrasted pluralism with factionalism. "The Democratic party," Wagner declared hopefully, "is a pluralistic party, as New York is a pluralistic state, and this will be a pluralistic campaign." Ada Louise Huxtable rejoices that pluralism is superseding the "destructively sterile" architecture of recent years, while a different kind of critic complains that "the fluff of pluralism" has muted "the chord of revolutionary discontent."[1]

For the most part current usage seems to refer to a condition rather than a theory: a condition of diversity, which prevents any one group or point of view from attaining preeminence. In the interest of clarification I will deal with pluralism in a stricter sense. As treated here it is not simply an attitude or a description of reality. It is a normative social theory. As such, pluralism attempts to explain and justify a feasible and desirable social order. It makes a serious claim on our understanding as well as our emotions. It deserves to be judged in terms of internal consistency and compatibility with other beliefs as well as empirical substance and social need.

The history of pluralist theories will, therefore, have to be examined in a wider context of ideas and values. We will have to take note especially of the interplay between pluralism and opposing theories of assimilation. It is customary today to denounce the melting-pot ideal as a false and even bigoted antithesis to the pluralist vision;[2] and it is true that ethnic pluralism arose as a protest against the losses some minorities were suffering under the stresses of assimilation. Pluralism could become a persuasive alternative only when general doubts developed that assimilation was the democratic way. Nevertheless, as we shall see, the rela-

1. Philip Gleason, "Pluralism and the New Pluralism," *America,* CX (March 7, 1964), 308–312; *New York Times,* August 12, 1972, p. 1; Ada Louise Huxtable, "In Love with Times Square," *New York Review of Books,* October 18, 1973, p. 45; *New York Times Book Review,* August 20, 1972, p. 28. See also the leaflet, "Come Home, Democrats," issued early in 1973 by the Coalition for a Democratic Majority and addressed "To all who believe in a pluralistic political process in which no single group or class enjoys a special moral status. . . ."

2. This is virtually a dogma among intellectuals today. For example, see W. H. Auden, "America is NOT a Melting Pot," *New York Times,* March 18, 1972, p. 31.

tion between assimilation and pluralism was not a simple dialectic of opposition. From the outset the belief that a democratic society should preserve the integrity of its constituent groups has unconsciously relied on the assimilative process which it seemed to repudiate; and now that assimilation has lost momentum, pluralism has lost its sense of direction.

Finally, we will discover that much of the disorientation in the present discussion of pluralism stems from increasing uncertainty about a cardinal assumption of pluralist theory, namely that the persistence and solidarity of ethnic minorities is essential to democracy. The general appeal of pluralism has inhered in its promise of extending democracy. In recent years, however, the most searching inquiries into pluralistic conditions have shown how extensively they serve to perpetuate inequalities. How much pluralism, and what kinds, a good society should have is a question no one has clearly addressed.

II

Pluralism in all its forms is a philosophy of minority rights. It arises when minorities become conscious of having a stake in the maintenance of their position within a larger society. A pluralist generally identifies himself with a social minority and writes in its behalf. But he also accepts minority status as a legitimate and perhaps even desirable way of participating in the larger society. Thus pluralism posits a situation in which minorities retain their solidarity and effectiveness; but it does not welcome all such situations. A pluralist wants to develop a mutually tolerable relationship between discrete groups and the social system in which they reside. Specifically, he seeks a relationship that will allow the individual groups both autonomy and unimpeded influence. He opposes assimilation on the one hand, because that threatens group survival; but he also opposes separatism, because that will exclude him from the larger society. Accordingly, pluralism addresses itself to the character and viability of an aggregate that has several components, and its special challenge arises from the attempt to define the aggregate in terms that none of its principal components need find unacceptable.

The belief that a well-ordered society should sustain the diversity of its component groups has, of course, deep roots in early American experience, but it became subordinated during the nineteenth century to the quest for unity. The building of a national republic gave central importance to the process of convergence, to the making of a homogeneous future from a heterogeneous past. The dominant American legend—what was later symbolized in the image of a melting pot—said that a continuous fusion of originally disparate elements was forming a single American people. In the attainment of oneness, rather than the persistence of separate identities, lay the promise of American life. After the Civil War, especially, a drive for national integration took priority over other group loyalties. American business and professional leaders built unifying networks of communications and social control. Intellectuals elaborated monistic schemes of thought, which enclosed the processes of nature and the achievements of man within an all-embracing, rational synthesis. If, as Henry Adams charged, his generation was mortgaged to the railways, it also gave its mind to a larger quest for unity, which Adams himself pursued through the eighties and nineties.[3]

Thus the pluralist ideology which emerged in the early twentieth century, though grounded experientially in the earliest facts of American life, represented a significant departure from conventional wisdom. Pluralism was, in fact, part of a profound intellectual upheaval, which Morton White has described as "the revolt against formalism."[4] Conceptually, it was a revolt against the monistic systems that prevailed in the late nineteenth century. It rejected their rationalistic spirit and their inclination toward a

3. *The Education of Henry Adams* (New York, 1931), 240. On the premium placed on unity in American intellectual life in the late nineteenth century see R. Jackson Wilson, *In Quest of Community: Social Philosophy in the United States, 1860–1920* (New York, 1968).
4. Morton White, *Social Thought in America: The Revolt Against Formalism* (Boston, 1957). I have dealt more extensively with this transition in "The Reorientation of American Culture in the 1890's," *Writing American History: Essays on Modern Scholarship* (Bloomington, Ind., 1970), 73–102.

stratified view of society. The antiformalists denied a privileged status to any fixed point of view or any social category. They accepted the multiformity of experience and the relativity of values. Their refusal of any single, all-embracing scheme of things acquired a pluralistic bent when it became a positive celebration of irreducible diversity.

Here the modern pluralist has echoed romanticism. The formalistic pluralism of the early republic, as expressed by James Madison, commended the instrumental value of *multiplicity*. Modern pluralism also champions *variety*. It rests on the romantic premise that differences are intrinsically valuable and should take precedence over conformity to a universal standard. In casting off the constraints of late-Victorian America, antiformalists sounded again the rallying cry of their romantic forebears: "*Vive la différence!*" It is significant that pluralism received its philosophical credentials from William James, the American philosopher who, more than any other, incarnated a romantic love of diversity, particularity, and uniqueness. James's late book, *A Pluralistic Universe* (1909), made the most careful statement of the case, though he had already, in *The Will to Believe* (1897), given wide currency to the term.[5]

For modern pluralism diversity has performed a special function, which was often missing in the romantic tradition. It has consistently worked against authoritarian claims to exclusive or preeminent wisdom. Since the democratic aspirations of the Progressive Era colored and shaped the entire revolt against formalism, modern pluralism was initially harnessed to an egalitarian ethic. Pluralists appealed for an appreciation of differences in order to rectify inequalities.

But there was always in pluralist thought an unrecognized tension between means and ends. Logically, an accentuation of differences should breed more inequality, rather than less. It should drive men apart, instead of bringing them together. The conditions under which the pluralist program could work were

5. William James, *The Will to Believe and Other Essays in Popular Philosophy* (New York, 1897), viii–ix. See also John Dewey's succinct article, "Pluralism," in *Dictionary of Philosophy and Psychology* (New York, 1902), II, 306.

more special than its advocates realized. The optimism of the early pluralists seems to have depended on an unstated assumption that a natural harmony underlies the conflicts and discords of life. Pluralists dispensed with any overall design, they renounced the struggle for an inclusive unity, because of an implicit faith that in some deep, unspecified sense it already existed. In an essentially friendly universe the parts can be true to their separate characters. Purposes can clash without rending.

These basic features of a pluralist philosophy—its celebration of differences, its hostility to existing inequalities, its implicit reliance on an underlying harmony—made it especially suitable to the defense of minority rights. Applied to society, pluralism provided minorities with a means of resisting absorption; they could now claim to constitute the very structure of the social order. From the point of view of the integrationist or the tender of the melting pot, minorities must appear subordinate and declining elements. Pluralism, on the other hand, defined the minorities as primary. The unity of the whole resided in their relations with one another. This was the pluralist's thesis, regardless of how he identified America's minorities. They might be regional or ethnic or—much later—religious groups.

For Frederick Jackson Turner the pluralist pattern inhered in regional (i.e., sectional) diversity. On ethnic issues the leading American historian of the early twentieth century was an assimilationist. He looked upon the West as a great melting pot of European peoples, and his whole approach to American history can be understood partly as a way of asserting the primacy of geography over race and culture. Turner's pluralism was an affirmation of sectional diversity as the dynamic principle in American life.

Other historians at the beginning of the twentieth century construed the main theme of American history as the gradual triumph of national unity over states rights and sectional differences. Sectionalism, in the conventional view, meant discord, disruption, even treason.[6] Turner, on the other hand, looked on

6. John Higham with Leonard Krieger and Felix Gilbert, *History* (Humanistic Scholarship in America: The Princeton Studies, Englewood Cliffs, N.J., 1965), 151–55, 158–69.

sectional differences as a continuing source of vitality for a democratic society. Born in a Wisconsin town in 1861, he never felt the scars of the Civil War deeply. For him national unity was an accomplished fact. But it posed new problems in the twentieth century. Under the imperatives of industrialization, unity might become a deadening uniformity. Would it perhaps obliterate the distinctiveness of his own beloved Middle West? Turner could not accept that prospect. Diversity would survive, he believed, through the socioeconomic contrasts and rivalries grounded in the principal regions of the country. To this vision Turner gave historical substantiation by showing that sectionalism was not ordinarily antithetical to nationalism but rather its matrix. American politics functioned through a complex, balanced interplay of at least three sections—North, South, and West—in which the characteristic strategies were bargaining and compromise.[7] Turner first explored this theme in *Rise of the New West, 1819–1829* (1906). He carried it forward, but with ever-increasing difficulty, in a posthumous work he was never able to complete, *The United States, 1830–1850: The Nation and Its Sections* (1935). Turner's story broke off, let us note, just at the point in American history when the sectional struggle was turning into a rigid dualism, for which his pluralistic theory did not allow.

Turner spoke for the Middle West at a time when homogenizing forces of national integration threatened its distinctive character. Similarly, the early advocates of pluralism in ethnic relations were defending self-conscious minorities whose survival seemed endangered by the pressures of assimilation. Just as Turner thought that American democracy depended on the persistence of sections, ethnic pluralists maintained that its enduring basis lay in ancestral cultures. Whereas Turner described the United States as a federation of sections, proponents of "cultural pluralism" called it a federation of nationalities. Turner tried to show that sectional differences could and should endure, since he identified with a section that might otherwise be submerged. His

7. Turner's sectionalism is discussed carefully, but in a critical vein, in Ray Allen Billington, *Frederick Jackson Turner, Historian, Scholar, Teacher* (New York, 1973), 135–36, 181–83, 215–32, 370–74, 465–70, and in Richard Hofstadter, *The Progressive Historians: Turner, Beard, Parrington* (New York, 1968), 94–111.

counterpart, Horace Kallen, argued for the indestructibility of ethnic cultures in an effort to resist the disintegration of his own.

No immigrant group brought to the United States an older, prouder heritage than did the Jews, and none seemed in early-twentieth-century America more exposed to an erosion of group identity. The great exodus from the *shtetls* of eastern Europe had already torn hundreds of thousands of Jews loose from traditional roots, and the very real prospect of a wider life in a more receptive milieu intensified the urge to cast off the burden of a distinctive heritage. Those who tried to do so encountered a rising anti-Semitism, often expressed in the belief that they were incorrigibly alien to American life. Nevertheless, there were enormous opportunities in America for Jews, particularly for those who could escape the anti-Semitic slurs. It was a Jewish playwright, Israel Zangwill, whose enormously popular melodrama, *The Melting Pot* (1908), offered the most ringing apostrophe to the glories of assimilation, though the play also revealed (through a veil of sentimental clichés) the searing conflicts that process created between generations. Wracked with internal divisions and assailed from without, the Jewish community in the early twentieth century might well have questioned its future in America.

In this situation the Zionist movement worked to rally Jewish group consciousness. In calling for the rebirth of a Jewish nation, Zionism affirmed a commonality of all Jews transcending religious, social, and political differences. In America it made its strongest appeal as an antidote to assimilation. By awakening the rising generation to the value of its ethnic heritage, Zionism proposed to save American Jewry from disappearance. As early as 1909 the outstanding American spokesman for cultural Zionism, Judah L. Magnes, was criticizing the melting-pot idea that national groups in America were destined to lose their special character.[8]

The chief author of the theory of cultural pluralism, Horace Kallen, was an early and active Zionist, deeply stirred by the

8. Arthur A. Goren, *New York Jews and the Quest for Community: The Kehillah Experiment, 1908–1922* (New York, 1970), 4, 23–24. See also Moses Rischin, *The Promised City: New York's Jews, 1870–1914* (Cambridge, Mass., 1962).

hope of a Jewish national revival. As a graduate student at Harvard University in 1906, he had a leading part in founding the Harvard Menorah Society. This was the beginning of an intercollegiate movement designed to overcome a "shameful ignorance of things Jewish" among Jewish students and thus to combat their impulse to forget or to hide their origins. In an early address to the Intercollegiate Menorah Association, Kallen propounded what would become a cornerstone of his thesis: people cannot successfully change their ethnic identity. Mixing occurs only in external relations, not in a man's inner life. "An Irishman is always an Irishman, a Jew always a Jew. Irishman or Jew is born; citizen, lawyer, or church-member is made."[9]

An antiassimilationist attitude would not alone have made Kallen a genuine pluralist, however. He also posited an intimate connection between ethnic separateness and national unity. Like Turner and like James, Kallen embraced the whole as well as its parts. An American nationalist as well as a Zionist, he believed that all the varied groups in America could coexist, each conserving and perfecting its selfhood, in a kind of natural harmony.

This belief did not come easily. Kallen arrived at it through a deep inner struggle between Jewish and American allegiances. Born in Silesia, he was brought to the United States at the age of five. He was raised in Boston, he recalled, on "the Hebrew Bible with its Judaist commentaries and the difficult and heroic economy of the orthodox Jewish home." But in the Boston public schools, visiting Bunker Hill and listening to teachers recite the precepts of Ralph Waldo Emerson, Kallen underwent during the 1890's the common second-generation experience: loss of religion and an uncritical enthusiasm for America. "It seemed to me that the identity of every human being with every other was the important thing and that the term 'American' should nullify the meaning of every other term in one's personal make-up. . . . Everything Jewish could be absorbed and dissolved in something

9. Intercollegiate Menorah Association, *The Menorah Movement for the Study and Advancement of Jewish Culture and Ideals* (Ann Arbor, Mich., 1914) gives the early history of the organization and, on pp. 84–86, the text of Kallen's address of 1913. My quotation, however, is from Horace Kallen, *The Structure of Lasting Peace* (Boston, 1918), 31.

quite non-Jewish and identical with the Yankee being as I knew it in Boston."[10]

Eager for that consummation, the youthful idealist was drawn to the inner sanctum of the Yankee world. There, in Harvard College, his simple Americanism received a series of shocks. A nearby social settlement, where Kallen worked for room and board, exposed him to socialist and anarchist ideas and to a maelstrom of ethnic aspirations. He began to participate in the romantic spirit of liberation, which affected so many of the younger intellectuals in the early twentieth century and reached a crest on the eve of the First World War. Kallen's thinking matured in that effervescent context.

Meanwhile, a more orthodox but no less exciting intellectual experience occurred in the classroom of Barrett Wendell, whose course on American literature yielded a startling new perception of the link Kallen was seeking between himself and America. Wendell, the very incarnation of genteel New England culture, was himself a conservative assimilationist, for whom English— and more specifically Puritan—traits constituted the American character. But the Puritans in turn, Wendell emphasized, modeled themselves on the Old Testament prophets. America began as another Israel. Wendell even entertained a curious theory that the early American Puritans were largely Jewish in blood.[11] Kallen thought he had escaped from a Hebraic past. Here what he was running away from suddenly became central to what he was pursuing. The stimulus of Wendell's course led him to a renewed study of Jewish culture and thus to Zionism. It suggested that one could remain an unreconstructed Jew while belonging to the core of America.

10. Horace M. Kallen to author, January 16, 1948; Horace M. Kallen, *Individualism, an American Way of Life* (New York, 1933), 5–8.

11. Edmund Wilson, *A Piece of My Mind: Reflections at Sixty* (New York, 1956), 97–98; Barrett Wendell, *Liberty, Union, and Democracy: The National Ideals of America* (New York, 1907), 8–11, 36. Kallen's indebtedness to Wendell, expressed in the sources cited in note 10 and even more strongly in a personal interview on December 22, 1947, appears also in the dedication of *Culture and Democracy in the United States: Studies in the Group Psychology of the American Peoples* (New York, 1924): "To Barrett Wendell, Interpreter of America and the American Mind, In Whose Teaching I Received My First Vision of Their Trends and Meanings."

The other major influence came from William James. Kallen's studies under the great Harvard pragmatist, begun as an undergraduate, continued through a Ph.D. in 1908. The young man then became a colleague during James's last years; he remained always a devoted disciple. By translating James's philosophy into social terms, Kallen gave a general reference to the newly discovered relationship between his Jewish and his American self. James intended pluralism to overcome an either/or choice between rival absolutes. Applied to the problem of national identity, it legitimized the intersection of comparatively independent loyalties. Kallen was especially struck by James's use of a powerful American metaphor. Echoing the aboriginal pluralism of American political institutions, James had described the universe as "more like a federal republic than like an empire or a kingdom."[12] Could not the same image apply to an American union of ethnic collectivities, in which each enjoys both the irreducible singularity and the full civic partnership Kallen had found in his own special heritage?

For the traditional American faith in assimilation through fusion, the young Jewish social philosopher substituted a federal or polycentric ideal. He summoned every ethnic group to be American by being true to itself, by preserving its own separate culture. His ideas seemed more radical than they actually were, because they crystallized at a time of sharply increasing ethnic tensions, when the melting-pot idea came under attack from those who thought it was too permissive as well as those like Kallen who considered it too exclusive. During the years just before the United States entered the First World War, when Kallen was teaching at the University of Wisconsin and enjoying the ethos of a state rich in minorities, an almost hysterical fear of "hyphenated Americans" seized public opinion. This was accompanied by a more or less racist belief that further assimilation would dilute the purity of an already fixed American type. Kallen was especially stung by demands, from some of his progressive colleagues, for tighter restrictions on immigration. When the prominent Wisconsin sociologist Edward A. Ross

12. William James, *A Pluralistic Universe* (New York, 1909), 321–22.

published a scathing assessment of the harm the newer foreign groups were doing to the United States, Kallen replied with a famous article in the *Nation* in 1915, "Democracy Versus the Melting Pot."[13] Summing up ideas he had nurtured for more than a decade, Kallen suggested that the current ethnic ferment showed the bankruptcy of the melting-pot theory. America faced more drastic alternatives: a regimentation that would stifle all minorities, or a new understanding of democracy as a federation of autonomous, self-realizing nationalities. "Democracy," he wrote a year later, "involves not the elimination of differences but the perfection and conservation of differences."[14]

In effect, Kallen called for an ethnic policy which would not depend on the classic American belief that all men are basically alike. To that extent he concurred with his most implacable adversaries, Anglo-Saxon racists like E. A. Ross. Both sides agreed that fundamental human differences would not dissolve in any melting pot. Both asserted that ethnic character was somehow rooted in the natural order. But Kallen contemplated nature's diversities with the benign gaze of a romantic. Whereas Ross saw everywhere a harsh Darwinian struggle between unequal species, Kallen observed a freely proliferating universe with room for all. "Nature is naturally pluralistic," he wrote; "her unities are eventual, not primary; mutual adjustments, not regimentations of superior force."[15] Kallen lifted his eyes above the strife that swirled around him to an ideal realm where diversity and harmony eternally coexist.

Perhaps even more important in giving the new ethnic pluralism its beneficent, idealistic flavor was Kallen's exclusive concentration on culture as the locus of group identity. Kallen distinguished sharply between "inward" experience, which is essential and irrefragable, and the outer sphere of public policy and economic life. The latter belongs to Caesar, but not the former. The state may intervene in external conditions to promote justice or equality; but the collective consciousness of each ethnic group

13. Vol. C (February 18–25, 1915), 190–94, 217–20; Kallen, *Individualism*, 11–12.

14. Kallen, *Culture and Democracy*, 61. Cf. Edward A. Ross, *The Old World in the New* (New York, 1914).

15. Kallen, *Culture and Democracy*, 178–79.

must remain free and spontaneous.[16] Kallen never admitted that cultural differences might flow from or reinforce social inequities. He took no account of the social barriers between groups. They belonged to the rigidities of an artificial environment, not to the essence of a people. In the theory of cultural pluralism, culture was primary, and it was innocent.

The incompleteness and the bias of Kallen's pluralism becomes obvious once we ask what role it assigned to the Negro. The answer is: none. The theory that preserving differences promotes democracy surely called for some special attention to the ethnic group whose differentness most Americans were determined to maintain. Kallen carefully evaded the problem. Although he purported to write about the group life of all of the "American Peoples," he drew his examples and arguments exclusively from the experience of European immigrants, particularly Jews. He liked to describe the American ensemble as an orchestra; but there was a fatal elision when he wrote that America could become "an orchestration of mankind" by perfecting "the co-operative harmonies of European civilization." Nothing in Kallen's writings gave away the magnitude of that elision. In the fullest statement of his argument there was only a single, obscure footnote on the point. "I do not discuss the influence of the negro," Kallen confessed in fine print. "This is at once too considerable and too recondite in its processes for casual mention. It requires separate analysis."[17] The pluralist thesis from the outset was encapsulated in white ethnocentrism.

Possibly that was inevitable. Could anyone have designed a pluralism that would have suited blacks as well as Jews, the minorities that were left behind as well as those that were thriving? Could anyone, for that matter, have built a pluralist philosophy on the black experience? From time to time some American Negroes adopted a separatist (i.e., black nationalist) attitude, but their desire for liberation *from* America should not be confused with the pluralist's goal of liberalizing America. The difficulties black writers confronted in looking at the United States from a

16. Kallen, *Constitutional Foundations of the New Zion* (New York, 1918), 9–12.
17. Kallen, *Culture and Democracy*, 226.

pluralist perspective may be judged from the efforts that W. E. B. Du Bois made to do so.

The foremost ideological spokesman for American blacks in the first half of the twentieth century, Du Bois was not a separatist, but neither was he consistently an unambiguous integrationist. Like Kallen, he struggled as a young man to reconcile his racial and his national identity, "two warring ideals in one dark body." "Am I an American or am I a Negro?" Du Bois asked in anguish. "Can I be both? Or is it my duty to cease to be a Negro as soon as possible and be an American?"[18]

In grappling with the problem he drew on some of the same cultural and personal influences that stimulated Kallen. Both men felt a romantic appreciation of the spiritual diversity of mankind. Both regarded culture in an exalted way, as the finest flower of group life; and in the tradition of Herder and other romantic nationalists, they interpreted each race or nationality as the custodian of some great idea or artistic gift. Moreover, as a student at Harvard, Du Bois took encouragement from the same teachers who also served Kallen so well. Although Du Bois received his Ph.D. in history in 1895, he remembered William James as his favorite teacher, closest friend on the faculty, and "guide to clear thinking." Du Bois studied with Barrett Wendell too, and basked in his praise. "God was good," Du Bois remembered, "to let me sit awhile at their feet and see the fair vision of a commonwealth of culture open to all creeds and races and colors."[19] Kallen could well have uttered the same thanksgiving.

In 1897, when he was twenty-nine years old, Du Bois published a little-known essay, "The Conservation of Races." As fresh and striking in its way as Kallen's paper of 1915, it anticipated much of the latter's argument. Like Kallen, Du Bois was fighting against the kind of assimilation that breeds contempt for one's origins. In reviving ethnic pride, both men emphasized the priority of the organic group over the individual. Whereas whites had always advised blacks to gain acceptance and respect by conforming as

18. W. E. B. Du Bois, "The Conservation of Races," *Black Nationalism in America*, ed. John H. Bracey, Jr., August Meier, and Elliott Rudwick (Indianapolis, 1970), 257.

19. Francis L. Broderick, *W. E. B. Du Bois: Negro Leader in a Time of Crisis* (Stanford, 1959), 15–31.

individuals to the values of the larger community, Du Bois argued that that was not enough. Individuals do not make history. The great changes in human affairs come about through the collective action of races. Blacks should take advantage of that fact by organizing, asserting, and developing themselves as a distinct race, destined to make a special contribution to the future of the world. Replying to the fear that such moves toward racial solidarity would only sharpen the existing cleavage in society, the young militant asserted that the pursuit of separate "race ideals" could be compatible with equal participation in the polity and economy of a common country.[20] Thus far Du Bois adumbrated positions Kallen would take. He too was groping toward a compromise between diversity and equality. Nevertheless, to describe Du Bois as a cultural pluralist blurs a crucial distinction.

Du Bois never visualized America as a genuinely multiethnic complex, in which a variety of groups could enjoy an equal status and maintain their cultural autonomy indefinitely. The situation of black Americans was too special to be relativized and too severe to be equated with that of other groups. The reality confronting Du Bois must have seemed not many-sided, but starkly dualistic: everything was either black or white. The cleavage might be lived with, even turned to advantage; it could not be accepted as a permanent good. Looking far into the future, Du Bois projected an ultimate fusion—a city of man, not a federation of peoples. "Some day on American soil," he prophesied, "two world-races may give each to each those characteristics both so sadly lack." He called for the maintenance of racial identity only "until this mission of the Negro people is accomplished, and the ideal of human brotherhood has become a practical possibility."[21] Here, in attenuated form, was the old ideal of assimilation.

Du Bois had little reason, either theoretical or practical, to see the United States as a nation of minorities. Although William James evidently made a strong impression on him in college, Du Bois was no pragmatic relativist. Fundamentally he had a dogmatic, absolutistic cast of mind. Truth was singular for Du Bois,

20. *Black Nationalism in America*, 250–62.
21. W. E. B. Du Bois, *The Souls of Black Folk* (Greenwich, Conn., 1961), 22; *Black Nationalism in America*, 261.

not plural. If this reflected his own temperament, it may also have expressed the special need of the American Negro to rely on nothing less than the universal premises of the Enlightenment for a viable connection with America. Certainly Du Bois did not have the opportunity, which Harvard gave to Kallen, of finding his own people enshrined within the self-image of New England's founding fathers.

Du Bois, in urging group effort and racial pride, was not offering a general philosophy of minority rights. He was speaking specifically to his own ethnic group with the overriding objective of combating a paralyzing sense of inadequacy and inferiority. Kallen, on the other hand, addressed a general audience, using his own ethnic past as a model for other groups in the conviction that assimilation threatened them in much the same way. Kallen wanted to save a special tradition; Du Bois was trying to build or to discover one. Before American blacks could adopt a pluralistic ideology, they would need a stronger group life and a firmer cultural identity. Du Bois contributed to those ends, and during the 1920's other Negro artists and intellectuals overcame some important constraints; but they still remained overwhelmingly preoccupied with problems of self-definition.

We may anticipate, then, that cultural pluralism would appeal to people who were already strongly enough positioned to imagine that permanent minority status might be advantageous. It was congenial to minority spokesmen confident enough to visualize themselves at the center rather than the periphery of American experience. Accordingly, cultural pluralism proved most attractive to people who were already largely assimilated. It was itself one of the products of the American melting pot.

Perhaps that is the principal reason why the theory did not prosper until the late 1930's. Ethnic hatred reached an all-time high in the riots, hysterias, and proscriptions that accompanied and immediately followed the First World War. This 100 per cent Americanism—an indiscriminate rejection of all deviant groups—would have to subside before a pluralist America could seem a real possibility. The great leap forward in assimilation, which followed the enactment in 1924 of a permanent immigration restriction law, would have to get well under way before the desirability of complete assimilation could be widely questioned.

III

Accordingly cultural pluralism made relatively few converts for two decades after the publication of Kallen's article; and those few seem to have been either fellow Jews, like Louis D. Brandeis,[22] or idealistic Yankee intellectuals. At the outset Kallen's theory struck sparks among some of the young, native-born writers who were engaged with him in an antiformalist revolt against a single standard of culture and civilization. Randolph Bourne, attacking a growing war spirit in 1916, seized upon the thesis as a weapon against the superpatriots. Bourne vigorously championed all "hyphenated Americans" in the hope that a genuinely cosmopolitan America could emancipate itself from Anglo-Saxon dominance and become the first international nation. These early pluralists shared Kallen's romantic idealism and his spirited cultural nationalism.[23]

After the war, that kind of idealism went into eclipse. Not only were most minorities unready as yet to espouse the pluralist vision, but most of the literary intellectuals no longer identified themselves with America. As we have seen, cultural pluralism depended on an underlying commitment to the possibilities of America as an inclusive community. In good Wilsonian fashion, Kallen accepted the nation as the means for attaining a wider international fellowship. Out of the shambles of 1919, however, came a different cosmopolitanism, which rejected national loyalty and all other traditional obligations. In contrast to the young idealists of 1915, who attacked only a narrow, provincial Americanism, the Menckenesque critics of the next decade regarded the United States as intrinsically, irredeemably provincial. "Patri-

22. *Brandeis on Zionism: A Collection of Addresses and Statements by Louis D. Brandeis* (Washington, D.C., 1942).

23. Randolph Bourne, "Trans-National America," in *The History of a Literary Radical & Other Papers*, ed. Van Wyck Brooks (New York, 1956), 260–84, and "The Jew and Trans-National America," *Menorah Journal*, II (December, 1916), 280; Norman Hapgood, "The Future of the Jews in America," *Harper's Weekly*, LXI (November 27, 1915), 511–12.

otism is bunk; superstition; prejudice," Lincoln Steffens wrote from France in 1919.[24]

Kallen enlarged his early statements of cultural pluralism in a book published in 1924, *Culture and Democracy in the United States*. There, for the first time in print, he used the phrase "cultural pluralism" to identify his thesis. But the book attracted only mild interest. Reviews at best were condescending. One leading critic, Brander Matthews, said, "As he is not an American by birth, Mr. Kallen is a little lacking in that native sympathy which makes it easy for native Americans to understand one another."[25] During the next decade Kallen devoted himself chiefly to other issues. Cultural pluralism remained in suspension until liberal intellectuals, in the late 1930's, reverted to Americanism.

Meanwhile the older assimilationist attitude—the belief in a voluntary fusion of many peoples into one—gained a new power and range in the period between the two world wars. As a social ideal, the melting pot had traditionally suffered from the same ethnocentric myopia that afflicted cultural pluralism. Amalgamation, as envisaged by whites, referred primarily to immigrant groups, secondarily to American Indians. That Negroes too might merge with the main body of the population only a handful of radical idealists had supposed. Now, however, while pluralists shrank from facing the terrible gulf between blacks and whites, assimilationists pressed forward. Through a sweeping attack on race prejudice the American intellectual community gave assimilation (or integration, as it was increasingly termed) a more universal import than it had ever had before.

From modest beginnings in the Progressive period, the repudiation of racial thinking mounted steadily until it became, in the 1930's, almost the hallmark of a civilized man. It was in its early development a cosmopolitan attitude; it grew easily in the disillu-

24. *The Letters of Lincoln Steffens*, ed. Ella Winter and Granville Hicks, 2 vols. (New York, 1938), I, 478. See also H. L. Mencken, *Prejudices, Third Series* (New York, 1922), 319, and Louis Hartz, "The Coming of Age of America," *American Political Science Review*, LI (June, 1957), 474–83. I have differed here from the approach of F. H. Matthews, "The Revolt against Americanism: Cultural Pluralism and Cultural Relativism as an Ideology of Liberation," *Canadian Review of American Studies*, I (Spring, 1970), 4–31, where Kallen and Bourne are placed in the context of alienation and "the 'irresponsibility' of the 1920's." The opposite, I think, was the case.

25. *Book Review Digest*, 1924, p. 318.

sioned, postwar climate of opinion, which was uncongenial to cultural pluralism. After the emotional orgy of the First World War, many enlightened people adopted a critical attitude toward all group egoisms. Unmasking the illusions of race and nationality offered serious scholars a constructive task in an era of negations. The task had a special appeal for social scientists, since it helped to establish the autonomy of their subject matter. In the earlier Darwinian era social groups had been thought to be explicable on biological principles. Now, to refute racial determinism was, in effect, to declare the independence of the social from the natural sciences. Thus, in an age of widespread "debunking," American social scientists emerged as the most powerful critics of ethnocentric beliefs. Social psychologists began to examine stereotypes. Historians focused on the ill effects of modern nationalism. Anthropologists exposed the fallacies of current racial theories.[26]

The outstanding pioneer in the study of race relations was Robert E. Park, who taught sociology at the University of Chicago from 1914 to 1929. Park did not become a settled academic scholar until he was fifty years old, and he never brought his ideas together in a single major work. But his wide-ranging essays established ethnicity as one of the central, exciting concerns of American sociology. Park came to the subject of ethnicity in a most unusual way. After studying sociology in Germany, he worked for a while as press agent for the Congo Reform Association, a missionary-sponsored society to stir public opinion on Belgian atrocities in the Congo. The study of Africa led Park to Tuskegee, Alabama, where he became Booker T. Washington's assistant and public relations man. When Park moved to the urban jungle of Chicago, he carried with him an appreciation of ethnic experience in a remarkable variety of environments.[27] Cultivating a genuinely open mind and a truly

26. George W. Stocking, *Race, Culture, and Evolution: Essays in the History of Anthropology* (New York, 1968), 262–69; Donald Fleming, "Attitude: The History of a Concept," *Perspectives in American History*, I (1967), 326, 334–36. See also Peter I. Rose, *The Subject Is Race: Traditional Ideologies and the Teaching of Race Relations* (New York, 1968), 72–74.

27. Fred H. Matthews, "Robert Park, Congo Reform and Tuskegee: The Molding of a Race Relations Expert, 1905–1913," *Canadian Journal of History*, VIII (March, 1973), 37–65.

cosmopolitan eye, Park looked always for interrelations, for comparisons, and for the bearing of ethnic patterns on all of the dimensions of modern society. More than anyone else, he tried to understand both Negroes and immigrants in the United States in the context of a global process that also affected European nationalities and Asian races in varying but related ways. Thus, under Park's auspices, the purely sociological study of race relations was launched as a comparative examination of multiethnic societies in various parts of the world. It transcended the normative, American-centered framework within which Kallen and his opponents had debated.

Or did it? When we look closely at Park's conceptual scheme, we discover an improved version of the classic American ideal of assimilation, now extended, as only a few radicals had done before, to include Negroes as well as immigrants. Park defined prejudice not as an exceptional or especially irrational phenomenon but simply as a kind of conservatism, a way of keeping what is strange and unfamiliar at a distance. Yet modern urban life inevitably throws people together, he pointed out. It widens their horizons while loosening their customary ties. In the long run assimilation usually occurs. "Every society, every nation, and every civilization has been a kind of melting pot and has thus contributed to the intermingling of races by which new races and new cultures eventually emerge."[28] Park believed that the process for the first time was reaching a global scale, most strikingly exemplified in the Hawaiian Islands. A new world civilization might be arising. In Park's sociology the melting pot was internationalized.[29] Its consequences, though often troubling and poignant, were not to be denied.

Park made a second significant modification in the assimilationist tradition. He not only gave it an international and fully interracial formulation; he also incorporated within it a quasi-pluralistic appreciation of ethnic solidarity. Influenced by Booker T. Washington's encouragement of self-respect among southern Negroes and perhaps also by Jane Addams's friendliness toward

28. Robert E. Park, *Race and Culture* (Glencoe, Ill., 1950), 192, 230–33, 346.
29. Ibid., 116, 149, 151.

minority cultures at Hull House, Park noted that group pride actually mediates the assimilative process. Indeed, the arousal of nationalist and racial sentiments is an essential phase in the mingling of peoples. By forming their own institutions and mobilizing their own collective consciousness, emergent minorities begin to challenge the existing distribution of power and status.[30] Park regarded mobilization as only the first stage in the cycle of ethnic relations—an encouraging sign of change rather than a permanent condition. He was therefore no pluralist. But he interpreted the problems of a multiethnic society in a way that took account of pluralist as well as assimilationist claims.

Consequently, Park could weave the conflicting aspirations of Negroes and immigrants into a single conceptual scheme without threatening the confidence of native white liberals. In the late 1920's, when Park and his University of Chicago colleague Louis Wirth developed the first courses concerned solely with racial and ethnic relations, they opened a scholarly counteroffensive against the Anglo-Saxon racists and 100 per cent Americans of the day. The latter insisted that the Negro and the immigrant comprised a single problem. The sociologists in effect agreed, but rejected an ethnocentric framework for explaining the problem. Against nationalists, pluralists, and racists, they raised the banner of social science and inscribed on it the old faith that all men are basically alike.

The pluralist challenge to that faith received very little notice throughout the interwar period. To most intellectuals who thought about the matter at all, it must have seemed but a difference of emphasis, so thoroughly was it overshadowed by a common opposition to the dominant racism of the day. Both pluralists and assimilationists wished to reduce the inequalities between American ethnic groups, though they chose different paths to that goal. Moreover, both approaches encouraged a common hope that inequalities would diminish as false ideas were corrected. In reacting against the gloomy determinism of the racists, in dispelling the anxieties of the superpatriots, liberal social thinkers of every persuasion diagnosed the race question as

---

30. Matthews, "Robert Park," 61–62; *Robert E. Park on Social Control and Collective Behavior,* ed. Ralph H. Turner (Chicago, 1967), xxxiii–xxxvii.

essentially a disorder in men's perceptions and beliefs. For Kallen the heart of the matter was the vitality of *cultures;* for Park it was the flux and interpenetration of *attitudes.* In either case, the truth would make men free from the bonds of prejudice. Looking back, we can see that both approaches, by interpreting ethnic problems as fundamentally attitudinal, rendered them somewhat insubstantial. Both underestimated the recalcitrance of institutions.[31]

Park's assimilationism may impress us as especially optimistic because of its pervasive emphasis on change. As patterns of communication widen, he argued, old taboos fade, attitudes change, and corresponding shifts in social relationships follow. Optimistic this was, but it was neither naïve nor parochial. What is truly regrettable is not that Park's immediate successors kept his faith in integration as a realistic long-range goal, but rather that they lost the broad, international vision which had raised his study of ethnicity to a universal level.[32]

Ironically, the book that probably had more influence than any other in shrinking the focus of scholarship to the American scene alone was the work of a European savant famous for his international studies. On its publication in 1944 Gunnar Myrdal's *An American Dilemma* instantly established itself as a landmark in race relations. It dominated the study of the American Negro for the next twenty years. Myrdal placed himself emphatically in the assimilationist tradition. He argued that assimilation was the normal experience of American ethnic groups, which the nation's basic ideals prescribed for all minorities. He rejected the claim urged upon him by the anthropologist Melville Herskovits, that American blacks had preserved over the centuries a distinctive African heritage, which they ought to cherish. Myrdal relied instead on the contrary findings of Park's illustrious student, E. Franklin Frazier: the Negro is to be understood as an American

31. A Dutch sociologist, Harry Hoetink, has commented perceptively on the excessive "sociologistic optimism" of American social science in *The Two Variants in Caribbean Race Relations* (London, 1967), 85–89.

32. Rose, *The Subject Is Race,* 75–79. Park's overemphasis on attitudes was pointed out in 1946 by his student, E. Franklin Frazier; but by then other influences, discussed below, were reinforcing that emphasis. See *E. Franklin Frazier on Race Relations,* ed. G. Franklin Edwards (Chicago, 1968), 39–40.

type and an American issue.[33] Faced with the rich detail Myrdal marshaled with such confident power, few noticed how narrowly American his approach was. He made no reference to black experience in other countries and no specific comparisons between Negroes and other minorities. The entire argument was set in the context of what Myrdal called "The American Creed." Thus Park's international melting pot was renationalized.

IV

An American Dilemma opened a new era in the study of ethnic problems. By then social scientists and others had driven the more obvious manifestations of race prejudice out of the high culture; and a fear of totalitarianism had awakened acute anxiety over national unity and created for the first time since the Civil War a really widespread guilt over the most appalling weakness in American democracy.

The new era was characterized, first, by urgency. Relieving ethnic tensions became, in cultivated opinion, an immediate imperative. The critical question was how to do it. "Action-research" on ways and means of combating prejudice and discrimination came much into vogue. The detached, speculative, evolutionary, cross-cultural, and basically quite assured sociology of Robert E. Park was swiftly eclipsed. Closely related to the pressing desire to assuage group hostilities was a second feature of the postwar era: a deep concern about national unity. Leaders of opinion wanted to bring about *The More Perfect Union*, to quote the title of a leading handbook on controlling discrimination.[34] Thirdly, most intellectuals were persuaded that the key to

33. *An American Dilemma: The Negro Problem and Modern Democracy* (New York, 1944), 930–31. Cf. E. Franklin Frazier, *The Negro in the United States* (New York, 1949), and Gunnar Myrdal, *Against the Stream: Critical Essays on Economics* (New York, 1973), 295–302.

34. Robert MacIver, *The More Perfect Union: A Program for the Control of Inter-Group Discrimination in the United States* (New York, 1948). The sense of crisis is evident in Social Science Research Council, *Annual Report*, 1944–45, p. 45. The SSRC Committee on Techniques for Reducing Group Hostility, which was appointed at that time, resulted in a report by Robin Williams, Jr., *The Reduction of Intergroup Tensions* (Bulletin 57, Social Science Research Council, New York, 1947).

unity, the linchpin of collective experience, lay in a set of ideals, norms, or values—an American creed. This ideational approach to social issues was so common that it virtually dominated the social sciences. Historians flocked to the writing of intellectual history; anthropologists fixated on the study of culture; sociologists depicted norms as the constitutive elements of any social system.[35] And students of ethnic relations attributed decisive importance to the problem of attitudes. "Prejudice"—particularly as it is conditioned by stereotypes and ideologies—became the focus of research.[36]

The 1500 pages of Myrdal's great work mentioned fascism or totalitarianism only in passing, but the totalitarian challenge to democracy surely accounts very largely for the special features of ethnic studies in the 1940's and 1950's. Was it not the fear of totalitarianism that made ordinary Americans anxious about national unity and guilt-stricken about their own racist heritage? Was not the totalitarian threat responsible for narrowing ethnic studies to problems immediately visible on the American scene, while persuading Americans to interpret those problems in terms of clashing ideologies? Totalitarianism convinced Americans that racial and religious divisions constituted the last, the most vulnerable, and the most vicious cleavages in a beleaguered society that was otherwise knit together by a sturdy web of ideals.

One might suppose that the strong commitment to national unity would also sustain an assimilationist approach to ethnic problems, an approach stressing the oneness toward which America was supposedly moving. It is true that for blacks assimilation remained the unqualified goal of most American intellec-

35. Robert F. Berkhofer, Jr., "Clio and the Culture Concept: Some Impressions of a Changing Relationship in American Historiography," *Social Science Quarterly*, LIII (September, 1972), 299–307; Richard A. Schermerhorn, *Comparative Ethnic Relations: A Framework for Theory and Research* (New York, 1970), 34–36, 127.

36. Arnold Rose, "The Causes of Prejudice," *Social Problems*, ed. Francis E. Merrill (New York, 1950), 402–25, and Ronald Lippitt and Marian Radke, "New Trends in the Investigation of Prejudice," *Annals of the American Academy of Political and Social Science*, CCXLIV (March, 1946), 167–76, are informative summaries of the prevailing theories. This emphasis was further accentuated in the 1950's by a series of studies sponsored by the American Jewish Committee, particularly T. W. Adorno et al., *The Authoritarian Personality* (New York, 1950).

tuals of all races. In the relationship between black and white all of the differences seemed impediments to unity and equality; the great object was to eliminate them. On a more general conceptual level, however, totalitarianism had the opposite effect: it stimulated appreciation for cultural pluralism. In fact, democracy was now widely redefined along the lines Kallen had sketched, so that an equation between democracy and diversity became a fundamental premise of political and social thought. In the postwar era, an explicitly pluralist theory of group relations attained its widest vogue.

It is not hard to see why Americans should have exalted the principle of diversity at a time when their understanding of themselves was so strongly conditioned by their polar opposition to a supposedly monolithic enemy. If the enemy was totalitarian, America would have to be pluralistic. But the enemy also demanded, as we have already noticed, a lessening of internal differences, a strengthening of national unity. The astonishing fact about the emphatic endorsement of cultural pluralism in the postwar years was not its occurrence but rather a general unwillingness or inability to assess critically its relation to the apparently contrary imperative of national integration. On the one hand, a movement for "intercultural education," beginning in the late 1930's, infused school curricula with a celebration of the cultural differences between ethnic groups. Popular journalists like Louis Adamic joined professional historians in denouncing the melting pot as a false ideal. The Supreme Court declared in 1943 that the Constitution protects the right to be different. And a wave of ethnic novels—particularly Jewish—gave some substance to pluralist claims.[37] On the other hand, the glowing

---

37. Stewart G. Cole and William E. Vickery, *Intercultural Education in American Schools* (New York, 1943); Francis J. Brown and Joseph S. Roucek, eds., *One America* (New York, 1952); Alexander Alland, *American Counterpoint* (New York, 1943); David F. Bowers, ed., *Foreign Influences in American Life: Essays and Critical Bibliographies* (Princeton, 1944); Milton R. Konvitz, "On the Right to Be Different," *Freedom and Experience: Essays Presented to Horace M. Kallen*, ed. Sidney Hook and Milton R. Konvitz (Ithaca, 1947), 60–61. The reciprocal relation between pluralism and assimilation in literature is the central theme of Allen Guttmann, *The Jewish Writer in America: Assimilation and the Crisis of Identity* (New York, 1971).

invocation of group differences was almost always linked with a denunciation of discrimination, meaning a failure to judge every individual on his own merits without regard to his group membership. The traditions of pluralism and assimilation blurred into a rosy haze, in which differences were praised in principle but never looked at very closely lest one fall into the cardinal sin of prejudice. Scholars described ethnic loyalty as having great psychological significance for those whom it bound together. Ethnic hostility, on the other hand, was generally traced to external circumstances, either environmental or ideological.[38] The best authorities on intergroup relations admitted that positive goals were vague and inconsistent. Their own attempts at clarification accomplished almost nothing beyond the suggestion that cultural pluralism might be considered a middle way between complete assimilation and a compartmentalized society.[39]

Almost alone, the Columbia University sociologist Robert M. MacIver made a significant effort to give that middle way some conceptual coherence. Born and educated in Britain, MacIver began wrestling with the problem of the one and the many under the stimulus of English political theorists who wanted to break up the concentrated power of the modern national state. While sympathetic with their attack on the state, MacIver took pains to mark out its essential sphere. His early writings in the 1920's developed a fundamental distinction between culture and coercion. Culture is the spontaneous, creative expression of a community; the state is its system of regulation and control.[40] Although MacIver's concern about ethnic minorities came later, he was already making explicit the liberal, idealistic view of culture that Kallen had taken for granted.

In the 1940's MacIver plunged passionately into the struggle

38. John Higham, "American Anti-Semitism Historically Reconsidered," *Jews in the Mind of America*, ed. C. H. Stember (New York, 1966), 239–43.

39. Williams, *Reduction of Intergroup Tensions*, 11–12; Goodwin Watson, "The Problem of Evaluation," *Annals of the American Academy of Political and Social Science*, CCXLIV (March, 1946), 179–80.

40. Robert M. MacIver, *The Modern State* (Oxford, 1926), 161–63, 180; George Kateb, "R. M. MacIver," *New York Review of Books*, March 25, 1965, p. 25. Cf. Harold J. Laski, *Authority in the Modern State* (New Haven, 1919).

against ethnic injustice. At the same time his theoretical interests fixed on the opposition between democracy and totalitarianism. His crowning work, *The Web of Government* (1947), offered an interpretation of democracy as a unifying framework which allows a maximum of cultural diversity. Democracy explicitly sanctions the limited role of the state; it puts the common interest—the community—first. In doing so it assists, instead of hindering, "the difference-breeding processes inherent in modern civilization."[41] Those spontaneous processes will be thwarted either by uniformity or by an unmitigated pluralism in ethnic relations. Through democracy, unity and difference can grow hand in hand.

It was a noble faith that MacIver expounded. Perhaps it came close to expressing America's best possibilities. It combined Kallen's appreciation of ethnic diversity with Myrdal's insistence on the preeminence of a common culture. MacIver built on the pluralist tradition but tried to release it from captivity to minority interests. On that score he ultimately clashed with Jewish defense agencies that had earlier sponsored his work.[42] Nevertheless, MacIver's theory of ethnic democracy lacked a certain toughness. It rested on the same soft assumptions we have already noticed in the thinking of his liberal predecessors and contemporaries. In company with so many social scientists of the 1940's, MacIver assumed the primacy of culture, the centrality of values, in the constitution of society. "All social relations, the very texture of human society," he wrote in the first pages of *The Web of Government*, "are myth-born and myth-sustained."[43] The ethnic problem, therefore, is fundamentally one of myths or attitudes. Secondly, MacIver was optimistic about correcting those attitudes because he believed that democracy was still evolving and that the general course of history backed his hopes. Although MacIver's reconciliation between unity and multiplicity was actually quite vague and insubstantial, it gained plausibility from a sweeping interpretation of modern history as a

41. *The Web of Government* (New York, 1947), 58.
42. Leon Bramson, "Introduction," *Robert M. MacIver on Community, Society and Power: Selected Writings* (Chicago, 1970), 17-20.
43. P. 4.

continuing proliferation of more and more groups, loyalties, and cultures. Only the flexible ways of democracy, said MacIver, can contain and accommodate these multiplying differences. Ultimately, it was the contrast between democracy and totalitarianism that sustained MacIver's basic postulates. The totalitarian challenge fed both his ideological passion and his faith in a democratic synthesis of many cultures.

During the course of the 1950's, the ideological fervor of American intellectuals rapidly cooled. As the years passed, totalitarianism seemed less and less monolithic; democracy seemed less and less dependent on the triumph of a specific set of beliefs. Internal political debate, as well as international polarization, lost its sharpness. Some intellectuals theorized that the fundamental conflicts of industrial society had been solved; perhaps "the end of ideology" was at hand.[44] Consequently, the tendency to locate social dangers and social solutions in attitudes or ideals began to decline. Social scientists shifted from a primary interest in ideas to a primary interest in institutions, or from the study of culture to the study of behavior. Significantly, the failure of liberal idealism in the 1950's brought no lessening of interest in ethnic differences, no restoration of the melting pot as the model of American ethnic relations. But the meaning of pluralism underwent a profound change. Instead of designating a theory of culture, the term pluralism came to designate a theory of power.

The waning of *cultural* pluralism may be traced, on an empirical level, in its failure as a guide for research. If America was in fact a patchwork of ethnic subcultures, which were somehow distinct, equal, and at least potentially harmonious, scholars should be able to describe them and to specify their relations to one another. For the most part, efforts to demonstrate the persistence of ethnic subcultures produced either trivial or negative conclusions. It was of course not difficult to show that people recently transplanted to America, or segregated within it, maintain some peculiarities of their own. A longer-range approach, however, typically revealed an erosion of distinctive customs and

44. Raymond Aron, *The Opium of the Intellectuals* (New York, 1958); Daniel Bell, *The End of Ideology: On the Exhaustion of Political Ideas in the Fifties* (Glencoe, Ill., 1960).

ways of life with each successive generation. The most ambitious attempt to prove the toughness and continuity of an Old World culture was Melville Herskovits's *The Myth of the Negro Past* (1941). But widespread criticism of his research techniques helped to convince the academic community that he found only what he was looking for.[45] A settled disbelief that American blacks retained any ethnic culture estopped further research. Meanwhile most studies of white minorities indicated that these too have tended to lose their internal cohesiveness. After a massive investigation of "Yankee City," W. Lloyd Warner concluded in 1945 that only the color line was withstanding the pressures of assimilation. Otherwise, "The future of American ethnic groups seems to be limited; it is likely that they will be quickly absorbed." The dean of American anthropologists gloomily agreed. Studies of acculturation, said A. L. Kroeber, repeatedly demonstrate that "when a bulldozer meets the soil that nature has been depositing for ages the bulldozer always and promptly wins."[46]

There was certainly some extravagance in these judgments. Nonetheless, they bring out the difficulty of emphasizing diversity at a time when homogenizing tendencies were indeed strongly at work in American culture. For a while in the late 1950's an intermediate position spelled out by Will Herberg offered a shelter for cultural pluralists. The American ethnic group, Herberg conceded, does eventually lose its separate identity. But its functions are taken over by a religious community. Religion is the truly lasting dimension of culture and the foundation of American pluralism.[47] The plausibility of this view depended in good measure on the so-called return to religion of the Eisenhower years, a phenomenon which may in itself be

45. Norman E. Whitten, Jr. and John F. Szwed, "Introduction," *Afro-American Anthropology: Contemporary Perspectives*, ed. Norman E. Whitten, Jr. and John F. Szwed (New York, 1970), 25–30.

46. W. Lloyd Warner and Leo Srole, *The Social Systems of American Ethnic Groups* (New Haven, 1945), 283–96; Alfred L. Kroeber, *An Anthropologist Looks at History* (Berkeley, 1963), 139.

47. Will Herberg, *Protestant-Catholic-Jew: An Essay in American Religious Sociology* (Garden City, N.Y., 1955); Franklin H. Littell, *From State Church to Pluralism* (Garden City, N.Y., 1962); John F. Wilson, ed., *Church and State in American History* (Boston, 1965), x.

understood as a final attempt to give contemporary experience an ideological construction. When the religious revival ebbed in the early 1960's, the only way of saving some kind of ethnic pluralism was to waive all cultural claims and locate the ethnic bond in the sheer facts of behavior.

This is approximately what Milton Gordon did in his important book, *Assimilation in American Life*. Instead of accepting the usual assumption that ethnicity inheres in culture or ideology, Gordon pointed out that a group will still retain its own associational life after it has lost a distinctive culture. Ethnic identity is primarily structural rather than cultural. Crudely stated, what counts most is not what you think but whom you associate with. This was sociologically illuminating, but it left the moral status of pluralism uncertain. Suppose pluralism turns out to preserve social barriers while ethnic cultures disintegrate? Gordon wrote within the pluralist tradition but closed on a note of caution and perplexity: fluidity, moderation, and "the option of democratic free choice for both groups and individuals" should be our basic long-range goal.[48]

V

The shift in the focus of ethnic studies, which Gordon's book highlighted, was confirmed by a more general change of outlook among political scientists and sociologists. As ideological debate subsided in the 1950's, there was less inducement to perceive one's own society as a system maintained by common values. Instead, it looked more like a field of competition between interest groups. The students of interest groups became known as pluralists, since they argued that democracy works by dispersing power through a multitude of autonomous organizations and interests. Democracy depends not so much on an overarching political creed as on a rough equilibrium between many contend-

48. Milton M. Gordon, *Assimilation in American Life: The Role of Race, Religion, and National Origins* (New York, 1964), 264–65. Another transitional book was Nathan Glazer and Patrick Moynihan, *Beyond the Melting Pot: The Negroes, Puerto Ricans, Jews, Italians, and Irish of New York City* (Cambridge, Mass., 1963), which notes a sharpening of group consciousness and gives considerable attention to political and economic conflicts.

ing groups. It rests, in John K. Galbraith's pungent phrase, on "countervailing power." This kind of political pluralism, derived originally from James Madison and Alexis de Tocqueville, filled the ideological vacuum that developed in the 1950's. In Edward Shils's eloquent treatise, *The Torment of Secrecy*, pluralistic moderation is explicitly contrasted with extremism, totalitarianism, and ideology.[49] Gordon's "structural pluralism" was in no sense an outgrowth of political pluralism; it dealt with different phenomena. But both registered the same underlying change in priorities, the same exhaustion of ideology. The old pluralism, from Kallen to MacIver, was an ideal, regarded as especially appropriate for the United States but as yet unrealized. The new pluralism was a condition, embedded in successful institutions. The old pluralism had taken for granted—though it was never able to articulate—a common standard and purpose. The new pluralism dissolved the "ought" in the "is."

As a result, pluralism lost most of its normative content. Most American intellectuals are still antiformalists, still swayed by romantic values, still desirous somehow of upholding both equality and diversity. Doubtless that is what the continuing allusions to "pluralism" in our rhetoric mean. As a coherent theory of American society, however, pluralism could no longer inspire belief when the status quo it purported to describe became hateful. The rending events of the 1960's made untenable the belief that a happy balance between competing groups had been attained. Two alternative possibilities suggested themselves. Either America is not pluralistic after all, or pluralism itself is repressive. In either case American experience ceased to provide a model for intergroup relations.

The first alternative—denying the reality of American pluralism—was proposed by C. Wright Mills. In Mills's *The Power*

49. Edward A. Shils, *The Torment of Secrecy: The Background and Consequences of American Security Policies* (Glencoe, Ill., 1956), 231–36. See also John K. Galbraith, *American Capitalism: The Concept of Countervailing Power* (Boston, 1952); David B. Truman, *The Governmental Process: Political Interests and Public Opinion* (New York, 1951); Robert A. Dahl, *A Preface to Democratic Theory* (Chicago, 1956). An excellent account of this development is in Edward A. Purcell, Jr., *The Crisis of Democratic Theory: Scientific Naturalism and the Problem of Value* (Lexington, Ky., 1973), 235–69.

Elite all the various groups in American society have lost their traditional autonomy to a dominating, ethnically homogeneous clique. Pluralism is a nostalgic description of yesterday. A related view of American power as monolithic took hold of many black intellectuals, who were embittered by the inability of the civil rights movement to improve ghetto conditions. According to Harold Cruse, the white Anglo-Saxon Protestant elite has thwarted the pluralist idea by manipulating and subduing every minority.[50]

In the 1960's other radical intellectuals chose the second alternative—interpreting pluralism as a repressive condition and a delusive theory. These scholars and critics have looked skeptically at the actual functioning of pluralistic systems. They have tried to demonstrate that a polycentric system, which is held together by power relationships rather than a common set of norms, cannot dispense justice or serve the common good. In this vein, Theodore Lowi and Robert Paul Wolff accept the political pluralists' assertion that power is distributed in the United States among many competing groups. But, they continue, government is thereby immobilized. Sweeping changes are precluded, and special interests preempt the authority that rightly belongs to the people as a whole.[51] Thus the sustained analysis of pluralist theory in the 1960's turned hostile. A Rousseauistic vision of democracy reasserted itself. Did this mean that the pluralistic society for which ethnic spokesmen and liberal intellectuals yearned would in actuality be a honeycomb of reaction and privilege?

Logically, radical criticism should have extended to pluralism in ethnic relations. By appealing to universal principles and to

50. C. Wright Mills, *The Power Elite* (New York, 1956), 242–68; Harold Cruse,.*The Crisis of the Negro Intellectual* (New York, 1967), 456–57.
51. The sustained critique by Henry S. Kariel, *The Decline of American Pluralism* (Stanford, 1961), was followed by Robert P. Wolff, *The Poverty of Liberalism* (Boston, 1968); Michael Paul Rogin, *The Intellectuals and McCarthy: The Radical Specter* (Cambridge, Mass., 1967); Theodore J. Lowi, *The End of Liberalism: Ideology, Policy, and the Crisis of Public Authority* (New York, 1969); William Gamson, "Stable Unrepresentation in American Society," *American Behavioral Scientist*, XII (November–December, 1968), 15–21; Darryl Baskin, "American Pluralism: Theory, Practice and Ideology," *Journal of Politics*, XXXII (February 1970), 71–95.

centralized authority Lowi and Wolff pointed toward assimilationist goals. They have been careful, however, not to say so.
Their object was to attack a system that had been defined as
pluralistic, not to propose another system. The depth of alienation in the 1960's deprived both models of ethnic relations—
assimilation as well as pluralism—of credibility. Assimilation
could hardly offer an attractive prospect if the host society were
adjudged a failure. "Do I really *want* to be integrated into a
burning house?" James Baldwin asked.[52] On the other hand,
pluralistic arrangements are unacceptable if they simply divide us
from one another. Who wants to live in a house which the occu-
pants are tearing apart? On the principal problem of social relations in the contemporary world—the nature of a decent
multiethnic society—radical thought simply had nothing to contribute.

In the absence of any overall vision, we now observe a spreading assertion of group consciousness on a strictly expediential
basis. Some sociologists today are less inclined than was Gordon a
decade ago to concede that cultural differentiation is declining.[53]
But ethnic mobilization does not have the salience it acquired
during the riots and protests of the late 1960's. Instead, the development of specialized media and an increasing tolerance for
diversity of every kind are permitting more and more differentiation within, outside, and across ethnic boundaries. Each group—
whether it be bicycle enthusiasts, black lesbians, or the Lords-
town assembly-line workers—cultivates its own solidarity with-

52. James Baldwin, *The Fire Next Time* (New York, 1963), 108.
53. The attack on Gordon is central to John Horton, "Order and Con-
flict Theories of Social Problems as Competing Ideologies," *American
Journal of Sociology*, LXXI (May, 1966), 701-13. Other insistent demands
for ethnic recognition are in Stokely Carmichael and Charles V. Hamilton,
Black Power: The Politics of Liberation in America (New York, 1967);
Charles Keil, *Urban Blues* (Chicago, 1966); L. Paul Metzger, "American
Sociology and Black Assimilation: Conflicting Perspectives," *American
Journal of Sociology*, LXXVI (January, 1971), 627-47; Michael Novak, *The
Rise of the Unmeltable Ethnics: Politics and Culture in the Seventies*
(New York, 1972); Vine Deloria, *We Talk, You Listen: New Tribes, New
Turf* (New York, 1970). This new hard line ethnicity has alarmed many
Jews, including Harold Isaacs, "The New Pluralists," *Commentary*, LIII
(March, 1972), 75-79, and Robert Alter, "A Fever of Ethnicity," *Com-
mentary*, LIII (June, 1972), 68-73.

out guidance or resistance or even much disguise from any ideology. At least for the time being, pluralism has been largely superseded by a new particularism, which encourages a heightened solidarity within any segment of the population that can define itself as somehow distinct.

Nevertheless, on a conceptual level my report does not end on an entirely negative note. The decline of an idealistic approach to ethnic relations—the concern with power and status rather than norms—has had one salutary effect. It has freed ethnic studies from the narrowly American framework that enclosed them in the 1940's and 1950's. So long as pluralism was regarded as the expression of democracy and a fulfillment of American values, there was little incentive to examine multiethnic societies comparatively. Once pluralism became understood as a structural or behavioral pattern, with no necessary relation to democratic ideology, its functioning could be studied in a broader international context.

Like the critics of American political pluralism, social anthropologists and political sociologists in recent years have been asking what happens when disparate groups are held together by power rather than a common culture. Michael G. Smith, Pierre van den Berghe, and others have developed a highly unflattering portrait of what they call plural societies, i.e., states in which two or more ethnic groups with distinct cultures and institutions live under a single political and economic system. Most plural societies, the anthropologists point out, are tyrannies ruled by one of the constituent groups. Others are often disrupted by open conflict and plagued by instability.[54] The most broadly based study to date of ethnic politics reaches a somber conclusion: ". . . is the resolution of intense but conflicting preferences in the plural society manageable in a democratic framework? We think not."[55]

54. A succinct summary of this development is in Pierre L. van den Berghe, *Race and Ethnicity: Essays in Comparative Sociology* (New York, 1970), 13–16. For detailed studies see M. G. Smith, *The Plural Society in the British West Indies* (Berkeley, 1965), and M. G. Smith and Leo Kuper, eds., *Pluralism in Africa* (Los Angeles, 1968).

55. Alvin Rabushka and Kenneth A. Shepsle, *Politics in Plural Societies: A Theory of Democratic Instability* (Columbus, Ohio, 1972), 217.

Through the comparative study of plural societies as they exist in Africa, the Caribbean, and elsewhere our understanding of ethnic relations is regaining the cosmopolitan breadth it lost around the time of the Second World War. Smith, van den Berghe, and their associates say little about the United States and generally deny that their own pluralism is anything but an analytical concept. Still, it gives an ironic perspective on our domestic rhetoric and behavior. The old theory of cultural pluralism was an expression of American nationalism and a consequence of the assimilation that it deplored. It stressed values to the point of obscuring realities of ethnic status and power. The new particularism, concentrating exclusively on those realities, disdains any idealistic appeal. But the best current scholarship is revealing the indispensability of what pluralists first took for granted and later tried to do without, namely an underlying consensus about basic values. Apparently, a decent multiethnic society must rest on a unifying ideology, faith, or myth. One of our tasks today is to learn how to revitalize a common faith amid multiplying claims for status and power.

Chapter Ten

Another American Dilemma

A season of struggle and hope, of turmoil and guilt, in American racial and ethnic relations has passed. In its place has come a time of apathy, cynicism, exhaustion, and near despair. The civil rights movement has collapsed, a victim at least in part of its successes. The demands for ethnic power and recognition, which exploded in the wake of the civil rights movement, have used up the hectic energies of posture and intimidation. This is a moment, then, for reflection and reconsideration. It is most especially a moment to reckon with an impasse in our thinking about ethnicity. Until the rigid opposition between two ways of looking at ethnic problems is overcome, it is hard to see how further advances can take place. The conflict between those contending points of view is paralyzing because it divides the creative minority of Americans who actively seek a more just social order.

The clash is old and familiar, though (as I shall argue later) most American writing on ethnic relations seeks to suppress or avoid it. One form of the basic dilemma occupied the New England Puritans. For them the problem of the one and the many centered in the difficulty of maintaining a unified society while guarding the purity of independent congregations. On another level the issue crystallized in the structure of the American Constitution. The founding fathers not only left us the problem of reconciling national supremacy with state and local rights; they provided a matrix for dealing with it. The importance of reconciling ethnic diversity with national unity is no less crucial, but much less attempted. The Constitution laid down no explicit guidelines for adjudicating issues of social integration—we have no court of ethnic rights—and an appreciation of the complexities in this troubled area is rarely met. Here the dilemma is both sociological and moral. It has to do with what we are and what we wish to be; with the possibilities of our social heritage and circumstances, and with the kind of identity we would like to have.

I propose, first, to state the crux of the dilemma as we confront it today; second, to review two characteristic strategies American intellectuals have used to escape from the dilemma, and finally to suggest a third strategy which may not suffer from the shortcomings of the other two. Doubtless there are other fruitful approaches to the perplexities of a multiethnic society. I intend not to be exhaustive but to concentrate on the leading tendencies in American liberal thought in the twentieth century. In proposing a third formulation I do not suppose I am settling anything. Fundamentally the issues of ethnic life are never settled. But a clear grasp of unacceptable alternatives and some sense of direction can help us to move beyond the constraints of received opinion.

The essential dilemma, of course, is the opposition between a strategy of integration and one of pluralism. Although the contrast has many dimensions, it can be summed up as a question of boundaries. The integrationist looks toward the elimination of ethnic boundaries. The pluralist believes in maintaining them. Their primary difference, therefore, concerns the scale and character of the community each takes as a model. Integration is pledged to the great community which is yet to be realized: the brotherhood of mankind. Pluralism holds fast to the little community: the concrete local brotherhood which is rooted in the past. Integration in its modern form expresses the universalism of the Enlightenment. Pluralism rests on the diversitarian premises of romantic thought.[1]

From this fundamental distinction others flow. In the United States both integrationists and pluralists claim to be the true

1. Leonard J. Fein, "The Limits of Liberalism," *The Saturday Review*, LIII (June 20, 1970), 83–85, 95–96; Wilson Carey McWilliams, *The Idea of Fraternity in America* (Berkeley, 1973).

champions of democracy; but democracy means different things to them. Consistent with its universal criteria, integration lends itself to a majoritarian emphasis. The integrationist expects a simple majority to approximate the general will. Pluralism, on the other hand, is always a philosophy of minority rights. It represents an effort to generalize the particular claim of a small part of society. It resists the conformity that majorities encourage; it is likely to dispute the legitimacy of any simple majority. Pluralism conceives of democratic politics as a process of building coalitions between minorities.

The democracy of integration is an equality of individuals; pluralist democracy an equality of groups. For the assimilationist the primary social unit and the locus of value is the individual. What counts is his right to define himself. He must therefore be free to secede from his ancestors. This is exactly what happens in the process of assimilation: individuals or families detach themselves one by one from their traditional communities. For pluralists, however, the persistence and vitality of the group comes first. Individuals can realize themselves, and become whole, only through the group that nourishes their being.[2]

The priority one side assigns to the individual and the other to the group affects their respective views of what binds a people together. For integrationists the linchpin of a rightly ordered society is a set of ideals, a body of principles, in our own case what Gunnar Myrdal called an "American Creed." A people who aspire to universality and consist largely of detached and mobile individuals will rely heavily on the beliefs they hold in common. Indeed, they may share little else, for all who subscribe to the official creed should be received into membership. The pluralist cares much less what people believe; he wants to know who they are. The most important social bond is inherited, not adopted; the work of ancestors, not of abstractions. In a multiethnic society, therefore, the assimilationist stresses a unifying ideology, whereas the pluralist guards a distinctive memory.

When the two positions are stated so baldly, the undesirability of either—at least without heavy qualification—becomes manifest. For one thing, both positions are unrealistic. Assimilationism

2. Michael Novak, *The Rise of the Unmeltable Ethnics: Politics and Culture in the Seventies* (New York, 1972).

falsely assumes that ethnic ties dissolve fairly easily in an open society. On this score the melting-pot idea—the standard metaphor of assimilation—presents the same weakness that vitiated Frederick Jackson Turner's frontier thesis. Just as Turner underestimated the toughness of the entire social heritage that pioneers carried westward, so the melting-pot theory fails to appreciate the durability of their ethnic allegiances. Even Mary Antin, the most ecstatic of assimilationists, who claimed to "have been made over," to be "absolutely other than the person whose story I have to tell," could not exorcise the past. "The Wandering Jew in me seeks forgetfulness," her autobiography confessed. "I am not afraid to live on and on, if only I do not have to remember too much."[3] Other immigrants, of course, never wished to forget. Many people resist for generation after generation the assault of technology and modern education on their sense of ethnic selfhood. No ethnic group, once established in the United States, has ever entirely disappeared; none seems about to do so. People are not as pliant as assimilationists have supposed.

Pluralism makes the opposite mistake. It assumes a rigidity of ethnic boundaries and a fixity of group commitment which American life does not permit. Although immigrants like Mary Antin could not forget the past, some of their children and more of their grandchildren could detach themselves from the old ethnic base. All American ethnic groups perpetuate themselves, but none survives intact. Their boundaries are more or less porous and elastic. All of them lose people who marry out and whose offspring cease to identify with the rejected strain. This is so patently true that loud assertions of pluralism almost invariably betray fears of assimilation.

Pluralism encourages the further illusion that ethnic groups typically have a high degree of internal solidarity. Actually many of them are unstable federations of local or tribal collectivities, which attain only a temporary and precarious unity in the face of a common enemy. On top of sharp localistic differences, an ethnic group is likely to be split along religious, class, and political lines. For example, the American Dutch, a relatively small immigrant group, belonged in the nineteenth century to three

3. Mary Antin, *The Promised Land* (Boston, 1912), xi, xiv.

rival churches (Reformed, Christian Reformed, and Roman Catholic), many distinct speech communities (Zeelanders, Groningers, Friesians, Gelderlanders, Limburgers, Noord-Brabanters, East Friesians, Flemings, Utrechters, people of Graef-schap, and those who spoke the Drenthe and Overijsel dialects), and totally dissimilar generations (colonial descendants versus nineteenth-century immigrants). No American ethnic group, Arthur Mann has pointed out, has created an organized community capable of speaking for all its members.[4]

In addition to being unrealistic, both integration and pluralism are morally objectionable. From the point of view of the individual, integration is an ethic of self-transformation—an Emersonian summons to "shun father and mother and wife and brother when my genius calls me." It teaches a rejection of one's origins and a contempt for those parts of the self that resist transformation. It sacrifices love and loyalty to autonomy and mastery, only to find those elusive goals dissolving in a pervasive conformity. In sum, for individuals outside the mainstream the process of assimilation is identical with the pursuit of individual success. It gives an edge to private ambition and a spur to personal aggrandizement. In actuality only a thin line separates Mary Antin's idealistic renunciation of the past from the queasy evasions of the traveling salesman in William Faulkner's *The Sound and the Fury*:

> "I'm not talking about men of the jewish religion," I says, "I've known some jews that were fine citizens. You might be one yourself," I says.
>
> "No," he says, "I'm an American."
>
> "No offense," I says. "I give every man his due, regardless of religion or anything else. I have nothing against jews as an individual," I says. "It's just the race. You'll admit that they produce nothing. They follow the pioneers into a new country and sell them clothes."
>
> "You're thinking of Armenians," he says, "aren't you. A pioneer wouldn't have any use for new clothes."

4. Henry S. Lucas, *Netherlanders in America* (Ann Arbor, Michigan, 1955); Arthur Mann, "The City as a Melting Pot," in Indiana Historical Society, *History and the Role of the City in American Life* (Indianapolis, 1972), 18–19.

"No offense," I says, "I don't hold a man's religion against him."

"Sure," he says, "I'm an American. My folks have some French blood, why I have a nose like this. I'm an American, all right."

"So am I," I says. "Not many of us left."[5]

Here assimilation becomes a species of disloyalty.

Moreover, assimilation lays a stigma of failure on those who remain loyal to ancestral ways. The integrationist's assurance that individuals need only an opportunity to prove their worth has led innumerable underachieving ethnics into a blind alley. They must conclude either that they are indeed unworthy or that the proffered opportunity was fraudulent. The result is either self-hatred or alienation from society. It can frequently be both.

The liabilities of a pluralist ethic are equally severe. Whereas assimilation penalizes the less ambitious and successful groups and individuals, pluralism limits the more autonomous and adventurous. To young people fired by curiosity and equipped with a cosmopolitan education, the ethnic community can be intensely stultifying. It is likely to be suspicious, narrow-minded, riddled with prejudices. Pluralism adjures the young to realize themselves through the group to which they belong; but many have little sense of ethnic identity and in any case will not forego individual opportunity in the interest of ethnic separateness and cohesion. While assimilation sacrifices the group for the sake of the individual, pluralism would put the individual at the mercy of the group.

The dangers of the latter course became manifest in the light of proposals from some pluralists for giving legal protection to ethnic differences. Harold Cruse would amend the Constitution to secure the rights of racial and ethnic groups. The Indian activist Vine Deloria has offered somewhat more concrete proposals for "tribalizing" American society by giving corporate bodies full control over local communities.[6] The threat such

5. William Faulkner, *The Faulkner Reader* (New York, 1954), 143–44. Copyright 1929 by William Faulkner and renewed 1957. Reprinted by permission of Random House.

6. Harold Cruse, *The Crisis of the Negro Intellectual* (New York, 1967), 317, 394; Vine Deloria, *We Talk, You Listen: New Tribes, New Turf* (New York, 1970).

arrangements would pose to the equal rights of individuals is only part of their difficulty. Raising the walls around unequal ethnic groups must surely sharpen conflicts between them while vitiating the common principles on which all rely to regulate their intercourse. A multiethnic society can avoid tyranny only through a shared culture and a set of universal rules which all of its groups accept. If integration is unacceptable because it does not allow for differences, pluralism fails to answer our need for universals.

The record of American intellectuals in clarifying the issues of race and ethnicity is less than notable. Polemics we have in abundance, but on this subject no contributions to democratic theory compare in depth or complexity with the writings of Hamilton, Madison, Dewey, and Niebuhr. Faced with the antinomies I have outlined, all but a very few theorists have simply elaborated one side of the argument. The other side is either repressed or relegated to some inactive region of consciousness.

Even before pluralism emerged as a distinct alternative to earlier conceptions of the American ethnic pattern, American spokesmen adopted simplistic positions on the subject. In the nineteenth century the question of ethnic boundaries was argued in terms of the advantages of purity or of intermixture. Controversy centered on the merits of a unitary culture, deriving from one dominant source, as opposed to a syncretistic fusion of diverse cultures. Today we honor especially the few idealists like Wendell Phillips who were genuinely all-embracing in their commitment to the mingling of races and peoples in the United States.[7] What troubles the modern reader is the assurance of such writers that every ethnic group will contribute something valuable to the amalgam without neutralizing any of the other ingredients. In this tradition there is no admission of sacrifice, strain, or loss.

Only among a few novelists and dramatists in the early twentieth century do we begin to glimpse the poignant complexities that underlay the cheerful enunciation of unambiguous ideals. Fiction has projected inner conflicts which discursive argument

7. See Gilbert Osofsky's fine essay, "Wendell Phillips and the Quest for a New American National Identity," *Canadian Review of Studies in Nationalism*, I (1973), 14–46.

continues to hide. Of all modern statements of the assimilationist position, the most influential was Israel Zangwill's play, *The Melting Pot*. It gave general currency to the image which has since dominated assimilationist thinking. On close inspection, however, the play reveals a riptide of conflicting values and emotions.

Before Zangwill's play opened on Broadway in 1908, the analogy between the United States and a "melting pot" was rarely if ever drawn.[8] Earlier tributes to America's power of assimilation had implied that the process occurred effortlessly and spontaneously. There was no point in conceiving of America as a melting pot if one supposed that the country was as yet unformed and that every current of immigration could alter it in some notable way. The traditional view of assimilation did not require a crucible—a rigid, preexisting institutional matrix—for if America was the pot what contribution could newcomers make to it? A melting pot also implied a tender; it suggested that assimilation needs control and supervision. It was an industrial image, fraught with the menacing heat and the flaming intensity of a steel mill. In the climactic speech of the play the hero shouts, "These are the fires of God you've come to . . . into the Crucible with you all! God is making the American . . . he will be the fusion of all races, the coming superman."[9] The message was rapturous, but it came in an ambiance of fiery Apocalypse. Both the symbol of the melting pot and the rhetoric surrounding it betrayed the mounting tensions Zangwill wanted to allay.

The story, too, was full of ambiguity. It told of a young Jewish violinist, David Quixano, whose parents had died in a Russian pogrom. Having emigrated to New York, he is writing a great symphony that will celebrate the American spirit. At a settlement house he falls in love with Vera, the daughter of a Russian army officer who had herself become a revolutionist before escaping to America. Their determination to renounce the "blood hatreds" of Europe nearly founders when David discovers that Vera's father was the fiendish slayer of his parents. In the

8. Philip Gleason, "The Melting Pot: Symbol of Fusion or Confusion?" *American Quarterly*, XVI (1964), 20–46.
9. Israel Zangwill, *The Melting Pot* (New York, 1909), 37–38.

end David's American ideal triumphs. The symphony, now completed and wildly acclaimed by its first audience, revives his faith in the melting pot. But others pay a price for that epiphany. "Those who love us *must* suffer," David sternly declares. "It is live things, not dead metals, that are being melted in the Crucible." Vera recognizes that even she must take second place in David's life, that his music and his "prophetic visions" come first.[10]

Thus ideals conquer memories; the abstract community of the future prevails over the tangible communities of the past. Zangwill took care, however, to blunt the painfulness of the choice. Fundamentally, what made David's willful and visionary behavior tolerable was the uniqueness of his artistic genius. It is your destiny, Vera told him, to stand "above the world, alone and self-sufficient." David's beloved uncle reinforces the point. Acquiescing reluctantly in David's flouting of ethnic loyalties, Uncle Mendel concedes that geniuses are exceptions. Through the romantic cult of the genius—a law unto himself—Zangwill enabled his audience to accept integration as a lovely, inspiring theory without having to face squarely the dilemmas it posed for them.

While imaginative writing began to reveal the complexity of ethnic experience, polemicists continued to simplify it. Consider, for example, John Collier's passionate plea for the group rights of the first Americans, *Indians of the Americas* (1947). As U.S. Commissioner of Indian Affairs in the 1930's, Collier was largely responsible for the enactment and execution of a pluralist program to revitalize tribal power and identity. Collier's program did strengthen the corporate life of the tribes; but it also had some contrary effects which his book completely bypassed. The "New Deal for the Indians" made available to them modern techniques of administration and land utilization. In that sense it was assimilative. Collier saw that his efforts entailed assimilation as well as preservation of native culture. "I was often gripped in anxiety," he confessed late in life, "that this spiritual center of Indian life might be lost if we carried the Indians too far along with us."[11] Yet *Indians of the Americas*, his major book, never mentioned

10. Ibid., 157, 196.
11. John Collier, *From Every Zenith* (Denver, 1963), 203.

the problem. It was a sustained hymn to the deathless continuity of Indian culture.

The tendency of writers to seize exclusively on one side of the American ethnic dilemma is especially striking in recent discussions of black power. The classic text by Stokely Carmichael and Charles V. Hamilton rejected integrationist goals because they sap the black community's leadership while benefiting only the few who are lured away. *"Before a group can enter the open society, it must first close ranks,"* Carmichael and Hamilton declared. "By this we mean that group solidarity is necessary before a group can operate effectively from a bargaining position of strength in a pluralistic society."[12] The reader is led to suppose that ethnic groups have advanced in America only through a collective struggle against other groups, in spite of the fact that some of the most disunited and individualistic elements in our society—native white Protestants and Jews—have been the most successful. Moreover, when native white Protestants have mobilized self-consciously against others, as in the Know-Nothing movement and the southern Confederacy, they have usually been thrown for a loss. Pluralism works for some of the people some of the time, but not for all of the people all of the time.

In view of the obvious shortcomings of both the assimilationist and the pluralist models, a few students of ethnic problems have tried to combine the two. Let us call such intermediate schemes "pluralistic integration." Until some entirely new model turns up, pluralistic integration seems to offer the most promising approach; so we should observe carefully how it has been attempted. What nexus can be forged between individual rights and group solidarity, between universalistic principles and particularistic needs?

Robert E. Park, the first outstanding modern student of race relations, offers a clue. Comparing immigrants, blacks, and European peasants, Park proposed in the 1920's an evolutionary cycle that tends to recur (he thought) wherever different peoples meet. An initial phase of competition arouses nationalistic and racial sentiments, through which an emergent group acquires the self-consciousness to challenge the existing distribution of status

12. Stokely Carmichael and Charles V. Hamilton, *Black Power: The Politics of Liberation in America* (New York, 1967), 44, 51.

and power. This brings a new accommodation between the contending groups. Once the accommodation is reached, a slow process of mutual assimilation can go forward. Thus ethnic mobilization and assimilation are alternating phases in the long history of widening human contacts. Group solidarity becomes a temporary but essential stage in the progress of assimilation.[13]

Another, not altogether dissimilar vision possessed Robert Mac-Iver, the principal spokesman of ethnic democracy in the 1940's. Writing in an era dominated by the challenge to totalitarianism, MacIver was especially concerned to reconcile unity with diversity, liberty with order. He described an "inherent tendency" in social evolution toward more and more differences, loyalties, and associations. Democracy, by affirming the common welfare with a minimum of coercion, gives maximum scope to the spontaneity of culture. A democratic ethos keeps institutions flexible and men responsive; it prevents difference from turning into separation. While Park construed integration and differentiation as successive stages of a dialectical process, MacIver described a way of life in which they could grow together.[14]

Fundamentally, both men relied on a common theory of history. Their writings gained persuasive force from a belief in progress. Park's benign determinism and MacIver's idealistic voluntarism offered the same assurance that a more and more humane adjustment can develop over the long run between particular communities and the great community. The problem of the one and the many, insoluble in theory, will be solved in history. Unfortunately for these optimistic assessments, the progressive interpretation of history on which they depended lost credibility in the 1950's. Evolutionism was in general rejected in history and the social sciences.

MacIver's faith in the harmonious unfolding of cultural diversity looked particularly naïve as the challenge of totalitarianism was succeeded by the challenge of technological uniformity. Instead of advancing confidently against the totalitarian enemies of diversity, American intellectuals found themselves enmeshed in the more subtle but more pervasive totalitarianism of modern civilization itself. Internationally, the era was dominated by the

13. Robert E. Park, *Race and Culture* (Glencoe, Illinois, 1950).
14. See above, pp. 221-23.

slogans of modernization. Everywhere the plastic sterility of the "international style" replaced local idioms. Rootless urban slums appeared where tribal villages had stood. In the United States television, bureaucracy, and suburbia seemed even more destructive of ethnic differences; and the first significant advances toward racial integration in American history apparently confirmed the belief that assimilation pure and simple would be our destiny. Many American intellectuals still preferred some form of pluralistic integration, but their sense of history—to say nothing of their own feelings of deracination—deprived the wish of all conviction.

In the last decade we have encountered diversity with a vengeance. It is too soon, of course, to say whether the return to ethnicity is a temporary reaction, a mere interlude in the onrush of modernization. Still, it presents an opportunity to reassess the course of history. If the sharpened ethnic assertiveness that erupted in the late 1960's is more than a passing phenomenon, it may indicate that modern history supports the theory of pluralistic integration after all, though not in quite the form either Park or MacIver suggested.

Even to consider this possibility will require a conception, clearer than we have yet formulated, of what a system of pluralistic integration might be. In contrast to the integrationist model, it will not eliminate ethnic boundaries. But neither will it maintain them intact. It will uphold the validity of a common culture, to which all individuals have access, while sustaining the efforts of minorities to preserve and enhance their own integrity. In principle this dual commitment can be met by distinguishing between boundaries and nucleus. No ethnic group under these terms may have the support of the general community in strengthening its boundaries. All boundaries are understood to be permeable. Ethnic nuclei, on the other hand, are respected as enduring centers of social action. If self-preservation requires, they may claim exemption from certain universal rules, as the Amish now do from the school laws in some states. Both integration and ethnic cohesion are recognized as worthy goals, which different individuals will accept in different degrees. Ethnicity varies enormously in intensity from one person to another. It will have some meaning for the great majority of Americans, but intense meaning for relatively few. Only minorities of minorities, so to speak, will find in ethnic identity an exclusive loyalty.

Obviously pluralistic integration depends on a lack of precision in social categories, and a general acceptance of complexity and ambiguity. Does history give us any reason to suppose that so messy a pattern can develop enduring vitality in a world pervaded by technological rationality? I think it does. Already in some degree our situation approximates the model of pluralistic integration. Indeed, the diversity of the origins of American society provides a substantial historical base for such a pattern, although the early development of an absolute distinction between races presents an enormous obstacle. In order to take seriously the possibility that group consciousness may become more universal and less absolute, it is not necessary to suppose that a complete restructuring of American society must occur. A more modest hypothesis may be sufficient: namely, that *the trend toward a rigid, absolutistic definition of roles and identities, which arose in the eighteenth century, is now being reversed.*

This is too large a topic to do more than touch upon here. I can only suggest that modern racism, which is the principal hindrance to pluralistic integration, was itself an expression and a result of the rigidification of social boundaries during a particular era of European and American history. Prior to modern times western man—guided by a richly elaborated world picture— seems to have lived in a hierarchy of multiple, overlapping, indistinct categories. The boundaries of the nation, the family, the age group, and the individual were vague. Even the concept of mankind was imprecise when monsters, angels, and legendary creatures also peopled the imagination. Beginning in the seventeenth and eighteenth centuries, all of these categories became much more separated from one another. "The new society," writes Philippe Ariès, "provided each way of life with a confined space in which it was understood that the dominant features should be respected, and that each person had to resemble a conventional model, an ideal type, and never depart from it under pain of excommunication."[15]

15. Philippe Ariès, *Centuries of Childhood: A Social History of Family Life* (New York, 1962), 415. See also Margaret Hodgen, *Early Anthropology in the Sixteenth and Seventeenth Centuries* (Philadelphia, 1964).

No simple explanation will account, of course, for modern racism. It arose during the great age of discovery, amid dazzling advances in science, knowledge, and freedom. Why, at such a time, did European civilization increasingly associate the physical characteristics of peoples with ineradicable inequalities of culture, morality, and status? Part of the answer must be sought in the ancient institution of slavery, now revitalized by new economic forces and warped into a strictly racial form of exploitation by overseas expansion. Racism also owed much to religious, social, and sexual predispositions in northern Europe. A complex of attitudes, emerging especially in Protestant countries, promoted greater freedom and equality among individuals, and thereby made inequalities between nations and races immeasurably more difficult to deal with.

Still, in its most essential aspect, as a rigidly categorizing habit of mind, racism may require some further probing. Neither slavery nor Protestant culture helps us greatly in understanding Voltaire's insistence that Indians and Negroes are unrelated to whites and incapable of civilization. Nor do the usual interpretations of modern racism explain the obsession with purity of blood (*limpieza de sangre*) in Spanish Catholicism during the sixteenth and seventeenth centuries, when religious and lay communities sought to root out anyone with a trace of Jewish ancestry.[16] It may be that the emerging classification of people by race was part of "a general tendency towards distinguishing and separating" which has characterized both modern philosophy and modern life.[17]

In the United States the absolutization of social identities may have reached an apogee in the late nineteenth and early twentieth centuries. Differentiation between the sexes was carried to an extreme. The privatized family offered itself as a refuge from and antithesis to the world outside its limits. An intense demand for purity arose in the nineteenth century. A "wall of separation"

---

16. Albert A. Sicroff, *Les controverses des statuts de "pureté de sang" en Espagne du XVᵉ au XVIIᵉ siècle* (Paris, 1960); Thomas F. Gossett, *Race: The History of an Idea in America* (Dallas, 1963), 3–53.

17. Ariès, *Centuries of Childhood*, 314. See also S. L. Bethell, *The Cultural Revolution of the Seventeenth Century* (London, 1951).

grew between church and state, between Protestant and Catholic, between sinner and "teetotaler," between black and white. In the latter decades of the century, as the interdependence of an urban industrial society was increasingly evident, the purity ethic became more and more defensive. A fear of infection, sharpened by the germ theory of disease, replaced a hope of purifying the world. It was in this context that national and racial identities acquired an absolute character. After the First World War a policy of "isolationism" in foreign affairs was a culmination of a 200-year trend toward cultural and social apartheid.

Since that time we have witnessed what may be only the beginning of a profound shift of direction. Robert Jay Lifton has described the emergence in the 1960's of a new personality type, which he calls Protean Man and associates with a capacity to change roles and to relate flexibly to changing experience.[18] What he describes may be not a generational trait but rather part of a wider cross-cutting and interpenetration of group identities. The appeal of pluralistic and relativistic perspectives among American intellectuals in recent decades provides one indication of an increasing ability to tolerate ambiguity. Another is Robert Venturi's bold repudiation of purity and consistency in architecture. "I like elements which are hybrid rather than 'pure,' compromising rather than 'clean,' . . . inconsistent and equivocal rather than direct and clear. . . . I prefer 'both-and' to 'either-or,' black and white, and sometimes gray, to black or white. A valid architecture . . . must embody the difficult unity of inclusion rather than the easy unity of exclusion."[19] These words might equally be applied to some contemporary sensibilities in the areas of sex, race, religion, and ethnicity. In the 1973-74 television season the hero of A.B.C.'s most popular serial, *Kung Fu*, was neither black nor white, but a half-Chinese secularized monk.

In a cultural setting which seems so uncongenial to simple stereotypes and fixed allegiances, what can we make of the vaunted "return to ethnicity"? Does not the strenuous reassertion

18. Robert Jay Lifton, *History and Human Survival* (New York, 1970), 311-31.
19. Robert Venturi, *Complexity and Contradiction in Architecture* (New York, 1966), 22-23.

of ethnic pride at the present time partake of the very rigidities our culture is supposedly overcoming? Must not Protean Man elude the claims of ancestors as well as the coercions that would demean or obliterate them? Again, answers lie in the future. But it can be suggested that the lasting significance of the ethnic revival of the late 1960's may have to do with the strengthening of nuclei rather than the guarding of boundaries. Certainly a very large part of the ferment in contemporary ethnic life aims at revitalizing the nuclei of ethnic groups that have needed new symbols and new leadership. That is what Black Power and Black Studies are largely about; what explains the Chicano movement and accounts for the Second Battle of Wounded Knee; what inspires the appropriation of federal funds for "ethnic heritage" programs; what lies behind the annual festivals, reunions and parades of many otherwise indistinguishable Americans. In a society as fluid as ours—a society moreover in which so much that is crucial transcends ethnic categories—the quality of ethnic life depends to a very large extent on the quality of the nuclei. Pluralistic integration implies that invigoration of the nuclei can relieve the defense of ethnic boundaries.

In the 1950's, when assimilation was advancing so rapidly, there was much concern over the oppressive featurelessness of a standardized mass culture. Today the weakening of social boundaries does not suggest a further descent into uniformity, but rather a multiplication of small audiences, specialized media, local attachments, and partial identities which play into one another in ways we cannot yet understand.[20] Many who are concerned about ethnic justice feel pessimistic about the ability of our society to develop the necessary appreciation of diversity. But it is possible, in view of the trend I have sketched, that our greater problem in moving toward pluralistic integration may come in rediscovering what values can bind together a more and more kaleidoscopic culture.

20. For various indications of the growth of cultural differentiation see the report on religious trends in the *New York Times*, January 7, 1973, p. 55; "The Arts in America," *Newsweek*, LXXXII (December 24, 1973), p. 40; Richard Maisel, "The Decline of Mass Media," *Public Opinion Quarterly*, XXXVII (1973), pp. 159-70.

Acknowledgments

The opportunity I had in 1973–74 to reconsider my earlier ventures into American ethnic history, and to endeavor in this book to reach a more coherent understanding and a more consistent point of view, owed most to two sponsors. For the time I had free from teaching responsibilities I am indebted to the National Endowment for the Humanities and to the Institute for Advanced Study, Princeton, New Jersey, which also provided me with exceptional conditions for scholarly work. Among the many institutions that assisted my research in previous years I remember with special gratitude the University of Michigan, where I benefited from the support of the Committee on Comparative History and the Horace H. Rackham School of Graduate Studies. I am also obligated to the American Jewish Committee for indulging the intrusions of an outsider, whose interpretations were not always what leaders of Jewish defense organizations wanted to hear. A small conference on anti-Semitism, which the Committee convened in New York in 1964, was for me a particularly important intellectual event.

The individuals whose criticism or encouragement contributed to one or more chapters include David Herbert Donald, Felix Gilbert, Orest Ranum, Fred H. Matthews, and Moses Rischin. I am also indebted for assistance at particular points to four former students: Sondra Herman, Raymond Detter, William Joyce, and Josef Barton.

Chapter 1 is an elaboration of my essay, "Immigration," in *The*

Comparative Approach to American History, ed. C. Vann Woodward, copyright 1968 by C. Vann Woodward, Basic Books, Inc., Publishers, New York. Chapter 2 is based upon "American Immigration Policy in Historical Perspective," which was part of a symposium on "Immigration" appearing in *Law and Contemporary Problems*, XXI (Spring, 1956), 213–35, published by the Duke University School of Law, Durham, N.C., copyright 1956 by Duke University. Chapter 3 reprints, with additional material, "Emma Lazarus, *The New Colossus*," from *An American Primer*, ed. Daniel J. Boorstin and published by the University of Chicago Press (copyright 1966 by The University of Chicago). Chapter 4 first appeared as my introduction to the Harper Torchbooks edition of Abraham Cahan's *The Rise of David Levinsky* (New York, 1960). Chapter 5 is derived from "Anti-Semitism in the Gilded Age: A Reinterpretation," *Mississippi Valley Historical Review*, XLIII (March, 1957), 559–78. Chapter 6 is an adaptation of "Social Discrimination Against Jews in America, 1830–1930," *Publication of the American Jewish Historical Society*, XLVII (September, 1957), 1–33. Chapter 7 is a new version of "American Anti-Semitism Historically Reconsidered," in *Jews in the Mind of America*, by Charles Herbert Stember et al., copyright 1966 by The American Jewish Committee, Basic Books, Inc., Publishers, New York. Chapter 8 is reprinted from *Journal of American Ethnic History*, I (Fall, 1981), 7–25. Part of the argument was earlier stated at a conference at the Hebrew University of Jerusalem in December, 1976, and published as "Disjunction and Diversity in American Ethnic History" in *The American Experience in Historical Perspective*, ed. Shlomo Slonim (Ramat Gan, Israel, n.d.), 79–97. Chapters 9 and 10 were written specifically for this book; but the former was originally presented to the annual conference of the Canadian Association for American Studies in October, 1972, and the latter was discussed at a conference at the Center for the Study of Democratic Institutions in May, 1974, and printed in *The Center Magazine*, VII (July–August, 1974), 67–73.

Index

abolitionists, 179
Adamic, Louis, 77–78, 222
Adams, Brooks, 109–10, 161–62, 163
Adams, Henry, 109–10, 162, 201
Addams, Jane, 217–18
agitators, 107–8, 111–13, 115, 148
agrarianism, 159–63, 166, 167–69, 172–73. *See also* Populists
Ahlwardt, Hermann, 112
Alaska, 8
aliens, 54–56, 60; deportation of, 41, 52, 60, 62; illegal, 68–69
American culture. *See* culture, American
American Federation of Labor (A.F.L.), 49
American Jewish Committee, 133
American Jewish Year Book, 172
American Protective Association, 106
Americans, 5, 8; and anti-communism, 60, 61, 171; as anti-restrictionists, 31, 40, 42, 44, 62, 63–64; and ethnic groups, 8–11, 43–65 *passim*, 77–78, 105, 144–47, 150, 155–56, 165; fears of, 39, 48, 52, 58, 155–56, 164–65, 208, 213, 220; as a heterogeneous people, 3–4, 16–17, 28, 31, 42, 60, 77–78, 165, 174, 185, 201, 225; as a homogeneous people, 3, 28, 32, 37, 44, 201, 204, 226, 229; and individualism, 24, 25, 172; national identity of, 20, 28, 31, 42, 46, 77–78, 186–87, 188–90, 208; and 100 per cent Americanism, 53–54, 164–65, 170, 174, 213, 218; and practicality, 189–90; as reformers, 37–38, 42–43,

48, 62, 102–3; as restrictionists, 31, 37–42, 43, 44–58, 61–63, 74, 76, 115, 208. *See also* culture, American; nativism; racism; society, American; United States
Andover, 131
Anglo-Americans, 185
Anglo-Saxon race, 46–47, 50, 56, 150, 218
anthropology, 47, 216, 221, 226, 231
Antin, Mary, 236, 237
anti-Semitism, 95–174 *passim*; and Christianity, 148–49; and conservatism, 95–96, 154, 155; decline of, 171–73; and democracy, 153, 154, 163; duality in attitudes of, 101–3; and economics, 95–96, 97–98, 100–101, 102, 103, 104–5, 108, 109, 119–20, 136, 147, 158–63, 166–69; in employment, 169–70; of German immigrants, 114; of German Jews, 105; ideological, 99–117, 123, 146, 147–51, 159–63, 166–68; of Irish immigrants, 114; Jews' role in, 103, 120, 124–25, 145; and nationalism, 137, 150–51; and nativism, 131; and neoliberalism, 97–98, 104, 106; and New Deal, 104, 106, 108, 170; in New York City, 114–15, 121, 123, 138, 169; and nonproductivity, 160–62, 166; outlawing, 133, 140, 171; of patrician intellectuals, 109–10, 115; and Populists, 97–98, 102–3, 109, 115, 163; and quota systems, 138–40, 168, 171; and racism, 113, 115, 149–50, 152; in real estate, 134–36,

In JOHN HIGHAM's early experience as a child of midwestern parents growing up in the densely immigrant world of New York City's public schools and streets, ethnic complexity and contradiction were compelling realities. With those realities the American history he was taught had little connection. Much of his interest as a scholar has been in finding the connections.

In addition to writing about ethnic conflicts and identities, Higham has also studied his own profession. His book, *History: Professional Scholarship in America* (2d ed., 1983, published by Johns Hopkins), is the standard authority. A former president of the Organization of American Historians, Higham teaches at the Johns Hopkins University. In recent years he has lectured extensively in Europe and Asia.